My Father's Blood

MICHAEL C. ROBINSON

Published in the United States by Claire Aldin Publications
Visit the website at www.clairealdin.com

Cover design by Britney Slater of Initial Brands, Inc.
Visit the website at www.ibrandcorp.com

Scripture quotations are from the Holy Bible, King James Version (KJV), in the public domain, unless otherwise noted.

The author has tried to recreate events, locales, and conversations based on memories of them. In order to maintain their anonymity, in some instances, the names of individuals, and places have been changed. Some identifying characteristics and details such as physical properties, occupations, and places of residence, may also have been changed for privacy.

ISBN: 978-0-9996840-4-7

"Pastor Mike has written an exhilarating book which illustrates his testimony and the lifelong effects that daddy issues can cause. As a minister, seasoned educator, and elementary school principal currently working in Flint, Michigan, I have personally witnessed the aftereffects a young person who is void of their father's approval can experience on a daily basis. It is the culprit of serious societal ills…but there is hope! God is a healer and Pastor Mike has assisted so many people in this healing transformation. My Father's Blood is a must read for the people of God and every parent who wants his/her child to walk in the power of God. Pastor Mike has taken his past hurts and outlined an actionable, prosperous future for those who are hurting and wounded. The power of God flows through his words and from these pages with "real-time" signs, wonders, and miracles awaiting each reader."

~Evangelist Brigitte Brown Jackson, Ed.S
Principal
Flint, MI

"Seldom do you find a story like this in which the subject of the story has lived to tell his own tale. In this read, you'll find that you identify with the traits of the protagonist as he struggles not only with the realities of living through one of the most notorious drug waves in Detroit history, but that this is just the external expression of deeper internal issues. This is the read that puts into words the things that anyone who has been in a dark period struggles to express. Moreover, it proves that even in the belly of the beast, anyone can see the light."

~Kimani Jeffrey, M.P.A.
City Planner

"This book is a raw and heroic story of why young people who make mistakes deserve another chance. It's been an honor and pleasure to personally witness Michael's transformation and his passion to help others move their lives in a better direction."

~Rita Cargile
Senior Account Executive

"I believe that every young person, no matter the background, needs to read this book. The real life application that is found within these pages will deeply impact and enrich lives for generations to come."

~Randall White, Jr.
Youth Commissioner
Park Forest, IL

"...A chilling and captivating story of a man whose identity transformed into the miraculous. This story gives the account of a hustling drug dealer who finds a passion for the gospel of Jesus Christ. Michael literally transcends through dark forces in his search of freedom. Not only was he saved from a life of destruction by preaching, he shares his testimony with the saved and unsaved he encounters along the way. Truly inspiring!"

~Nya Jordan, Professional Basketball Player
Le Harve, France

"Pastor Mike Robinson is a living miracle!!! His testimony is that regardless of where you've come from and what has happened in your life, the grace of Jesus can save, heal, and deliver you completely! Perhaps you have a loved one who needs divine intervention. The message Pastor Mike brings is *with God nothing is impossible*. M Believe it and see the miraculous!"

~Pastor Tony Kemp
Tony Kemp Ministries

"This book will change your life. Be prepared for the words to grab onto your heart and place a hunger in you to want more of God. Pastor Mike has a heart for people, and it shows not just in his words, but in his actions. I look at him as a spiritual father. Watching him through the years, I have seen him lead hundreds of people to God in the streets, on college campuses, at high schools, and God has used him to do great miracles. I encourage everyone, especially the youth, to read this book."

~Evangelist Tiffany Saunders
Iris Global Alumni (HS17)
South Elgin, IL

4

"This is no ordinary depiction of rags to riches. In *My Father's Blood*, Robinson leaves no stone uncovered while demonstrating the real life dangerous effects of a secretly, emotionally abusive family dynamic. This long awaited real life tale if full of the redemptive hope of the Gospel and its power in spite of great odds. This tale is true and raw. The best part of it is that it shows the truth really does prevail and we win!"

~Triette E. Cathey, MAPT
Author and Overseer
The Apostolic Realignment of Church Culture
and Fisherman Ministries, Inc.

"This book is a wonderful attestation to the fact that people can indeed change through the power of the love of God! Pastor Mike Robinson's candid testimony of redemption is proof that we can overcome *anything* regardless of the odds, and that our past mistakes do not define us. It is refreshing to know that there are those who are willing, unashamed, and bold enough to share the many adversities they have experienced…and how to triumph over each of them. This book is a must read for all those in need of restoration, emotional healing, and the courage to press through every trial. Pastor Mike Robinson is living proof that miracles still happen, that hopes and dreams can be recovered, and that the love of God really does conquer all!"

~Dorothy Dumas, BSCP

"In search of acceptance, appreciation, and love from his biological father, he found redemption, salvation, and eventual calling from his holy Father. An inspirational and spiritual leader of his flock, Pastor Robinson draws from these experiences to show the way to salvation to all he encounters."

~Jay Melton, God-father
Former Vice President
Random House

FOREWORD

How often do we want to please our fathers? How often do we seek acceptance, attention, and love from our fathers...even if it is misguided, misplaced, or imagined? How many black and brown boys want to know who their father is, why he didn't love him, and why he is not worthy of his love? The questions continue, *"If you know him, why doesn't he live under our same roof?* Whether he does or not, *"Why doesn't he have time for me?"*

These are the questions of far too many young black men and boys. Due to this lack of connection, lack of presence, and lack of love, it leads numerous youth to a never-ending spiraling abyss of dysfunction. Unfortunately, it creates direct pathway from the cradle to the penitentiary.

When did we as black men fall from grace or walk away from our responsibilities and obligations? When did we forget, or did we ever know or understand our progeny as descendants of kings and queens, rulers of great civilizations and cultures in our Motherland? How could we forfeit our heritage? How could we come to accept the belief that we were only *dependents* of America's slavery, products of the Jim Crow era, or rejects from the civil rights days? How did we accept a destiny as pimps, hustlers, drug dealers, or users and gang bangers? Has it really come down to being the unfortunate long-term residents of the federal or state penal institutions...or even worse, the early eternal residents of cemeteries and graveyards across this nation?

Michael C. Robinson was not a young man who should have failed his youth or sought the avenues previously described. He was the middle child of his parents. Both mother and father were educated, had long-term, steady employment, and by all standards, were living the American middle-class dream. In *My Father's Blood*, Pastor Mike takes you on a journey to a sunken place. He describes the separation of his parents and the revelation that while a great father, he was a terrible and abusive husband.

Although his parents ultimately reunited, a wedge was placed between him and his father which catapulted young Michael on his way to his personal earthly hell. The long walk to the penitentiary or grave included women of the night, slinging drugs, committing street crimes, being crowned "Big Baller of the Hood" and being thrown in prison. After six years in the federal penitentiary, he saw the light, and asked for God's guidance. He made a promise to God and never compromised on that promise. God never turned his back on Pastor Mike.

Angels have guided his steps from that day forward. The journey has not always been easy, but a 10,000 mile journey begins and ends with one step at a time. This book takes the reader through his journey, through dark and lowly places, from the highs of street life, to the bottom of prison.

As a judge, I have seen far too many young Mike's who did not seek or get the blessings of a second chance. They did not have the opportunity to fulfil their God given talents or dreams. In my humble opinion, *My Father's Blood* is a must read book.

~Judge K. M. Colley

PREFACE

Prepare to be immersed in a landscape filled with the raw emotions experienced daily by urban youth. Delve deeper to explore the cloak of victimhood which so many choose to hide underneath, unable to handle the intensity of life as it spins them in a whirlwind. Emerge with renewed purpose and undying love from your Heavenly Father as Pastor Michael C. Robinson peels back the layers of his life in a story so captivating that you won't be able to put it down until you read the very last word.

Pastor Mike gives you full access to his world as he pours out his heart on the pages that follow. Witness the transformation for yourself, but don't stop there. Allow his transparency to lead you in a closer examination of your own experiences. May it be evident to all who read this story that your Heavenly Father has so much more in store for you as you uncover the mystery of *My Father's Blood*.

~Dr. De'Andrea Matthews
President
Claire Aldin Publications

DEDICATION

This book is dedicated to everyone who has been a blessing and made a contribution to my life in any form or fashion:

- To my Savior, Christ Jesus, for shedding His blood for the unsaved world.
- To my wonderful church family, Ypsilanti Community Church and Kingdom Come Bible Missions at Eastern Michigan University.
- To My lovely family: my wife, Michelle; my mom, Berneice Robinson; my brother, Cordell; my niece, Misty, and my nephew, Lil' Kordell Robinson.
- Most of all, to my precious God-sister, who has been heaven sent in my family's life in general, and my life specifically, Carolyn "Kitty" Cannon. Thank you for how much you inspired me on the numerous occasions when I felt like quitting and throwing in the towel. You became *my* pastor and counselor when I couldn't talk to anyone else or share confidential matters. You inspired me, encouraged me, and ministered to me when I was at the lowest point of my life. I appreciate all of the wise advice that you shared with our family concerning my dad. When my own brother and I didn't see eye to eye, you took the liberty to counsel the two of us to get us back on one accord again. You've been there for Michelle for whatever she needed. You've been the sister I never had, the friend I always longed for, a wise counselor, and a soldier who fought with me on the battlefield. Last, but certainly not least, you inspired me all the way to completing this project, over and over again. I appreciate your faithfulness, persistence, and commitment for constantly encouraging me to travel down unchartered territories. Without your help…and constant annoying questions like *"What chapter are you on now?"*…I would not

have finished. Thank you for just being you and having the heart and compassion of Christ. I'm sure that's why God has empowered you to become a successful business woman, and the **CEO of Lyndsey's Linen and Chair Covers**, the best linen company in Michigan in my estimation. I love you, God-sister. Keep praying for me and I will continue to do the same for you.

~Michael C. Robinson

TABLE OF CONTENTS

INTRODUCTION

Finding a way to survive on the streets of Detroit was no small feat. Walking away from the dumpster that showed no signs of my earlier stomping victim, I hear a white man's voice tell me to put my hands on my head. Spinning around, there was no mistaking that .38 snub nose black revolver pointing at my head. Though my body extended far beyond my normal height, I could feel that officer squinting his eyes as hatred spewed from his furled lips uttering "look n***er, put your hands on your head". Moving ever so cautiously from hands in the air to planted firmly on my head, I rehearsed in my head the procedures to follow to show the officer that I was surrendering. That didn't keep him from raising his shirt showing me his nickel-plated revolver while exclaiming "This is my *registered* gun. If you don't put your hands on your head, I'm going to shoot you in your _____ _____ head, then go home and sleep peacefully tonight". Stammering a response, "oh, my head, officer, my head, yes sir", I continued with "my grandmother is on the porch over there. She sent me here to check on some commotion we heard, but if you kill me, she *know* I was back here, officer." Unfazed, he told me to shut the _____ up as his partner watched from the black special unit squad car.

I later found out the officers I encountered were the same ones responsible for the death of Malice Green. My friends and I had taught that guy invading our turf a lesson earlier. Sitting back afterwards near the corner of 24th and McGraw drinking Coronas, laughing, and enjoying the summer air seemed like a distant memory now. Knowing that officer had a registered gun *and* a throw away – it's a miracle that I'm alive today. What the devil meant for evil, God turned it around for my good. I was covered by the blood of Jesus that night when it could have been my own blood instead. This is my story.

SECTION ONE:

BLOODLINES

1974 – 1975

PAPA DIDN'T TAKE NO MESS

James Robinson stood about 5'9 tall, but in the eyes of his son, he appeared to be more than ten feet. He had an intimidating raspy voice which felt like it could make the earth tremble. His kids respected and honored him as if he was God, but not because of his stature or muscular physique as much as he controlled everything in his domain. Mr. Robinson was the man of their world and Papa didn't take no mess!

An athletic man, he had a powerful build. Mr. Robinson played every sport imaginable, but boxing and baseball were his favorites. He was very well known on the streets of Detroit. It seemed like everyone knew him and there was nothing that he could not do. He'd showcase his athletic abilities to get the other kids in the neighborhood interested in sports. Mr. Robinson wanted his sons *and* the neighborhood kids to be athletic. There was not one sport he had not conquered, including skating. In fact, he could have been a professional skater if he wanted. He danced and did tricks on skates! His kids were great skaters, too.

Mr. Robinson swam with finesse and rode a bicycle backwards with expertise. Talk about basketball! He could dribble and move a basketball around his body better than the Harlem Globetrotters. He taught many of the neighborhood kids how to hold a baseball bat, how to catch a baseball, throw a football, shoot a basketball and any other skills you could think of.

At 42 years old, Mr. Robinson was still playing baseball. In the evening, he would race the entire neighborhood of kids in the streets, leaving them all behind! Everyone thought he was the coolest ole man in the hood because he took time to play with his sons and the neighborhood kids. Excelling at sports is what he taught best.

Mr. Robinson came across as a hero in everything he did. One day while driving home, there was a car accident. The car had flipped over and landed upside down. Mr. Robinson did not hesitate. He immediately pulled his car over, jumped out and began removing people from the overturned, damaged vehicle. He single-handedly rescued the driver and passengers, including several children, just before the car burst into flames. Everyone was amazed at his heroics and he grew even bigger in the eyes of his middle son. Who wouldn't be proud he was their father? After all, he was the kind of man who was willing to put his life on the line for others.

James Robinson was the epitome of a *real* man. In the eyes of his three sons, he was fearless. The man was smooth, cool, had street smarts and this certain charisma. Women often called him handsome, which was the expectation for a man with the reputation for being one of the sharpest dressed guys on the streets of Detroit. When it came to fashion, he was known as a *"Dapper Dan"* because he wore 3G suits and alligator shoes. He shopped at Cousins and Sconicks and only wore the finest. James Robinson never left the house without looking his best since he had a reputation to maintain.

Mr. Robinson was indiscriminate about who he gambled with – the biggest hustlers, players, pimps, and even drug dealers, though he hated drugs and drug dealers. In his eyes, it was a sin, but when it came to gambling, all were welcome. Needless to say, Mr. Robinson was well-respected on the streets and he wanted his sons to know it, which is why he took them so many places with him.

There were three of us brothers. Tony was the oldest, Cordell was the youngest, and then there was me, the middle brother. Tony was two years older than me, and Cordell was five years younger than me. My name is Michael. Growing up, our names were irrelevant, because Pops rarely called us by them. He addressed us by titles, such as *"Come here, my man!"* or *"I'm talking to you, my friend"*, or *"Hey partner, when you gonna get to cutting that grass?"* That's how he interacted with us.

In truth, Dad was a hustler himself. He could outsmart some of the *slickest* of the slick in poker, shooting dice, three-card Monte, pool - you name it. He was a master at shooting dice and shooting a hand – he could shuffle the deck and set the deck at the same time! Yes, whatever it was, he dominated it and passed those tricks of the trade down to Tony and me. He taught us how to mark the cards with a grain of sand glued to our fingers. We even learned how to tell when a deck was already marked. We caught on quickly, and at a young age, I was already captivated by the hustler life style.

You see, James Robinson never did anything in a normal fashion; he was always *extra*. He *wanted* to be noticed. He wanted to be known as being cool, and having exceptional street knowledge. One time, an older cousin told me that my dad, when shooting dice, would throw the dice through his shirt and they would come out of his sleeve. Whenever he taught us sports, he used tricks to convey his point.

It was no surprise that soon Tony and I could out hustle most of the teenagers in our neighborhood. Tony was the epitome of my father. He watched, studied, and learned everything my dad did. At the age of 15, he would take my five dollars, and my little brother Cordell's two or three dollars, go somewhere for an hour or two and come back with well over a hundred dollars!

I can recall shooting dice and playing cards on the street corners. If my dad pulled up, he wouldn't chastise us; rather he'd smile and then grin about it. He would often tell the people in the neighborhood, *"Yeah, my sons are gonna be hustlers one day, but they gonna be doctors and lawyers, hustling other doctors and lawyers".*

Dad was a heck of a man. He was the greatest dad in the hood. He would shoot the breeze with us about his perspectives of life on the streets. He taught us that hustling was almost legal if you did it the right way. I idolized him so much that I felt if I grew up to be like him, I could conquer the world!

If we had trouble with other kids in the neighborhood, my dad taught us to stand up for ourselves. He was a boxer, so quite naturally, he taught us some of his skills of protection. Although he was our protector, he would never fight our fights for us.

My pops was also a comedian and he consistently used psychology and con games on us. He would trick us into laughing and talking about school and say things like, "*Now, you know you wasn't paying attention in class today.*" Unwittingly, I'd agree, laughing with him. Then the next words I'd hear would be, "*Now, I'm getting ready to tear your behind up for acting a fool in school!*" which he proceeded to do unmercifully. My father would beat us like he'd lost his mind. He used extension cords, broom sticks, his hands, or whatever was available and effective to knock us out. I remember getting a whipping over at my uncle's house when I was about five years old. My dad picked me up by my afro and drug me up a flight of stairs, grabbed an extension cord and beat me until he bust my skin open in various places. This was normal practice with my dad. His adrenaline would rise when he noticed you were in pain.

I will never forget how he beat my older brother, Tony, one day. He made him lay on his stomach naked, and he took a buckled belt and almost beat him to death. The belt had a piece of leather, then a buckle, a piece of leather, then another buckle throughout the whole belt. My dad beat him so badly that he had dark blue and burgundy bruises all over the back of his body.

Yes, Mr. James Robinson had many layers. He was athletic, charismatic, and tough. What a contrast! He was a very hard man, but at the same time, he was a good provider. His demeanor reminded me of the character James Evans on "Good Times", but he could hustle like *Sweet Daddy*. He worked at Chrysler and owned several after-hour spots. These after-hour joints were illegal clubs which served liquor and offered the night life. They were cool places to hang out, dance, gamble, and relax after the regular clubs shut down at 2:00 a.m.

My pops was what you would call "paid" in the hood. He was also our idol. When it came to material things, we never wanted for anything. He shopped for us at Hughes and Hatchers, Saks Fifth Avenue, and J.L. Hudson. We were among the few boys in the hood to wear leather and rabbit jackets. He made sure we were always dressed to impress. We even owned a mini bike. That was a rare thing in our community. Those amenities came with a high price. We were held to a higher standard than most boys our age. We learned early on that we had to represent him well. We were not allowed to make mistakes and when we did there was hell to pay!

My father lived his whole life trying to impress others and there were times he used his boys to do just that. We would get a whipping if our afro was even out of place! Our shirts and suits had to be wrinkle-free and our shoes had to be shined to perfection. We learned to tie a tie by the time we were seven years old; and of course it had to be tied impeccably. We were expected to be *extra* perfect because the life we lived was full of extra material things. The most extraordinary things we received were merciless whippings with sticks, extension cords or anything he could get his hands on.

My father was controlling and overly demanding of us; but I still wanted to be just like him. In my eyes there was nothing he *couldn't* do. He was perfect and he expected perfection from his offspring. Everyone looked up to him. Everyone respected him. I believed we had the best dad in the neighborhood...never mind the beatings and the whippings. Who would trade in a dad like that?

After all the compliments and accolades I heaped on him, there was a problem I sensed early on. I looked up to him with awe; he looked down at me with indifference. I tried to mimic his hustling game on the street and be just as good as he was. My efforts never won me 100% approval from him. I believe that was because I was a sickly child in my early years, suffering from severe asthma and eczema. Not only that, but because of my condition I didn't inherit his athletic abilities at an early age like my brothers. In his eyes, I was the pitiful, sickly child. For that reason, I felt he treated me differently than the others. Though he never said it out loud, he conveyed to me a one-word underlying message: Insignificant. The impression of being unimportant to my hero made me afraid and this fear made me a risk-taker. I soon began to do dangerous things to get his attention, because I suffered from rejection. Maybe, too, it was because I was the middle child. Studies prove that the first child is always considered the "know-it-all" child, the natural leader, the attention getter or just the trophy child. The baby child on the other hand becomes the pampered child, the competitive child, even the clown child. The baby is the one who can get all the attention because this is the one that should get everything and that gets away with everything. With the first and last positions filled, the middle child is the least favorite, and almost an afterthought because all the energy is focused on the first born and the baby. I became the one who was easygoing, independent, and secretive. There were times I felt life was unfair; so I put all my efforts into trying to be accepted by my loved ones, instead of being overlooked by them. I wanted that acceptance so very much that I was willing to buy love, sacrifice for it, and I tried to be loved by any means necessary.

I was considered a copy-cat and the daredevil of the family. If I wasn't copying everything my brother Tony did (because my father seemed to love him so much), I was taking stupid risks. Armed with my father's rejection only made me relentless! I wasn't afraid to try anything! While our neighborhood friends were jumping off porches, I was jumping off roofs and buildings! I found myself fighting the biggest and the oldest kids in the neighborhood. I played harder, jumped higher, and gave my all, even with asthma. I couldn't understand why the other kids grew tired so fast and they weren't sick like me.

I tested the limits; and this behavior often kept me confined to the house for "my own good." It made me angry. I wanted to play and go outside with the rest of the kids. I thought that if I did well and held my own then maybe, just maybe, my father would see me as strong and athletic as Tony. Maybe he would approve of me. Sadly, no matter how tough I was or how hard I tried, I was never able to get the love and recognition from my father that I so desperately craved; and that I believed he willingly gave to my brothers. I felt that I was invisible to him.

YOU'RE ALL I NEED TO GET BY

It was totally different with my mom. She was always there, always present, and in the moment. My mother, Berneice Robinson, was a beautiful woman. She had a caramel brown complexion and black shoulder length hair that she dyed light brown. Mama was medium height.

My parents met each other at a young age; she was twelve and he was sixteen. They grew up in the same neighborhood on the north end of Detroit. Even though my father ruled our home and his personality was larger than life, my mother was the yin to my father's yang. She wasn't a quiet wallflower. She was smart, quick-witted, and outspoken. She made sure that she got her point across to anyone who challenged her. For the most part, my folks did the best they could with the little knowledge they possessed regarding raising three boys on the streets of Detroit.

My parents loved one another, yet they were total opposites. He was the muscles of the operation, and she was the brains. My father's objective as a parent was to have his boys work hard, learn the hustle game, and play sports with the potential to obtain athletic scholarships for college. He had little concern for academics. On the other hand, my mother wanted us to totally focus on education and academics.

You see, my mother graduated from high school at the age of fifteen. She was considered a childhood genius in her family. After high school, she obtained her bachelor's degree in education from Eastern Michigan University at eighteen years old.

She became a high school Spanish teacher but quit because of the difficulties she faced instructing students that were so close to her age. Not only that, but my dad was threatened by her teaching. He was insecure of her teaching young men her own age. As a result of these difficulties, she obtained a job at the Wayne County Tax Department and worked there until her retirement. Mother took pride in her ability to pass any test, but for the record, she was street-smart, too. She more than likely picked it up from my dad. She knew how to recognize marked cards and could always think fast on her feet, but she was most proud of her intelligence. It was who she was. Her intellect allowed her to hold a conversation with anyone. She would tell us boys how much competition there was in the world; and that we would need to be prepared for any exams that came our way. She wanted us to do extremely well, whether the test was given in the classroom or in real life. She wanted us to be the best, and not just the best, but better than the others. The reason she gave us was because white people are privileged in this country and we are not.

Mom and I had a close relationship. She was my main caregiver since I was always sick. My asthma was so severe and on numerous occasions, I stayed in the hospital. Mom stayed right there with me.

Talk about a hero. She was my wonder woman. She took care of the family and worked a full-time job, too. It was unusual for a woman to have a full-time job like that when I was growing up. Our friends' mothers were always home while their fathers went off to work every day. Because both our parents worked, we didn't have much adult supervision. We did, however, have ample time to get into trouble.

I recognize now that my mother had a lot pressure on her. She took it in stride because she looked at her roles as wife, mother, homemaker, and bread winner as a test for her shine and be the best!

During summer vacation, Mom left me and my brothers home alone while she went to work. My oldest brother was twelve, I was ten, and my younger brother was around five, at the time. She left strict, detailed instructions to never open the door for anyone. Why she thought it would be alright to leave three young, mischievous boys home alone, I will never know.

One particular day, a man from the Detroit Water Department needed to enter our home to read our water meter that was in the basement. My older brother, Tony opened the door to let him in, disobeying my mother's strict rules. My younger brother Cordell and I went into the other room. We pretended to be dogs and began barking and banging on the bedroom door as if we were going to break the door down. The water meter man was terrified and asked if the dogs were secure in the other room. Tony reassured him that the dogs were secure and they could not get out. We continued howling, barking and growling like we were going to tear that man limb from limb! The water meter man ran down stairs, read the meter, and then was out of our house like lightning!

I mentioned before that I was a sickly child. My constant bouts with asthma required frequent medical treatments. I went to the hospital so much that all the nurses knew me. A diagnosis of asthma in those days was very critical. They didn't have the convenient treatments that are available today. In fact, when I was very young, a neighborhood friend died at the age of ten after having a severe asthma attack.

The hospital saw me at least once a week and I was admitted at least once a month. The story was told to me that when I was an infant, I had a severe asthma attack and my father felt it wasn't necessary to take me to the doctor. He kept telling my mother that I would be alright. My mother defied him and took me to the hospital. When the doctor examined me, he told Mom that if she hadn't gotten me there, I wouldn't have made it through the night. It's important to note that the enemy will always try to destroy a young life when God has a call upon that person. After that near fatal incident, she always kept a close watch on me. Mom was everything to me.

IF THE TRUTH BE TOLD

This incident reminds me of the time when Herod made the proclamation to kill all of the young boys under the age of two years old because he knew that a king had been born. That king was Jesus. The enemy heard the prophecy that a king had been born and it was his job to highjack the prophecy. The scripture says in *1 Peter 5:8, your adversary the devil walks about like a roaring lion, seeking whom he may devour.*

As a child, I used to watch the educational television program *Animal Kingdom.* What I noticed was that the lion always looked to hunt the baby zebra, baby buffalo, baby elk, etc. The enemy's objective is to seek the life of the young. The devil wanted to take my life, but God wanted to give me life. In my home, I was the only child with asthma, and I was the only child that dealt with the spirit of rejection. Satan devised a plan to destroy me before I got started. He wanted to abort my God-given destiny and to intercept my purpose and my future!

Don't get discouraged when the enemy has put a child high on his hit list, because there is something that God has destined for that child's future! Be encouraged.

COME AND GET THESE MEMORIES

It was the summer of 1974. Brand-new Fleetwood, Brougham, and Eldorado cars lined the driveways and down the street. Between my family and the other hustlers who lived on my grandparents' street, it looked like the parking lot of a Cadillac dealership. I was nine years old at the time, and it was mesmerizing to see these players, hustlers, pimps, and pushers stepping out of their caddies dressed in bell-bottom pants and Roberto hats. Now tell me that wasn't cool.

I could hear Curtis Mayfield's "Super Fly" theme song playing in my head, because what I saw reminded me of scenes from the movie. That's how I remembered the family gatherings. My uncles and aunts slow rolling up to Grandpa Buck and Grandma Alice's house in their shiny new Cadillacs and dressed to the max!

During the summers, my brothers and I stayed at our maternal grandparents' house. Grandpa Buck had a serious drinking problem, but it didn't keep him from retiring from Ford Motor Company. It also didn't keep him from providing and protecting his family. Grandpa Buck would literally kill for Grandma Alice. He was known for getting drunk and pulling out his shotgun, threatening anyone in the neighborhood. He was fearless. We loved going to Grandma Alice's house. Her spirit was so alive in that home. She was a beautiful, spirited, brown-skinned, small framed, woman made from real, certified grandma stock. She grew up in the small country town of Bolivar, Tennessee and she possessed an abundance of southern charm and hospitality.

Grandma Alice was the most loveable person in the entire world! She had an uncanny ability to look beyond a person's faults and see the area where they needed the most help. When it came to her children and grandchildren, I'm sure she had her favorites, but you never knew it. Her favorite would be the one who needed her the most, at that time. I have so many memories of her home being filled to capacity with family on the holidays. Anyone visiting on the holidays could smell the aroma of cakes and sweet potato pies when the door to her house opened. At those holidays, the grownups would be talking and laughing, while the children would be jumping over the banisters and playing outside. She cooked everything from scratch. She would buy fresh peas and green beans from the farmer's market and snap them open. We knew that going to grandma's house for dinner meant there would be more than enough food to eat. We'd always be able to take food home, too.

Grandma Alice even canned jelly preserves and other things. She was one of a kind. She never had a driver's license so family members had to drive her around. On Sundays, she faithfully took the bus to church so she wouldn't be late to serve in her honored position as an usher. I even had an aunt, Aunt Alberta, who sang in a local quartet group called the Trumpleletts.

She welcomed everyone to her loving home. My brothers, cousins, and I spent a lot of time in the heart of the ghetto where she lived on Martindale Street. We loved being there. When my father would be too hard on us, I would call her. She was our protector and our advocate. Dad had much respect for her. She was the only one who could tell him off and make him back up off of us.

Martindale Street was always blazing. Grandma Alice lived on the same street as Butch Jones and Raymond Peoples, founders of the well-known Detroit drug gang, Young Boys Incorporated (YBI). On Martindale, we could do whatever we wanted; so I hung out with the older teenagers. My youth was centered on the street life, the thug life. There were notorious Detroit-raised gangsters making a name for themselves at that time. Often, we'd hear wild stories about the criminal element of Detroit. Grandma Alice's house was located within the 10th police precinct, where the 1967 Detroit riots began. In our day, Detroit was known as the "Murder Capital of the World" for at least 10 years!

Criminals and murderers, like Chester Campbell, who was the most villainous hit man in the country, lived in Detroit. He was

26

believed to have murdered over 200 people! People were afraid to even mention his name. They called him the "Black Angel of Death" or the "Undertaker." It was rumored that he worked for the Italian mob and other Detroit gangsters. He was more than willing to handle any problems or people who needed to be silenced.

Then there was Frank Nitti, a drug kingpin who operated mostly on the eastside of Detroit. Nitti and his gang, "Murder Row", was believed to have been involved in a triple beheading along with numerous other murders on the streets of Detroit.

Gee "The Fat Man" Jackson and Courtney Brown were other Motor City drug kingpins who made a name for themselves by being ambitious and slinging heroin while looking good doing it. They were seen on numerous occasions attending events dressed in fur coats and costly jewelry.

There were many of my other uncles and family members also living in the fast lane by selling drugs, pimping, running numbers, and just plain hustling. Oh, the things we saw and outrageous criminal stories we heard as young boys hanging out on Martindale Street!

Looking back, it felt like I lived in one of those old gangster movies. I was way too young for the things that I saw and experienced, but this was life growing up on the streets in the "D." At nine years old, Grandma Alice had me and some of her other grandchildren running numbers.

She ran numbers for my uncle, Big Harry. She was known as the "Numbers Lady." Running numbers was the illegal public lottery. People didn't buy them in the store. They paid the numbers man or woman. People placed bets on numbers with small amounts of money. If they won they would get a high return for the amount they played. No one could use the phone at Grandma's house from 9:00 a.m. until after 3:00 p.m. The phone line had to be free for people to call in their numbers. I loved making the money drop when someone hit the numbers. I would get paid twice, once by Grandma then again by the winner. I would earn at least five-dollars, which was a lot of money for a young boy. My cousins and brothers would argue and fight over whose turn it was to make the winning money drops.

Grandma made me laugh because she was overly paranoid. Every time a police car would roll down the street she'd run and hide the number books and money. She acted like she worked for a drug cartel. Her greatest fear was being raided by the police. In her paranoia, they were looking for her. No matter the risk, the love of money kept her and everyone else in the game.

Unknowingly, I was groomed by my family to survive on the city streets. Dad didn't have a liquor license, but he ran his after-hours operations like a bar. His operations were very lucrative, and he'd be gone almost every weekend and some weeknights. I knew that Mom didn't like him being gone like that, and she would accuse him of cheating. But his reply was that he had to work weekends to bring in extra money for the family, playing poker. Playing poker required him to have to spend countless hours at the poker table. He was a true hustler.

Dad's job at Chrysler allowed him to play it smart. He used his legal job as his steady income, while his side hustles allowed him the freedom to live the life that he wanted, full of materialistic things that made him feel like a man.

Growing up as I did around my dad and family hustling, I thought it was my destiny to hustle. From a child, that seed was planted in me as I witnessed the illegal business worlds of my family. My family wasn't alone in hustling. It was happening all over the city of Detroit. Black people were hustling legally and illegally.

Overall, Detroit was a great place to live if you were black. Times were changing for the better. There were black-owned party stores, beauty shops, nail salons, night clubs, and we were building churches. In November 1974, we made national headlines as Detroit elected its first black mayor, the Honorable Coleman A. Young. We were all glued to the television set. Families all over Detroit watched as history was made. Coleman A. Young made us look good. He was a young, intelligent, black man who brought pride and promise to the City of Detroit. We were proud. When he became mayor, people were outside in the neighborhoods yelling with excitement. Even at nine years old, I could recognize the definite transition of blacks coming to power in Detroit. Our new mayor began to open doors wide for black people to get to the next level. At that time, we were one of the few cities that had people of color climbing to the top of the political ladder and owning businesses.

As with any significant change in leadership, some people in the city of Detroit were afraid of the changes taking place. Black people were finally getting their '*piece of the pie.*' White and Jewish communities began leaving the city in droves. Other ethnicities were moving out of the city at record speed, too. But we stayed. Black folks were on the rise.

INNER CITY BLUES

One day, while visiting my Uncle 'Sugar Chile' Robinson's house, I was sitting down trying to catch my breath at Miller Junior High baseball field. My uncle had been a child prodigy at seven years old, playing the piano and singing with greats such as Count Basie, Frank Sinatra, Sammy Davis Jr., and Billie Holiday! As a child, he helped paved the way for many black entertainers. He made movies and traveled the world. He was the first black entertainer to ever perform at the White House for President Harry Truman!

We were proud of our uncle's accomplishments. He even took time out to form and coach a Detroit Eastside baseball team. My brother was on the team and they had just finished playing a game. I was exhausted. My asthma had flared up because I tried so hard to keep up with everyone. While I was laboring to draw in air, I looked across the field and saw a man get out of a car. There was nothing unusual about that. He was leaning into the car talking to the driver from the passenger side. Suddenly, shots rang out! The man who had exited the car had been shot by the driver. Everyone turned around in amazement and the next thing I knew we were all running at top speed across the street as the driver fled the scene. The man lay on the ground in a pool of blood!

A little girl rode up on a tricycle screaming *"Dad, Dad!"* *"Run and get your mother,"* the man said faintly to his daughter. After what seemed like hours, the Emergency Medical System (EMS) came and one of the men asked the man, *"Who did this to you?"* He said, *"I don't know, but they said they were going to kill me."*

The man was obviously trying to protect his family, by not revealing the shooter. Sadly, the man stopped responding before they took him away. I was only nine years old and now I was a witness to what appeared to be a bloody murder. The smell of blood, the little girl crying, and the look of that man covered in blood made me numb. I was confused and shocked. *"This can't be real"*, I thought.

At such a young age and living in Detroit, I saw a lot of violence, even while visiting my Grandma's neighborhood. There were gang fights, people stumbling around high on drugs, and drunk from alcohol. Men beat their wives and girlfriends; teens ran from the police. People were cruel and had no respect for life.

There was even a purse-snatching ring. Three thieves would scope out women leaving the bank. One thief would snatch the purse, and then his crony would pretend to be a Good Samaritan and run to that woman's rescue. He was called the wingman. If she mentioned that she was alright because she put her money in her bra then the wingman would snatch the money from her bra and run.

Growing up in the "D", we had to watch out for gangs. My brothers and I would go downtown to the Adams Theatre and watch Bruce Lee movies. We had to be careful because we were in the gang neighborhood of the Errol Flynns and Black Killers (BKs). It was dangerous to be caught out after 8 p.m. So, we went to the early showings, and were gone long before the gang members got to the movies with their girlfriends.

Sadly, at the early age of 10, I was smoking and selling weed. I sold a joint for a dollar. My brother, Tony, gave it to me. I didn't know where he got it from, either. There were times when I would be so high out of my mind that I'd walk over to my grandma's house instead of going home. She thought that I was just tired from the walk. There was a time when some friends of mine asked to buy a $10.00 bag of weed. I told them I didn't have anything but $1.00 joints. I found out that my brother, Tony, was a big hustler right then. The person wanting to buy the weed asked me where my brother was. I told him that Tony didn't have that much weed either. He laughed out loud and said: *"Your brother is the weed man around here."* I didn't know that Tony was selling a lot of weed until that moment.

As a youth, I learned work ethics from my family - good and bad. Running numbers as a kid was just a way that I earned money. I even worked on an ice cream truck to make extra money. Normally, the ice cream lady paid me $5 a day, but most of the times, I only received $2.00 to $3.00 because she knew I would sometimes hide money from sales in my socks.

By the time I was 12 years old, I would hang at the local grocery store on the weekends assisting women by carrying their groceries for them. On Fridays and Saturdays, I could earn up to $40.00 a day. People were very generous after they cashed their checks. I would take my younger brother Cordell with me. He'd hold the money as I collected it.

We had to play it smart, too. Older guys would come from the Herman Garden projects and take the money from younger guys like me carrying groceries. So, I devised a plan. I would have Cordell posted somewhere watching me. I would motion him over every time I felt like I should put some money up. The older guys didn't suspect him holding the money; he was just a young kid playing outside the store. If the older guys decided to shake me down, they would only get a few bucks. As soon as I felt he had enough money, I sent him home on the bus. That was my hustle and I made it work. If the street life taught me anything, it taught me to hustle, have a good work ethic, and to think faster than my enemy. But what we saw as children—how my family lived, how our father interacted with our mother and more, influenced us positively and negatively. Soon the street mentality and the negative influences would affect the way we behaved.

IF THE TRUTH BE TOLD

It's amazing to me how one generation can have an influence on the next generation whether good or bad. Generational blessings and generational curses can both have an effect on a child's life. The monkey see, monkey do attitude is a trick the enemy uses frequently. A person who becomes comfortable with seeing certain things becomes comfortable with doing those same things. He or she becomes a product of their environment.

The Bible says that "iron sharpens iron" and it produces negative and detrimental results or positive and constructive results. Just as God molds and makes His people on the Potter's wheel, to make and mold you, the enemy, too, has a counterfeit wheel to do the exact same thing. Sadly, I was on the enemy's "potter's wheel" and he had some iron sharpening my iron.

SECTION TWO:
ISSUES OF BLOOD
1975-1978

IT'S A SHAME

I woke up to yelling, screaming, and the sounds of thumping on the floor. I got out of bed quickly to see what all the noise was about, but deep down inside I knew. I ran into the hallway which faced my parent's bedroom and I saw my mother crying. Her face had turned red and was beginning to swell. I was in disbelief. The next few seconds were a blur.

I saw my father raise his fist and hit my mother in the face again and again with uncontrolled anger. I was devastated. In a rage, I ran into their room, leaped on my father, and began pulling, punching and kicking him with all of my strength. I wanted to kill him, but it was only so much that a nine-year old could do. He was stronger than me! This was not the first time my father had hit my mother. He had even been arrested for domestic abuse several times before, but each time she got him out of jail.

They fought constantly. Every time my brothers and I would try to defend her. She would fight back, too. She would never just lie there and take it. My mom would throw a punch harder than him! She was tough. She could probably beat any woman her size. She always put emphasis on standing up and protecting yourself. She had *killer* in her blood! So, my father was always in for a fight. This is what made their fights so intense. She wouldn't back down! At those times, when we were pulling and hitting on him trying to protect our mom, he never tried to retaliate. I believe it was because he knew he was wrong.

He was jealous and always accusing her of seeing someone else. Due to his indiscretions, he no doubt saw himself in her. For instance, they were in a bowling league and he would accuse her of flirting or dating any man that spoke to her. Of course, because of her beauty, men would go out of their way to be kind to her, speak to her, or buy her a drink, but my father would take those actions to the extreme in his mind.

If someone asked her to dance when they went out, we would hear the arguments late into the night. He hated her friends and hated it even more when she socialized with them. He would often follow her. My pops became a certified professional at finding fault in the innocent.

When he did find fault with her, he would beat her. I was tired of him hitting her, tired of the yelling and accusations, just plain tired and angry! I was aggressive. When they would fight, I would go after him with a vengeance. I was unstoppable. I wanted to hurt him, like he hurt her. I wanted to make him suffer and cause him severe pain.

Even though I wasn't his favorite, he still showed enough interest to make me think of him as a great father. But as time went on, I began reasoning within myself: *He was my hero? How could my dad harm my mother? Was my father really this 'super dad' that I had made him out to be?* The images of him punching my mother in the face played over and over in my mind, this incident in particular since he was more violent than I'd seen him before. He was merciless; I began to see him in a different light and that light grew dimmer and dimmer.

What a life for a young boy. Sure, my family lived the middle-class life with ease, but we weren't happy. As a matter of fact, often, I was in a rage. Yes, I would be dressed 'fresh' every day at school. My dad drove a Caddy and my parents owned their own home. We lived well in our immaculate, perfect home with its plush carpet, new furniture and well-manicured lawn. Everything on the outside appeared to be perfect, but it wasn't because inside of me there was a huge void. Our neighbors respected and thought very highly of my father *and* our family; but it was all a cover-up, a lie. Only we knew the truth of our home life. As a result, we kept up the pretense. We were "Masters of Disguise."

Dad had a side to him that many on the outside never saw. He became more physically abusive to my mother day by day. In a distorted way, I knew that my dad loved my mom, but he was narcissistic, demanding, and jealous when it came to her. After so many incidents of his abuse, he was disgusting in my eyes. It got to where there was never any peace in our home. He was like a big spoiled child that threw temper tantrums when things didn't go his way. He was like Dr. Jekyll and Mr. Hyde. One minute, he was being controlling and manipulating, and the next minute he would be happy, sad, and then frustrated. We walked on egg shells.

I suppose because of my illness, he considered me as being the weakest link, so my aggression that particular night defending my mom caught him by surprise. Besides, with all of my hospital visits, my father didn't want to take on the frustrating responsibility of spending the night at Children's Hospital in the ER with me every time I got sick. Though my weakness was no doubt a disappointment to him, he soon realized that I had no problem challenging his authority when he would physically attack my mom. I believe that my aggressive behavior created additional animosity between us. I could not be controlled or stopped.

IF THE TRUTH BE TOLD

I didn't know my father's behavior was rooted in insecurity. Insecurity is a spirit and it's derived from fear. This spirit gets the better of us because we struggle at identifying who we really are. Satan is a deceiver; and he makes us think right is wrong and wrong is right. That's deception 101. He deceived my dad because my dad didn't know who he really was. As a result, he based his strengths on temporal and unimportant things. A good way to identify insecurity is when people strive for a certain image such as success, money, cars, clothes, and even talent in an effort to get the praise of people. We want to please changeable and wavering people, when we should aim to please Almighty God.

True and certain identity is found only in Christ. I didn't know that in the beginning, so the devil had me confused and searching. Now I know the devil is already a defeated foe; what he meant for evil, the almighty and all-knowing God would turn it around for good.

People in the world are searching for peace of mind. Some erringly look for it in drugs, alcohol, women, and in recreational activities, such as golf. But true, lasting peace is found only in Jesus Christ, because He is the Prince of Peace. Literally, the chastisement of our peace was laid upon Him. Any other peace is artificial or counterfeit. As I think about it, God doesn't mind people being miserable, because that misery leads to those same people seeking restoration.

R.E.S.P.E.C.T.

It got worse around our house. Dad worked and gambled mostly every weekend. Even though we were a two-income household and my father bought a new Cadillac every other year, he said that our family could only afford one car at the time. He drove to work every day while my mother would catch the bus to work.

It became more evident that because of my asthmatic condition, my father had a hard time accepting me and he treated me like I had a disability. He constantly pointed out that I overly exaggerate my condition. To be honest, there were times when I did use my condition to get my way, especially when I was being disciplined or on the brink of getting a whipping. I knew that if I cried hard enough and began to take deep breaths, my mother would stop my father from beating the brakes off of me. Still, I was a young boy and my condition was real. I felt like my father despised me at times.

I wanted so desperately to please my father. Every time I would try to win his approval he had a way of crushing my hopes. I just couldn't understand why he was as cruel as he was. *Was it because he did not receive love from his father?* I knew that he loved his family, but he would have outbursts of anger and he definitely didn't know how to show love. *Was it because society showed him that being a man meant that he had to be tough? Was it because he learned that men should not show or express their feelings? Could it be that I was dealing with insecurity myself?* Whatever the reason, my favorable impressions of my father diminished. I wasn't the only one with a diminished view of him. I was ten years old when the divorce papers came in the mail. We knew what they were. The papers from the lawyer came in thick, white envelopes and they usually came during the week. Our job was to get the mail before our father came home from work and put the papers up for my mother.

Mom had secretly planned to divorce my father and leave our home, but the court papers began coming in the mail before she could move out. One Saturday morning my father got the mail and saw the divorce papers. He woke all three of us boys up and read the divorce papers to us. The more he read the angrier he became! He told us that my mother did not love us and that she was trying to ruin his life.

After he finished reading the papers, he told us that he was going to go and wake our mother to ask her why she was ripping our family apart. He woke her up by pulling her out of the bed and at the same time punching her in her face. She woke up from her sleep screaming in agony, *"What the hell is wrong with you? Why did you hit me!?"* she yelled. We all ran into their bedroom. Mom had had enough. She openly expressed her anguish and disgust. But for all her unhappiness, Dad tried to downplay his actions as if hitting her was no big deal and that my mother was over exaggerating. He was a very manipulative person, telling us that she caused it and that she was faking when she fell on the floor. If my mother had any

38

doubts about divorcing him, they faded when he hit her that night. Their separation was eminent.

She moved out with my youngest brother, Cordell. She found her own place in a two-family flat. Poisoning us during this bitter episode in our family, my father told Tony and me that Mom didn't love us and she wanted to be with another man. That's why she didn't take us with her. We believed him. Our mother had left and only taken Cordell with her. What else could it be? Dad convinced us that our mother hated us. But the truth was she had to leave us with him because he wouldn't let her take us. She also didn't want him to find out where she lived for fear of his harassment and violence against her.

Bitterness set in and its roots grew deep down in me. It was because of his abusive treatment of my mother that she left us there when she moved out. I was bitter in my soul to the point of revenge. Bitterness took over my life like a festering and putrid wound; anytime he would do or say something to trigger the bitterness, it would infect the wound even more. The bitterness in me was so strong that I carried an uncontrolled and unforgiving evil with me daily. I had a chip on my shoulder. It was just waiting for him to knock it off so that I could do him bodily harm. When he would hurt my mother, I could feel her pain and I really wanted to make him feel what I was experiencing. I don't know how my mother endured this hardship with my father for so long. Maybe it was another test she thought she had to pass.

I hurt so much because before Mom left our home, I was with her all the time, due to my illness. She was very protective of me. When she left a part of me left, too, and I changed. Dealing with rejection and bitterness, I became more rebellious.

Dad had a lot of nerve. He was so intent on getting my mother back that he relaxed whipping us so much. He was a little easier to live with. What was interesting is that at the same time, I no longer experienced severe asthma attacks. Maybe it was because I no longer had my mother to take care of me. I don't know. It could have been that God was just healing me. I was growing up to the realities of life, but I deeply missed the comfort of my mother.

I began to see the world through different eyes. I saw my father for who he really was and how his manipulation, insecurity, and control ruined our family. I still loved him, but I was damaged by having an absent mother and living with a desperate father and no one to tell these secrets to.

IF THE TRUTH BE TOLD

Selfishness entered through the doorway of our house at some point in time. The Robinson's home desperately needed God's DNA, even though at the time we didn't know it. I wondered in later years if God had used that ugly situation to set us up for His glory. I don't know, but I do know that selfishness is the exact opposite of love. Hate is not the opposite of love. Selfishness breeds hate, and allows hatred to exist. Every self-centered person is capable of hating everything around, except for themselves. Selfishly pushing our own agendas forward makes life about 'me and me only.' Selfishness never takes the time to examine or consider someone else's feelings or needs. I believe that our whole house had become so thirsty for survival that we became selfish in our own ways to the extreme. We were trying to survive! Survival techniques make you only look out for yourself. That is why Jesus said to deny yourself. Just as selfishness entered through the door of our house, love was pushed out of the same door.

KEEP ON TRUCKIN'

After my mom moved out, our living conditions changed drastically. We could no longer live in our beautiful home until the divorce proceedings were final. So, we had to move in with our

Uncle Sugar Chile on St. Aubin and Leland Street near Mack Avenue and Chene. Uncle Sugar Chile had been a legend in his time.

His glory days gone, Uncle Sugar Chile was simply called Frank or Shug by his associates. He lived above a party store that he purchased, but that had gone out of business. Even though the store was closed, he still lived above it with his sister, Dorothy, in a three-bedroom apartment. Tony and I moved upstairs with them.

My father decided to bunk with our Uncle Gee who had taken the small room next to the party store downstairs and turned it into a studio apartment. There was a bed, bathroom, small kitchen, and a couch. Looking back, I believe my father moved in with Uncle Gee so he could live the life as a bachelor and come and go as he pleased.

Everything went down in Uncle Gee's crib! At our young ages, we saw a lot. Uncle Gee had connections to all of the low life's in Detroit. He sold dope, he hustled, he was a pimp, and more. If it was immoral, Uncle Gee did it. He was a gangster. We saw guns pulled on people, dope fiends getting high, and once we even saw a guy get pistol whipped! Uncle Gee didn't play. Actually, his wife was a gangster, too. She was the first lady pimp I had ever seen. We had to walk by Uncle Gee's apartment to get out of the building.

There were snacks and candy in the closed store below us and we feasted on them along with the rats. Most of it was stale, but we didn't care. Living with our uncles was thrilling. As the days went by, the hustler life appealed to me more and more.

Dad grew distant. According to the rumors, he was living the single life, and dating some of the women at the Chrysler plant where he worked. It was odd because he was still obsessed with reconciling with my mom. Over the next year, my father made every attempt and went to great lengths to win her over and to get his family back together. He was persistent and very resourceful. He was determined to find out where my mother was living and he was willing to go to any extreme.

One day he borrowed my Uncle Shug's car to follow my mother from her job to find out where she had moved. He disguised Tony, me, and himself in wigs! We followed her and found out where she lived. Later on that night, we went back to her place and pops sent us to knock on the door to try to get her to let us in. He told us that he would be down the street. He told us if she asks where I am, *"Tell her that I'm nowhere around. I promise you she won't let you in because she no longer wants to be involved with you all anymore or myself. She is determined to ruin all of our lives!"*

Well, when Mom refused to open the door for us, we became very hostile and we called her things that I refuse to repeat. My mother was very hurt by our disrespect; yet, she never held our actions against us, because she knew that Dad was poisoning our minds against her. We felt ashamed afterwards but, we just wanted our mom to come back home.

My father became so desperate to get her back that he even told my mother different stories to get her to come home. Some of them were really outlandish. For example, one night while we were visiting with mom at Grandma Alice's house, the phone rang. The caller asked if my mother was there. My grandma gave the phone to my mom. The caller then told my mom that they were calling from a phone booth and that Dad had been shot. The man on the phone told her that she needed to come to Oakman and Grand River right outside of Federal's Department Store to see about him. The man said that the ambulance had been called, but it wasn't looking too good, he might die.

Naturally, my mom was upset and she was on her way out of the door when my Grandpa Buck stepped up and stopped her from leaving. He said, *"Don't you see this is a trick Berneice? It's a lie! Nothing is wrong with him. He's just trying to convince you to come to where he is."* Grandpa Buck stood in the doorway and said, "You are not leaving this house over my dead body!" Grandpa Buck was right. There was never any record of him being shot or even going to the hospital.

Dad was relentless. On another occasion, he sent a letter to my mother, via my grandmother's home address. The letter was on hospital stationary. It said that he'd been diagnosed with cancer. Yep, he tried to get her to come back to him by making her think he was dying once again. When that didn't work he went to see the 'Voodoo Lady!' The 'Voodoo Lady' had my dad sprinkle holy water and garlic over the door to keep the devil out. She told him to get a brush with my mother's hair in it so she could make up some concoction. All while he was doing this stuff he'd tell my brother and me, *"She lied to me. She wants another man."* We were young, but we knew that he didn't trust her because he was unfaithful and running around on her. That insecurity was working overtime. Well, the concoction that the voodoo lady cooked up was supposed to hurt Mom. He told us, "Every time she is in the presence of that man her head is going to hurt badly." He tried everything, but it didn't work. He even tried to emotionally scar her. He'd take us to court with him during the divorce proceedings. I'm sure he was trying to appeal to her emotions by dangling the family in front of her. Mom, on the other hand, always came alone. When that didn't work, he brought some woman he was seeing at the time. Well, that backfired too. My mother's attorney pointed out to the judge that my father was accompanied by his new girlfriend in court and he wasn't even divorced yet!

Despite his best attempts to get her to come back home my mother refused to give in to his antics. She was free from being under his control. She was safe, maybe even happy.

IF THE TRUTH BE TOLD

Freedom costs; what is a man willing to pay to be free? The price for true freedom is much higher than any man can pay. But the good news is that Jesus has already paid the price for our freedom. We constantly seek love, joy, and peace in alcohol, drugs, relationships, material things. It's a void we are trying to satisfy. God has placed this void in all of mankind so that He alone can fill it. David said, God is my strength, my refuge, my present help in the time of trouble. Our family was in trouble. We went everywhere searching for what we thought we didn't have. We knocked on every door but the door to Christ. My mother was searching for this freedom; and my father was desperately searching for this same freedom, too.

AIN'T TOO PROUD TO BEG

My father was still working on devising a plan to get back with my mother. He had a friend at Chrysler named Brother Darrell. Brother Darrell got an opportunity to minister to Dad about having a relationship with the Lord and the responsibilities of the man and woman who follow God. Dad's friend took time to persuade him that he and his wife needed Jesus in their lives. He told him that the devil's job was to separate his family, and that Satan came to kill, steal and destroy. Listening earnestly to his friend, a light went on in his head. My father believed that if he followed Jesus, Jesus would reunite his family. He was desperate, he wanted his wife back!

My father agreed to give his life to the Lord. Afterwards, he immediately asked his friend and his wife to speak to my mother about the Lord, too. Dad's hardest test was if he was going to give up all that he acquired from the street life to regain his family? I questioned in myself, *did he realize what it would cost him? How would this affect the household?*

So, the dilemma my father faced was either to make the sacrifice to change or accept a divorce from my mom. Something in me wonders even now if, after consulting an attorney, my father

44

knew he had more to lose had my mother divorced him. Now I know why he would always sing that song, "It's cheaper to keep her!" He would have had to pay alimony and child support. As a result, he may not have been able to sustain the image of having the fancy clothes and driving a new car every other year.

I couldn't help thinking, *was he really going to sell out to God and sacrifice his fast and profitable lifestyle? Or was this just another one of his schemes to get my mom back and become the center of our universe again?* Well, in truth Pops changed his life and did a 180-degree turnaround. We joined a Pentecostal church and he became a man of God. He was spiritually connected. He stopped gambling and running around with women and partying. He gave up the after-hour joints and changed his friends. He stayed home at night with us.

He took us to church every Sunday. I can recall asking him why I couldn't hang with my friends as much. He told me, *"Son, we are living our lives for the Lord now and God wants us to do things that are pure and righteous. So, we had to give up those impure and unrighteous things. The Bible says separate yourself from amongst them!"* My father actually counseled me like a father would counsel his son. He was really making a change and I could see it.

My father meant the world to me again, though I did have concerns about giving up everything for the Lord. Since my father said we would do it, then that's how it was going to be and I was not going to stand in his way. I wanted to change, too. It's amazing how a father has influence over the entire household.

I realized that God was really doing something in my dad's life and Dad wanted his family back together. I liked the new man he was becoming. It appeared that my father, mother, and their church friends did have a conversation about the Lord. Her return wasn't instantaneous; however, she did begin attending church services with us. She strove to build a sincere relationship with the Lord. She grew closer to the Lord and she learned her role and responsibilities as the woman of the home. She wanted to do the right thing and honor the Lord with her life and family. Yet, she took her time and observed my father's actions. My father began to treat my mother with dignity and respect.

My mother saw the changes in his behavior towards her and realized that not only was he attending church, he had even given up his street life and his afterhours joints. Mr. James Robinson now had brand new friends who were impacting him positively and showing him the way of holiness.

My mother changed too. She had a sharp tongue and would let you have it if she felt disrespected. After joining the Pentecostal church she developed more patience as she increased in the knowledge of Jesus. It was different for us because we had never really been members of a church. The last time I even remembered attending any type of church services on a regular basis was at the Mosque. My father was heavy into the Muslim lifestyle and culture. Now, as church members, my brothers and I really enjoyed church services. It was exciting and Jesus was bringing our family back together!

After some time of observing my father's behavior, Mom returned home and stopped the divorce proceedings. We began attending church as a family. Our whole entire life shifted again. My mom and dad were filled with the gift of the Holy Ghost and they spoke in tongues! We found out that speaking in tongues was speaking in a heavenly language. God uses your voice to speak His language. We were now living a new and different reality.
My father pulled it off! He got his family back together. He went from serving the devil to serving Jesus! I was impressed.

OVERDOSE OF THE HOLY GHOST

It was my younger brother, Cordell, who saw the telecast of "The Hour of Power." Pastor Bonner was a preaching machine at the Church of Our Lord Jesus Christ, which later became Solomon's Temple, located at 2341 E. Seven Mile Rd. Cordell asked our parents if we could please visit. He said, "If I go to that church I would receive the Holy Spirit." We would watch Pastor Bonner on television every Sunday before we would go to our own home church.

We were in the process of looking for another church home because there were problems going on at the one we were attending. Cordell, like me and my brother Tony, wanted an overdose of the Holy Ghost that my mother and father had received. We would go into the prayer room, get on our knees and pray that Jesus would baptize us with his Holy Spirit, but we would never receive this gift that they made such a fuss about. For some reason, we would always leave the prayer room disappointed and tired, which was just another form of rejection to me. My parents said yes to Cordell's request and we went to the Church of Our Lord Jesus Christ on Sunday, May 21, 1978. I can still remember the service. I was 13 years old, Tony was 15, and Cordell was 7. The service was charged with the Holy Spirit. It was like there was an electrical current flowing through the service.

The presence of the Holy Spirit was stronger than I had ever felt since we had been attending church for the last few months. The power of God was present to destroy the oppressive yokes from the people's lives! Pastor Bonner ended services with an altar call and asked people to come down front to surrender their lives to God.

We felt God tugging on us to go up to the altar. Cordell kept his promise and stood up and following his lead, sure enough we all walked briskly down to the altar together, which was at the front of the church. We were ready. I'll never forget that day! The altar workers ushered us into the prayer room. There were four of us in there, three boys and another man. After only a few minutes, the report went back to the church that there are four young men in the prayer room and three of them are already speaking in tongues.

My mother heard the report and began to scream and praise God out loud right in service! She said that she knew at least two of her sons had received the baptism of the Holy Ghost. The Holy Spirit fell down on all of us so hard, just like that rushing mighty wind in the book of Acts. It was electric.

We all received the baptism of the Holy Spirit and now we were speaking in a heavenly language. From then on, we were known as the "Three Hebrew Boys," because we were all biological brothers who got filled with the Holy Spirit at the same time. We found favor with Pastor Bonner. I believe we held a special place in our Pastor's heart from that day forward. The Three Hebrew boys were young men in the Bible who were taken captive during the Babylonian reign over Jerusalem. This story can be found in the book of Daniel. Those three boys refused to worship the golden idol that the Babylonian king had built because of their convictions. They would only worship the one true and living God. However, because they disobeyed the command of the king to worship the idol, the three boys were thrown into the fiery furnace to die.

The furnace was heated seven times hotter than normal. It was so hot that the guards who threw them in the furnace died while putting them in. Well, the three Hebrew boys survived. When the king looked in to see their demise, they were walking around in the furnace, and another man was there who looked like the Son of God! Suffice it to say, the Hebrew boys were released because their God proved Himself to be the only true GOD! The boys came out untouched by the fire and heat; they didn't even smell like smoke! So we felt honored to be called The Three Hebrew Boys.

The next Sunday, we joined the church. Our whole family stood before the congregation. Everyone from every age group stood up clapping and welcoming our family into the church. It felt good to meet all of the young people at the church who genuinely were happy to meet us. We felt like we were home. Moses (Tony)

Coleman Jr., personally welcomed me into the church and we later became the best of friends.

Pastor Bonner took us under his wing and was very concerned about our family and our spirituality. He reached out to our family with support with the love of Christ. I enjoyed going to church. Tony and I eventually joined the Joy Bells choir; it was a well-known 100 voice choir, full of young people ages 15 to 35.

There were so many young people there. We were also a part of the *Young Men for Christ* a group led by Terrance Coleman, Moses' older brother. He was an excellent mentor and spiritual teacher to the young men in the ministry. To top it off, my father was appointed to the Deacon board by Pastor Bonner, after we had been attending for a while. My mother joined the Radio Choir, so we were all one hundred percent active in ministry.

Pastor Bonner loved us. There were times he would interview us on his television broadcast. Yes, the "Three Hebrew Boys" would sit and talk with Pastor Bonner on television. I remember him asking us how it felt to be saved and his chuckle after I told him, "I was thankful that God had delivered me from sin." It was true. Although, I was only 13 years old, I witnessed and experienced sin first hand. I gambled, stole, smoked weed, cussed and even tried to drink liquor at times, but now I was delivered. I found that having a relationship with the Lord brought me a sense of peace in my once chaotic world. And despite my illness and limitations I was finally accepted. I had real joy. My family was together and now we had a place where our souls could find rest. I realized that God had a better plan for my life.

IF THE TRUTH BE TOLD

Jesus said, "By their fruit you shall know them". Then, the Apostle Paul said in Galatians 5:22 that the fruit of the Spirit is love, joy, peace, patience, kindness, goodness, faith, gentleness and self-control. The fruit always reveals the root and I watched my father begin to express the godly characteristics that the Apostle Paul was explaining. I heard people in the church say things like, *"I can see the glow of Christ on you"*, and my father really did have that glow.

He told everyone he came into contact with about Jesus. He wanted to save the world. He was determined that no one in his household was going to hell. He talked about Jesus so much, you were going to either love Him or hate Him. He was the priest of our home and he became a true man of God.

SECTION THREE:

BLOOD CLOTS

1980-1982

THERE'S A GHOST IN MY HOUSE

We sat in Pastor Bonner's office as my father tried to explain himself, once again. I had to seek the Lord and the counsel of our Pastor, because my father was gunning for me. Yes, we went to church every Sunday, but my father's disdain for his family had steadily increased. My father would belittle and ridicule us. He had become as mean as a junkyard dog.

It could have been because I asked too many questions. I was the one who stirred the pot or ruffled the feathers in our home. I sincerely sought out help for our family. We finally found a safe haven at the Church of Our Lord Jesus and Pastor Bonner actually took the time to listen to our family concerns.

We were under so much pressure to please my father, because he had started to revert to his old controlling ways, but this time it was worse. Internally, my father was miserable. It was true; he had gotten rid of his old habits of clubbing, chasing women and hustling. He no longer smoked, drank or hung out; neither did he physically challenge my mother any more. He became a different sort of person— he was religious and with that came severe verbal abuse.

Our whole world as young boys had already turned upside down. Things were different. We could barely hang out with our friends any more. We had an early curfew. We could no longer talk to our friends or girls on the telephone after 8:00 p.m. That was difficult because up to that point we were accustomed to having lots of freedom to experience the "thug lifestyle" in the streets.

With the change in our lifestyle, we were known in the neighborhood as church boys. That still wasn't enough for Dad. I think he'd bitten off more than he could chew. Yes, this transition was difficult for us, but it appeared to be a natural death for him.

Misery was written all over his face. His scrutiny, especially of me, worsened. He walked around the house mad at the world and yelling at everyone for any little thing. He was like a mad man. One could assume that maybe he had some convictions, because he no longer did the things he used to do; but it appeared that part of him may have still desired that life. He found fault in anything and any one. He was always right and never wrong.

With no regard for our feelings or self-esteem, he would openly embarrass us. He had become cruel and unsympathetic. I thought to myself, *was he rebelling against God? It sure seemed like it.* I guess we all do that when we accept Jesus as Lord but only give him access to certain areas of our lives. We are quick to tell God what we want, but we don't ask Him what He *requires* of us. Thus, the inward struggle begins and continues until we completely surrender.

Life had become unbearable, so I sought out help. I was always the one who wanted to have family meetings to discuss things. I would even get an outside party to talk to him to prove to him that he was wrong to treat us the way that he did. I went to Pastor Bonner for counseling several times regarding issues with my father. Pastor Bonner would call us all in as a family for counseling.

In front of Pastor, he'd deny everything. So, one day I took my tape recorder and taped my dad while he was yelling at everyone in the house. It was his normal routine, so catching him in the act wasn't hard to do. The hard part was getting him not to notice that he was being recorded.

I felt it was my duty to prove to Pastor Bonner that my father was behaving terribly, because it was affecting my mom. I remember her saying that she never wanted to come home after work. She said she felt like driving off the freeway overpass and ending it all, instead of coming home. Mom said the only thing that kept her from going through with the plan, was that she wanted to raise her children. It's amazing how you can feel the presence of evil spirits, just as you can feel the presence of the Lord. The closer she would get to the house the more she felt the oppression of the evil spirits. We all felt it. Demonic spirits have the tendency to turn up the heat seven times hotter suggesting evil plans to get you to end your life.

I had to do something. My father's behavior was affecting all of us. I took the tape recorder to Pastor Bonner and he was astonished. That day during our family counseling session, Pastor Bonner reprimanded my dad hard. He told him that he would eventually push his boys out into the streets, if he continued to be so overly demanding on us. Because he respected Pastor Bonner, my father would accept the scolding from him and maintain his cool for about a week, but soon after he would return to his scornful ways.

It was my father that made this choice. He chose to have his wife and family back under the same roof. He chose his religion over the street life that he was used to. He chose to live a holy lifestyle and raise his boys up in the church. However, he was going about it with a fury.

He became unbearable and once again my mom was living a life of agony and despair. Our family was living as *religious* as could be. We went to church, but there was no peace in our home. *Was the change I saw before authentic or was it just to get my mom back?* He was like Dr. Jekyll and Mr. Hyde and I couldn't take it anymore.

IF THE TRUTH BE TOLD

My father always quoted these scriptures: *"Wives submit yourselves unto your own husbands, as it is fit in the Lord. Children obey your parents in all things: for this is well pleasing unto the Lord."* He neglected to mention these scriptures; *"Fathers, provoke not your children to anger, lest they be discouraged. Husbands love your wives and be not bitter against them."* Those scriptures addressed the alignment of a good Christian family. Our home "almost" had biblical alignment, but almost isn't good enough.

My mother was submissive to my father and we were obedient to our parents. Dad didn't live up to his portion of the scripture. He was using a tactic called "Bibliomancy." Bibliomancy means to use the scriptures to control people. It is a form of manipulation and witchcraft.

He was determined to provoke his children to wrath and to condemn everyone in the household. Condemn means to disqualify you from service. I saw my father take on this self-righteous spirit which meant whatever you do is right and if someone is not doing what you are doing, they are wrong. We were always wrong, although we were trying to do right and impress him. Because we were trying to please our dad to the extreme, we were not pleasing our Heavenly Father.

RUNAWAY CHILD RUNNING WILD

One day I was on my way to play open basketball at Detroit Mackenzie High School and Dad just started arguing. He had his reasons for arguing, but there was no point in my reasoning. That particular day, he refused to let up. He started accusing me of wanting to leave the house to go sell drugs or have sex with girls. He always accused me of that to provoke me or make me feel guilty.

The irony of all of it all was that I loved God so much that I didn't want to follow what everyone else was doing. Plus, I was only sixteen years old! Even though I knew other dudes my age were having sex, I still refused to go down that path. I wanted to be accepted and pleasing to God. Besides that I was afraid of the repercussions from the Lord.

No matter what I said to defend myself, my father just kept on nagging me. I couldn't take it any longer. I lost it and told him, "Since you don't care about me, I should just kill myself." I just said that as an afterthought to get him to stop harassing me. I really didn't want to kill myself. *Did he really care if I did?* Instead of saying, *"Son, think about what you are saying, or don't do it,"* he looked me in the eyes and said, *"Boy you ain't gonna kill yourself. You're just bluffing!"*

That was it! I ran into the bathroom, grabbed a bottle of pills from the medicine cabinet, poured a handful in my hand, and put them in my mouth. I was angry and I was going to prove my point. I closed my mouth full of pills and realized that I had to make a choice. Either, I was going to spit them out and prove to my dad that he was right or I was going to swallow all of them. I grabbed a cup of water and washed the pills down. I swallowed all of them. Even then, he maintained that I was bluffing. I must have been out of my mind but living under that pressure was so difficult. I thought to myself, *why did I always have to go so far? What's wrong with me? Is he really my biological father? Do fathers' treat their children this way? Why is he harder on me than my other two brothers? Is it because I had asthma? Is it because I challenged him more when he and my mom would fight? There was something to his anger that I just couldn't figure out? If God is so loving, why are we being punished?*

These were the thoughts that constantly played over and over in my head. He scrutinized everything I did. None of it was right. He didn't recognize that he was destroying his family once again. It was ironic that the same person that God used to bring joy into our home the devil used to bring misery again. If I'd ever been in a spiritual battle, I recognized that was one.

After storming out of my house, crying uncontrollably, I had to speak to God. I screamed toward heaven, *"Lord, why am I going through this!? Where are you God!? I need help, I need direction! God, I feel empty. I feel like I am nothing. I have given my whole young life to you, but you allow my father to continue to belittle, reject, and hurt me. I can't take it anymore. I just want to end it all. No one will miss me anyway!"*

For so long I heard the loving "Jesus" preached in church, but at home I was being preached to about another Jesus. The 'Jesus'

56

that my father preached was always condemning, always judging, and always sizing me up. That 'Jesus' was looking for me to fail. Even my brother, Tony, told my father, "*I don't want the JESUS you serve. That Jesus is too religious*". After a time, Tony became distant. He was failing in school. He wasn't abiding by the rules in the house. He began to get in trouble for selling weed and displaying a rebellious attitude. While Cordell and I really loved being in church and were living a changed life, Tony seemed to go in another direction. He was so much like our father. He had to do things his way.

It had only been a couple of years, since my father had transformed into the best father in the world. He had changed his life around and was raising us up in the church. Now, his religious and domineering attitude was changing the entire atmosphere of our home. It had become a cold, hard place full of tension. I was suffocating! I hated being at home so much that I thought about committing a crime, just so I could be sent to juvenile to get out of the house!

After swallowing the bottle of pills, I ran out of the house and went to play basketball. In the back of my mind I thought, *Should I go to the hospital?* I even began to worry that I was quite possibly going to drop dead while playing. I played several games. I'd forgotten all about what happened earlier.

I'm sure that it was the grace of God that covered me and nothing happened, not even a stomachache! I had a peace of mind because I was away from the nightmare on Northlawn Street with Freddie Krueger being played by my father. Anytime spent outside of that house was a peaceful time.

After that event, it wasn't long before I'd had enough again. A few weeks had passed and I yelled at the top of my lungs, "That's it! I'm ready to blow this joint!" I grabbed my basketball and left the house in anger. Once again, I needed to get away. I wasn't going to take this brutality from my dad any longer. *I'm leaving and I'm never coming back,* I thought. *I wasn't even going to go to Grandma Alice's house, where I would sometimes go to get a break. Nope, my pops didn't care for me anyway so let him sweat and worry about me for once.*

It was a warm fall day, so when I left the house I decided to go shoot some hoops at the court not too far from our house. It had gotten dark and I had no idea where I would stay the night. I was shooting baskets alone when out of nowhere a huge barking, dog came running at me with big, ferocious teeth. With my ball in my hand, I crouched down low and waited until he got closer to me and then WHAM, I hit him smack dead in his mouth with the ball. He ran off yelping. For a minute, I thought I was a goner. That was my cue to jet and find safety and shelter. I felt the closest and safest place for me to sleep was on top of the Lutheran Church roof across the street from the basketball court. I was glad that it was early fall because had it been winter, I'd probably have had to go back home. I climbed up the church onto the roof, found a cozy spot, used my basketball as my pillow, and fell asleep.

Early that morning I was awakened by the misty rain and the cold dew that had already formed on my sweat suit. My clothes were damp and I smelled like the outdoors. I decided to head on home knowing that my parents had already left for work. *I know I said I wouldn't return, but now I am cold, wet, and tired. I'll just get some rest and leave before they return home,* I thought.

Later that afternoon, I was awakened by my father yelling, "I thought you were leaving? Get out of my house and go and sleep where you slept last night!" *Man, I must have overslept, because I was trying to be out of this house before my parents returned home. What a welcome home and a way to wake up! Here we go with the badgering.* My father ranted and raged. He kept going on and on about me leaving without letting him know where I had gone.

My head pounded agonizingly. I wished for earplugs to drown him out and to top it all off, I had nowhere to go. I snapped. I sprinted into the kitchen and reached underneath the sink and grabbed a bottle of bleach. I drank the bleach then lay back down in my bed. I was tired of existing like that.

I woke up in an ambulance transporting me to the hospital. My mother was sitting beside me. My father was nowhere to be found. I didn't think he would be there anyway. Thoughts of my dad faded as I kept throwing up blood. *Am I really going to die this time? Lord, I'm only sixteen and I'm too young to die. Kids like me do stupid stuff. Lord, please forgive me and save my life,* I pleaded sincerely to God and repented for my behavior. God heard me and my prayers were answered again.

IF THE TRUTH BE TOLD

The spirit of rejection had consumed me. Rejection is when a person feels neglected or unloved by the people who should love him or her the most. It makes you wonder at times what you did to cause the pain, or what you did to deserve that rejection. Rejection usually links up with the spirit of rebellion. The person experiencing this may resort to rebellious and reckless living just to gain attention from the one rejecting and withholding love. It even causes a person to attempt suicide in an effort to seek attention. Rejection leaves one feeling abandoned.

If the truth be told there is only One who can fill the empty void inside of us. While I sought attention from my dad, Jesus was seeking attention from me. He said, *"Come unto me all ye that labor and are heavy laden and I will give you rest"* (Matthew 11:28). I just didn't know how to receive His rest at that time.

TEARS OF A CLOWN

St. Martin de Porres in Detroit was the best school I had ever attended, and it was considered a sports school. It was known for sports and had a family atmosphere. Attending de Porres gave me purpose. I was blessed to be there in the first place. My parents were looking for a school to put Tony in because he had been kicked out of the Detroit Public School system. St. Martin de Porres was a Catholic school. Most attendees were there on athletic scholarships; because tuition had to be paid, my parents were only going to send Tony there. I asked my parents if I could go, too. My grandmother Alice sat down and talked to them about it, as well. She questioned why discourage Michael from going especially since he is doing well in school? They always discouraged me from what I wanted to do. I wanted to play the organ and I wanted to box, but that was shot down. I had an art scholarship to a school in Pennsylvania; my dad discouraged me from taking that, as well. So, I wasn't surprised by them rejecting my request for de Porres, but thank God for my grandmother. My parents listened and Tony and I both were soon attending the great St. Martin de Porres. Tony found out I was going to have a fight after school; he got to the guy before I did. When I got there, my brother and the guy were already fighting. All I got was a few kicks in. We went to school the next day and we were called to the principal's office over the school's public announcement (P.A.) system.

On the way to the office Tony said to me, *"Mike I'm always getting kicked out of school, so I will take the rap and there's no need for both of us to get in trouble."* I was speechless. That was the first time Tony ever stood up for me. I felt unconditional love from him for the first time. It was such a shocking surprise because normally he and I were always in competition with each other. He had favor in our house and I didn't. So I determined to outdo him and he was determined to suppress me. We must have fought each other once a week for at least seven years of our lives. He won all but one of those fights. When I finally won a fight, he didn't fight me anymore.

While attending St. Martin de Porres, I met some of the best athletes of my generation; athletes who went on to be professionals in the world of sports. St. Martin de Porres was the best school ever! The following year, Tony decided to drop out of school and he made up in his mind to take the GED exam. I decided to leave de

Porres, even though it was full of great talent. For the most part, it was because I was riding the bench for the basketball team and I needed more playing time. (The good thing is my brother Cordell became a basketball great himself. He was all state for three years and ranked the 88th best in the United States when he was just in the 11th grade.)

I convinced my parents to allow me to attend St. Hedwig High School, which was class D and I was better able to strive to be a basketball great. I looked for a starting job on the team. I was in the eleventh grade when I went to St. Hedwig High School, but they mistakenly put me in the twelfth grade. It would have been great to be a senior and graduate at 17 years old, but I wanted to play at least two years of high school basketball. Mom was with me when they made me a senior. I was going to say something about it, but she kicked my feet under the table, I knew what that kick meant. She wanted me to just roll with it and so I did. Since she graduated at fifteen she wanted me to achieve academically and take advantage of this opportunity.

When I think about it, none of the men on either side of our family within the last twelve years ever graduated from high school. Along with Tony, my cousins all dropped out of school. This was my opportunity to be the one to break the curse in our family. My father dropped out of high school in the tenth grade, so of course I wanted to make him proud.

Things remained just as chaotic as ever at home, but it didn't bother me as much. I knew that if I stayed focused I would be the first son to graduate from high school and to graduate early. Things were looking up for me. I wasn't sure about my career plans after graduation, but I knew I would come up with something. I was determined to be somebody.

That year flew by fast, and just when I thought everything was going good, trouble rounded the corner. The school found out that I was really a junior. My mother and I spoke with the principal. The principal stated that I could still walk across the stage with the graduating class, but I would not get my diploma until I went to summer school and completed additional credits. Mom and I accepted the principal's offer.

Everyone, even my dad, was at my graduation. Although he didn't congratulate me like most proud parents, I was happy that he was there. I walked across the stage and I was so surprised to find out that they did, in fact, give me my diploma; so I didn't have to go to summer school after all. I accomplished so much that year. I was so proud of myself. I was still riding high from getting my high school diploma early. I was planning on getting a summer job and I really had my future in mind. My mom convinced me to take classes at Wayne County Community College. She said that it would help me decide what career I was really interested in. I followed Mom's advice and went to community college. I was a little apprehensive about going to college, and I wasn't the best student but overall things looked promising for me.

YOU KEEP ME HANGING ON

Dang! Who is that?! I was mesmerized. She was short, about five feet with brown skin. She was drop dead gorgeous and had a smile that could wake a dead man! She was fine as wine. I couldn't take my eyes off of her. I met Mary at the skating rink. We were at our church's skating party and one of the girls in the choir brought her sister with her. They called for threesome skaters so I took the chance and walked up to her and her friend, winked, and asked if they wanted to skate. I had to get close to her.

She had a flirtatious way about her and it was easy to talk to her. We laughed and skated all night. I wanted to see her again and again. I would talk to her on the phone sometimes and I kept inviting her to church. Her sister, Sherry, attended our church. So, whenever I saw Sherry I asked when she going to bring her sister to church. She would always say she's coming next Sunday and then next Sunday would come, but no Mary. I wanted to see her again so badly.

After much prayer on my part, she started coming to church every now and then. No doubt her sister, Sherry, told her I was asking about her. I was extra nice to Sherry, making sure she was on my side. Sherry didn't have a choir robe, so I gave her mine so she wouldn't look out of place. Our robes were brown and I had a sweet Yves St Lauren, brown suit that blended nicely with our choir robes, so the choir director didn't mind me lending my robe to her. I also loaned her my robe to put pressure on her so she would bring Mary to church. Mary knew that I liked her; and shortly thereafter she started coming to church regularly and joined the choir.

One night, Mary received the baptism of the Holy Ghost—she was speaking in tongues. I praised God and shouted all over that church to the top of my voice! Everybody there knew that she was my girl, because I had never praised God like that before. She was saved, she was fine, and she was all mine! It didn't matter that she was three years older than me either; because our connection was the church and God had brought us together. When that happened, I wanted Mary to have my robe and Sherry could get her own, but after thinking twice I realize that wouldn't be a good idea.

Even though I had someone who cared for me, I felt the noose my father had around my neck tightened. My father hated the fact that Mary was independent, had a job, that she had access to transportation, and that she was my friend. Mary also had a three-year old daughter. Mary was 20 and I was 17 when we met. I lied at first and told her I was 20. When she found out my real age, it didn't take her long to get over me being younger than she was.
We were inseparable. She had a difficult home life, too. Her father was an alcoholic; and her mother left her dad and moved into a one room apartment. That meant that she and her sisters had to live with their father.

Mary had her own car and we began to see more and more of each other as things at home got worse. She helped create havoc in my house because she was grown and had a car. I would call her when my father became intolerable. She knew I was going through hell with my dad. I would call her and she would say, "Michael, I'll come and get you," and she would. I would start walking and she would meet me at our pick-up spot on the corner of Livernois and Davison. We would ride around all night. Some nights, we would just sit at the park until the police told us it was time to leave.

To have a drinking problem, Mary's father maintained a regular routine. Every morning like clockwork, he would leave the house around 7:00 a.m., go to the neighborhood liquor store; hang out all day with his friends and return home around 8:00 p.m. at night. His schedule never changed.

Mary became my escape. She loved the Lord as much as I did. We had so much in common in addition to the issues with our fathers. She understood me. She sought God's help as much as I did. From time to time when I needed her to come and scoop me up from the mad house I lived in, she would come. She needed an escape, too, from her dad's drinking problem. I could relax at her house. Mary gave me a sense of peace. She would make a palette on her bedroom floor with blankets and pillows; it was some of the best sleep that I would ever have. That also meant that we would have to drive around all night until morning, then head back to her house when the coast was clear. I would crash and go to sleep on her bedroom floor. We were not having sex, because we were so sold out for Jesus. We knew that fornication was taboo. We did, however, come close to fornicating more than once, but God kept us. I've always been the kind of person that if I believe in something, then I'm willing to die for it. I believed in living righteously.

This particular day was just like any other day at home. My dad was having his usual temper tantrum. I decided that I wasn't going to stay and take the tongue lashing. Thank God for my girl, Mary. As soon as he saw me making the call he started accusing me of having sex and being a whoremonger and a fornicator. He would have been surprised that I was 17 years old and still a virgin. Mary and I had only kissed each other. My father ranted, "If you leave the house with that girl then don't come back!" I packed my things and moved in with Grandma Alice. My grandma always received me with open arms.

I was no longer welcome in my father's house, but I had a safe haven at my grandma's house. I was also working construction for Bishop Bonner helping to build the youth center, at that time. He hired all of the young men who wanted to work.

I had a peace of mind at Grandma Alice's house. She was still the numbers lady getting her hustle on, but she was still concerned about my life. She loved my girlfriend. It didn't matter to Grandma that she was older and that she had a baby. Mary also found favor with her because her license plate was 720 and that was Grandma's favorite number. She would tell Mary, *"Baby, every time I see your license plate I hit the number."* She would even give us $15.00 to $20.00 each for being her lucky charms.

Grandma was a wonderful woman. And just like it appeared that my dad wanted to hold me back, Grandma wanted to see me succeed. I had become a man. I was in college taking courses and making a living. In fact, I worked a couple of jobs. I worked at McDonald's and then at Phillip's Shoes in downtown Detroit. As a salesperson, the store dress code required that I wear dress slacks, shirts, ties, or suits sometimes. I didn't mind the attire because this is what I wore to church all the time and I enjoyed dressing to impress. I was transitioning into manhood and I was determined to be someone that my mother, father, and other people could be proud of. That is why I wanted to work and attend school.

Soon living a life of purity and holiness would prove difficult. We were growing up, I was becoming a man and Mary and I were always together. One weekend, Mary's mom decided to go and visit her relatives in another state. She asked Mary to housesit her apartment. There we were alone in her mom's apartment with no supervision. One thing led to another and I had sex for the first time in my life with the love of my life. We felt so guilty afterwards, that we both immediately got on our knees at the foot of the bed and began to repent. We prayed hard and asked God to forgive us of our sins and we believed that He did. But we were young people and we had eaten forbidden fruit—the next day we had to repent all over again.

IF THE TRUTH BE TOLD

The spirit of rejection will always have you looking for a replacement. I believed at that time Mary was God sent to be that replacement. Mary was the band aid to some of the frustration and rejection I faced at home. She gave me hope and mollified the putrid wounds and bruises that were caused because of my father rejecting me.

SECTION FOUR:

BLEEDING OUT

1982-1984

HELPLESS

Things went well for me on my job at Phillips Shoes, until one of the guys introduced me to a way to steal from the store. The store didn't keep good track of their inventory. That made it easy to sell items and pocket the money. We only told the older dudes, because we thought that the younger customers would tell on us. So, I would sell a pair of shoes for half the cost and pocket the money. Then someone came up with a grand scheme to take the sales slips to pocket more money. When I took the sales slip, I got caught. My manager questioned that there was one missing. I denied taking it; but they watched me so closely that I became nervous and my manager eventually pressured me to quit.

I was still living at Grandma Alice's house. Everyone including my cousins would crash there like it was their home. Grandpa Buck got tired of this and started putting everyone out of the house, including me. I ended up at Auntie Shoo Shoo's house, who welcomed me with open arms. Since I wasn't working anymore I started hanging with my cousin, Black. I couldn't find a job anywhere. It was like the devil was telling me *"A man gotta do, what a man gotta do"*.

Black's lifestyle made me think there was a future in being independent. The thought of surviving without my dad's help gave me a feeling of victory. I decided to survive no matter what I had to do. My brother, Tony, was a small time drug seller at this point. He was driving some guy's car, picking up money, and dropping off drugs. Whenever he came around he'd mock me like I was nothing.

I needed and wanted to be independent. To be a man and take care of myself was the only thing on my mind. I wanted to work with Black, who was a small time drug seller, too, but couldn't. I wound up working in the most uncomfortable environment; I was scared out of my mind. But I knew I couldn't show it because there was danger all around me. I learned at an early age how to hide my fear and to adjust instantly. I could roll with the punches, but in that environment, I was paranoid. I didn't trust anybody. Those were hard knocks and I had to show everyone that I was a man.

Where I was, the smell alone would knock someone dead. The house was raggedy and unsanitary; electricity was on illegally, it was stolen from the neighbor's house to have the lights on. We used kerosene heaters to warm the place up. Desperate, because I needed a job and a place to stay, I landed the worst job that I ever had. To top it off, it was also illegal. I may have felt free from my dad's condemnation, but I felt condemned by the environment I was living in.

The place was called the "Hit House." It was where heroin addicts came to buy drugs and got help right there shooting up. The reason for it is that the dope fiends' hands were either too shaky because they needed a hit really bad or because they couldn't find their veins underneath their swollen skin. They would pay me two dollars to shoot heroin in their veins. I didn't make very much money, maybe $30.00 to $50.00 a day, but at least I had somewhere to live and that's all I needed at the time, because I was totally homeless.

I left there and went to another drug house—a crack house. I was selling crack through the door of the house. The addicts would stick $10.00 through the door and then I would pass a rock of cocaine in exchange for the money. There was no heat in the house and if we wanted to take a shower, we had to take it in cold water. I wore an army fatigue jacket to keep me warm and it was also my blanket. Strangely, this house was a lot safer because no one actually came inside.

I was still with Mary, but I had to prove myself to be a man. She'd come over from time to time and give me $40 or $50. I reminded her constantly that I was alright and that I was trying to build something for us. I knew, however, that the drug game wasn't for me. The drug dealer who owned the house didn't pay me. He just took advantage of me. I lived in a crack house, dirty and homeless. I got to where I was glad just to be able to buy a Coney Island or McDonald's breakfast. I was humiliated and ashamed, but I survived.

I hadn't spoken to my parents in almost a year. I was embarrassed for them to see me in that condition. I had lost a lot of weight because I wasn't eating well. I was six feet tall and weighed about 130 pounds. I barely bathed at all. I would just wash my face and brush my teeth. From time to time, I would catch a cab to Aunt Shoo Shoo's or Grandma's house to take a bath. Had my parents seen me they would have thought I was on drugs. My dad would have been glad to see me fail. I finally got enough nerve to talk to my parents and tell them the conditions I was living in. It didn't matter to my dad, he wouldn't budge. I was being taught survival 101.

I was really desperate during that time, living in conditions that were even deplorable for a dog to live in. I realized that this was not the life for me. I was feeling alone and hopeless. So, I took a meat clever and cut my wrist. I called home and spoke with my mother and told her what I had done. I told her how I tried to harm myself and I tried to manipulate her by crying. I wanted her to care, to come and take me home with her because I was so unhappy about living on the streets.

My mother came to pick me up, I messed up! Blood was gushing out of my veins like a water hose. I didn't know if I wanted to die or if I just wanted the attention. I really wanted to go back home so I could get back on my feet. I was even willing to put up with my dad's constant arguing and false accusations. Their home was a lot better than the places I was staying at.

She took me to the hospital. We lied and told the doctor that I had gotten into a fight at the store so they wouldn't put me on the psychiatric ward. In retrospect, the psychiatric ward was probably the best place for me. I pleaded with my mother and father to let me come home. My father said, "No." The reason was my negative influences should not be around my little brother, Cordell; therefore, it would not be in their best interest for me to return home. *Why didn't my mother take up for me? After all I am her child! I'm only 19 years old lost in this great big city looking for help.* The help I needed was in the house where I grew up. Once again, I was rejected.

I would call my mom on the phone and tell her that I just needed somewhere to live so that I could find a job and get on my feet. Her answer was always, "Let me ask him." Her response showed how great an influence a father has on the family. I knew that she tried to keep down confusion between my dad and me but, I was still hurt and shocked that she didn't fight for me. I realize now that she could only do so much. Maybe by her silence she thought my dad would come around.

So, I couldn't go back home. I remained homeless with just a handful of clothes. I had to find places to get washed up. I would go days without bathing. I had no dignity and no self- esteem. I felt lost. I was suicidal. I even thought about going to jail so I could get "3 hots and a cot," but I was too afraid to catch a case. I had never been in such a vulnerable place in my life.

I often thought about my family and how we lived a middle class life. I thought about how my father drove a new Cadillac, how we dressed and how well we ate. I found myself living in a place where the rats were as big as puppies. I had no place to go. I was living life at the bottom of the barrel.

IF THE TRUTH BE TOLD

I never felt so rejected in my life. I wished that my parents could see the inside of my heart, which was filled with pure humility. My heart was pleading and begging for repentance and acceptance. After being rejected once again, bitterness began to take root in my heart like never before. The question I still ask even today is, *"How parents can put their child out of a home who had graduated from high school, and had been employed, going to college at 17 years old, but was never prepared to live in society? Where do they go?"*

The scripture says to train up a child in the way he should go and when he is old he shall not depart from it. I wondered in the back of my mind if I received the proper training? How did the training I receive lead me to living in drug houses, alone and homeless? Was I prepared as a teenager to take care of myself?

BALL OF CONFUSION

Tony had moved and was living in New York. My parents readily helped him. They wanted to get him off the streets and assist him with his future. They gave him Mom's car and sent him to New York to live with Bishop Ronald Carter. We looked up to Bishop Carter as our godfather. They even gave Cordell a car when he graduated from high school, although he did have a basketball scholarship.

It is perplexing how they never help me with anything. I thought I had done everything right. I was faithful in church. I studied hard in school. I graduated from high school early and got a job. Yet, the only thing I received was a hand out the door.

Things started to look up anyway. Mary had just got a promotion on her job. She traded in her hooptie for a brand new 1983 Renault Alliance. We were happy about that. One day, she asked me if I wanted to ride out of town to New York to see my brother. That was great and exciting. I had some money and bought myself some fresh navy blue suede pants and a silk shirt, a white track suit, and some new tennis shoes. I was still working at the light weight drug house and managed to save $182.00. Mary had the majority of the money to make our trip a dream vacation. We were on our way to New York!

We were about three hours away from New York driving on Hwy 80 East headed to Long Island when I began to get sleepy. I told Mary that I would stop at the next exit and let her drive. Mary was angry telling me to stop right then. She fussed and cussed telling me to pull over because she knew I was too tired to make it to the exit. But no, I had to be the man and take charge. I wouldn't pull over. I kept driving and nodded off to sleep. We never made it to that next exit. Mary had fallen asleep, too. I awoke in time to see two of the tires were in the grass in the far left lane and the car was shooting smoke all over the freeway. I panicked and turned the wheel full force to the right. When the wheels left the grass and touched the cement the car careened out of control. I hit the guard rails on the right at full force. The impact made the car bounce back over to the left lane in the median. Mary's head and shoulders went straight through the front windshield. The force of the impact knocked her backwards into her seat. Blood was everywhere! She laid her head on my white track suit. The amount of blood that was gushing out of her head scared me. I took off my jacket and wrapped it around her head.

It was God's grace and mercy that a nurse saw the accident and pulled over. She jumped out of her car with her first aid kit and ran over to our car. She immediately began giving Mary much needed medical attention. She wrapped her head up in gauze. A trucker also pulled over and called 911, while the nurse took care of Mary.

The emergency truck took us to a nearby hospital in Pennsylvania. Despite the car being totaled, Mary and I were in and out of emergency in a short time, including x-rays. Mary suffered a head injury, but she was alright and all I had was a scratch on my finger! God had spared my life. I telephoned my brother to come and pick us up since he was only three hours away from Pennsylvania. He told me that he was on his way.

We didn't know anyone in Pennsylvania and we were stranded. We sat in the waiting room and waited on Tony to pick us up. Four hours later, he still hadn't got there. I called him again and he answered the phone. I was so angry and hurt. He hadn't even left the house. He never had any intention of coming to get us. It was at that moment I knew my life would never be an easy life. I knew that I would have to battle alone. I needed emergency help and I was still overlooked. The only way that I would survive in this world would be to fight my way to the other side. That accident on the way to New York was the biggest wakeup call in my life.

I called a friend of mine, Kevin, who lived in New Jersey. He was about two hours away. I hadn't seen or spoken to Kevin in years. He was dating a girl from Detroit, and it just so happened that she was there in New Jersey with him. They came to pick us up and took us to get something to eat. He also took me to Bishop Carter's house in New York to see my brother. I wanted to tell him how I felt, but since I was at the Bishop's house, I simply said, "Hello," and held my peace. When he saw my girlfriend's bandaged head he realized how badly we needed his help and how he failed us.

My friend, Kevin took us to the airport. Back then there was an airline called People Express; we had standby tickets, so we had to wait to get an empty seat. The airline representatives said that they would try to get both of us on a flight; but at the very least one of us would be able to get a seat. Kevin told me that I wouldn't get on that first flight, but I decided to wait anyway. Kevin went home. He did more for me than my family member did, and I appreciated it, too. Mary made it back to Detroit safe and my cousin picked her up at the airport and took her home. I spent the night at the airport. Sleeping in the airport was way more comfortable than sleeping in the drug houses! My flight left at 6:00 a.m. the next morning.

God was raising a soldier and I didn't even know it. God was preparing me because I was going to meet the devil in the wilderness just like Jesus did! With my sleeves rolled up and my combat boots on, I was determined to find my independence. I learned a hard lesson from that ordeal and I knew that I would have to depend totally on myself to make it in the world. I was back in the "D" by 7:30 the next morning thinking of a master plan.

One might think that Mary would have broken up with me after I totaled her car trying to show her I was a man. But she didn't. We remained together and I was so glad that she had insurance coverage and was able to get another car, because I was in no shape to help her at all.

IF THE TRUTH BE TOLD

God spoke to Jeremiah in 17:5, ***"Cursed are those who put their trust in man and who rely on human strength and turn their hearts away from the Lord."*** Here was one of the times in my life when God showed me that my help would never come from a mere human being. It was God who spared our lives when I went to sleep at the wheel. It was God who rescued us on the highway that night. It was God who sent the nurse and the truck driver to help us in our dilemma. It was God who sent Kevin to provide us transportation from the hospital to the airport. I would have been a fool to not realize that God mightily showed His hand in my life.

Even though I wrestled with myself and vowed to be independent and never depend on anyone but myself, it would take God to turn my situation around.

MY WHOLE WORLD ENDED

People all over the city of Detroit were going crazy. Everyone was filled with excitement and enjoyment. Downtown Detroit was flooded with people celebrating. The Detroit Tigers had just won the World Series. It was on every T.V. station. I remember that day so vividly because my Grandma Alice was a diehard Tigers fan and she never got to see that day. She had passed a few months before. She died from a sudden heart attack.

When she passed, I felt as if there was no one else in the world who truly cared for me and wanted me to succeed. After Grandma died, Grandpa Buck wouldn't let anyone live in their house anymore. He didn't even want people to come visit him much. It was alright with me because I had adapted to the streets. I knew how to survive and I was willing to do whatever it took to make it.

I learned to be a pretender and it was easy. I found that I had many masks that I could wear to get what I needed or to accomplish what I wanted. I wore those masks well, too. I learned at a young age how to make people think we had a "Leave it to Beaver" life all the while hiding the abuse, agony, and rejection happening at home. We masked our suffering by enduring it silently. No one could ever guess what I went through because I wore my mask expertly. Oddly, that routine helped me get through some of the most trying times in my life. I was so good at pretending that the times when I was afraid, my opponent didn't know it. Even in the streets, I used to fake like I was one of those gangsters that I grew up hearing about. I had so many people fooled. No one knew that I was the "Great Imposter/Master of Disguise". Sadly, because I was incognito for so long, I lost me - the real Mike, and became that ruthless, cold-hearted, uncaring, one-track, selfish, and money-getter guy. I must confess that I didn't like that man in the mirror who stared back at me.

When I lost my grandmother, I wanted to give up, too, because the person who loved me the most and who fought for me the hardest was gone. I was still on the streets living from place to place, working here and there in various dope houses, sleeping on the floor. The sun seemed never to shine in my life. There seemed to be only darkness.

IF THE TRUTH BE TOLD

In Isaiah chapter 61 verse 3, it says that God will replace the spirit of heaviness for a garment of praise. I was at that point in life where I could only feel the spirit of heaviness. That spirit of heaviness is like a person walking around with a cloud over his/her head and weights on their shoulders. I could feel the weights on my shoulders and darkness followed me everywhere I went. God knew I needed to be clothed with the garment of praise, but I couldn't find Jesus. I needed His protection and I wondered why He didn't send an angel down from Heaven to turn my life around. It felt as though I was cursed in all areas of my life. Sure, I wasn't in the church, but I was praying every night, and God was still watching me through it all.

NEEDLE IN A HAYSTACK

Living on the streets of Detroit involved more than just finding a place to lay your head. It meant being prepared and ready for anything to jump off.

I remember a terrible incident when a couple of friends and I grabbed a cab. We started arguing over who would sit in the middle. I lost the argument and had to sit in the middle seat. I was still fuming about it when my friend said, *"Mike, man just get in the cab so we can go!"* I reluctantly got in. I mean what man wants to sit in the middle seat, sandwiched between two other men?

Five minutes hadn't passed when a van pulled up on the driver's side of the cab and blocked it off. Another car pulled up on the passenger side and both cars opened fire on the cab we were in. When it was all over, everyone in the cab was shot except me! The cab driver was slumped over, the guy on my right was shot in the head and the guy on the left of me had been shot numerous times! I wasn't hit at all! God in His sovereignty had protected me even though I thought I was all alone in life.

I was numb with fear from that drive-by shooting. Everyone was shot *except* me. The cab driver was killed and the guy seated to my right was killed. The guy seated to the left of me had been shot numerous times, but he survived. It was then that I decided to take life seriously. I lived in a world that was new to me. I even reflected on how blessed I had been as a kid to have lived in a good home. I was new to the street game, but the guys I was with had lived in the streets most of their lives. They had grown up without fathers. I knew the value of life, but the people I was around didn't know life's value for themselves or in the lives of others. I determined to protect myself by any means necessary. It was all about survival after that dreadful incident.

My cousin, Black, hooked up with another drug connection. This time it was different. We hit the jackpot because we were dealing with major drug dealers, and the operation they ran was sophisticated. I was very impressed by the setup. We lived in a plush apartment in Detroit near the Eight Mile and Dequindre area. The apartment was fully furnished and had two bedrooms, two bathrooms, floor model televisions, and all the luxuries you could think of. No more sleeping on the floor, giving fixes to the heroin addicts or handing crack through the door. I was working for the big players. That was a turning point for me.

Our job was to sell 1/8 of a kilo of cocaine, which went for $5,500 dollars, at that time. The gig involved me, Black and two other guys. The rule was that two people had to be there at all times making everyone accountable and for security purposes. In addition, there was another apartment in the same complex that was called the stash house. The stash house was where we would keep the drugs and the money. So, the second person would take the money from the buyer and go to the stash house to get the drugs and leave the money in the stash house. That routine kept the money and drugs safe in case the Feds or police raided us. That setup would have even confused Elliot Ness and Melvin Purvis.

Not only that, but the apartments were in different names so they couldn't be connected to one another.

They were rolling about $60,000 a day and I made $1,500 a week. I didn't have to pay any rent, so I would buy clothes and bank my money. That gig lasted only a couple of weeks. My cousin saw that we were doing well and started having a party every night! He would invite women over and serve food, liquor, Dom Perignon, loud music, the works. Because of that the guys kicked us out and shut down their operation. We drew too much attention…technically, they drew too much attention. I was too naïve to know how this drug operation worked.

They told us that they were going to be out for a while and they would call us when they started back up. But we knew we were fired because we abused the process. I was so close to victory, but I was out on the streets again and broke.

My aunt let us crash at her house again. I began to think that 'bad luck' was my middle name. I had only been at my aunt's house a couple of weeks, when Black started to beat up on his younger brother. I said to myself, *I can't let this happen in my presence.* I tried to break the fight up by putting Black in a choke hold. He turned his anger on me. I let him go and said, "*Dog you need to leave your brother alone.*" He was two years older than I, and he could always beat me. But since I'd gotten older and bigger, he was embarrassed that I had overpowered him. He was so angry because I interfered that he ran to his car and got his commando machine gun. I looked at him and said, "*So you gonna shoot me now?*" Instead of shooting me, he fired several rounds into the ground.

Later he told my aunt that we had gotten in to it. To eliminate the confusion, she said that somebody had to go. I wasn't surprised that I had to leave and not her son. I thought to myself, *I can't believe this. My aunt is going to put me out when her son was the one that started this mess. Wow, I have to jet again. I can't win for losing. I guess my aunt had good reasons to put me out, which was for the safety of us all. Now, I'm about to be homeless again!* I had nowhere to go.

I called Mary, who was my bail ticket once again, and asked her to come scoop me up because I didn't have anywhere to go. She asked me *"where are you planning to go?"* She was taking night computer courses at Pershing night school. She let me use her car and I dropped her off at school.

I had an hour and a half to do what I needed to do. I thought to myself, *I don't care if I have to beg and plead. I've got to make that last gig work. I was making money and I had a clean decent place to live. Man, I'm going to do what it takes to get back in with those guys.* So, I went back to the spot. I sat in the car and talked myself into ringing the buzzer. I was still shocked that these dudes buzzed me in so that I could talk to them. I pled my case and told them I was all about the business. I said, *"I'm my own man and I'm all about the Benjamins. I'm asking for a chance to prove myself."* They looked at each other. It was like they needed me as much as I needed them. One of the guys asked if I could count money fast. Of course, I told him, "Yes," and I even threw in the lie that I worked as a bank teller for a while. It was a wrap. They hired me back on the spot. I was back!

I told them I needed one favor. Can I get about $10.00 or $15.00 dollars to put $5.00 in my girl's tank and get us both something to eat. One of the guys pulled out a fresh hundred dollar bill and said, *"Take this Mike, and just come back tomorrow with your clothes, take your girl out to dinner."* I said, *"No, I know that you are giving me this as my walking money. I really need a job. My clothes are in the car."* They started laughing because they knew I was serious. *I didn't have anywhere to go; my grandmother was dead and I couldn't go to my aunt's house or back home.* He said, *"Naw Mike, take the $100 and come back tomorrow."* I took it.

I filled up the gas tank, bought Mary something to eat and paid for us a motel room for the night. I dropped the money on my girl, like "BAM!" and told her with tears in my eyes, our lives are about to change!

SECTION FIVE:

HEMORRHAGING

1984-1987

BACK IN THE GAME

Practice makes perfect. My pops was a medic in the army, and a drill sergeant with us. He used that same military mindset to train us. He was a stickler for making sure we gave our all. He instilled in us – "*Always do your best*", although my best never seemed good enough. Yep, so I believed that if I gave my all then I could achieve anything. Although, I wasn't the best player on the basketball court, I knew the fundamentals of the game very well. Most players underestimated my drive and persistence, which made me a real threat.

I viewed my new opportunity carefully. Every day I practiced counting money. I not only became faster but I was accurate, too. My bosses were impressed. Who wouldn't want someone around that was going to make sure their money was always right? Although there were three other guys working, they didn't have the dedication I had nor were they as hungry as I was.

A poor man will do anything to survive. I was good at handling the money and being responsible for protecting another man's domain. I was as vicious as a junkyard dog. I was so good that they began to leave me alone and I would be at the spot handling business on my own. I was learning every aspect of how the operation ran. I didn't miss anything. I was making $1,500.00 a week selling 1/8 kilos of cocaine. Because I could count the money fast and with accuracy, I was definitely an asset to the operation.

They were happy with my performance and I was happy on the job. I was loyal and dedicated to my employers. I had always wanted somebody to appreciate me. Finally, I had somebody to appreciate me for what I brought to the table. Little did they know, I would have sacrificed my life for them, and maybe even have taken a life for them. They didn't know that they were saving my life, by giving me the acceptance I craved. I was getting my self-esteem back.

There was a regular customer buying four 1/8 kilos, which is a ½ kilo of cocaine. We were making an extra $500.00 because another man brought him to us. The outside guy told us to charge the customer $500.00 extra so that he could get a cut and he would split it with us. We sold the cocaine to the new customers for $6,000.00 instead of the regular $5,500.00. We were making an extra $1,500.00 - $2,000.00 in cash every time he came to purchase. That customer would visit two to three times a week. It wasn't long before the other guys got comfortable with me doing everything and because they were looking for freedom, they tried to play me. I was the new kid on the block, but I played them. I saw that they were disloyal and I used it to my advantage. The other guys left me there alone. They knew I would cover for them when the bosses asked where they were. One day, the new customer asked me if he could come and buy without the other guy being with him. I made a true hustler's decision and said, *"Of course,"* then started to sell to the customer when they weren't around, and used the extra income myself. I was counting money so fast I would get him in and out before anyone knew he had been there. I was making about $4,000.00- $6,000.00 extra a week off of him alone!

My whole life changed. Before, getting a hundred dollar bill was a blessing and now I was making over $20,000.00 a month. Mary and I were coming up. It was our intention to save $10,000.00, get married and then I would get a regular job. But the love of money became addictive. It changed all our plans. I remember the saying my father used to always repeat, *"The devil will paint you a pretty picture but never show you the other side."*

We had an expensive and luxurious lifestyle and couldn't let it go. The money came too fast. We had money in the bank and in the credit union. I was buying her nice clothes, taking her shopping at Somerset Mall, and we were taking weekend vacation trips. We lived on a whole different level. We went from rags to riches in a matter of months! I was smart about it though. I didn't let the other guys know that I was stacking money like that.

The other guys would ask if our buyer was coming around. I lied and said, *"No, I haven't seen him."* The truth was that I was selling to him whenever they would leave me alone in the apartment. I was stacking bread and laying low. My brother Tony, who was back at home with my parents because he had fallen on hard times, started calling me and asking me for money. He saw from my clothes and me always driving different rental cars that I was doing good. Before, he made it a point to belittle me when I was living in the crack houses, but the tables had turned and he needed me.

I also moved up in the ranks fast and these cats didn't mind. It was enough to share and go around. I wasn't a pawn on the chess board anymore. I saved up about $100,000 in a few months. I was ambitious. I wanted to make some real money. I took $28,000 from my stash and I contacted some of my connections. I seized the opportunity to expand. It was time to start my own operation.

IF THE TRUTH BE TOLD

For the most part Satan uses two tactics to destroy God's people. He makes them suffer for not having enough of something, or he gives them too much of something to destroy them. He used both tactics against me. I went through hell by not having enough then he gave me too much because he was out to destroy my life and I didn't see it. Again, he painted a pretty picture but never showed me the other side.

WHAT'S GOING ON?

My two cousins Jerry and Black were "starving" (that's what we called being broke). My brother was still living at home with our parents. The people I was working with had shut down the operation for a few months because it was "hot". (The police were watching us.) They said they would call us when they were ready to crank back up. Normally, we would go our separate ways for a little while, spend money, and hang out. We were free to do whatever we wanted to do, during our down times. Mary and I got an apartment together.

My cousin, Jerry, had a wife and family and they were barely making ends meet. By the time the operation was shut down, there was no one else that I trusted to make it happen for me. I put the money up, bought a few ounces of cocaine, and my cousins, my brother and I went into business together. It was a win-win situation. I had the loot and they knew the spots where we could sell.

I setup a meeting with Tony, and my cousins Jerry and Black. I told them we were going to go back in business and make some real money this time. I had the money and I decided we were going to open up a couple of crack houses around the city. I was dealing with a lady I used to rent cars from. I never thought it was smart to be recognized by the police from the car you drive. So while people were buying Benzs and Vettes, I was getting rental cars. I was paying more for rentals, but I could switch cars monthly just for that reason.

We opened up two crack houses. Black and I rode together, and Tony and Jerry rode together. Tony and Jerry were the lieutenants of the organization and they were responsible for collecting the money and dropping off the drugs to the houses. It's amazing how jealousy and envy kick in when you work with family. Tony and Jerry allowed jealousy, envy, and greed to play a major part of our so-called drug empire. Black and I were in a raid on the eastside buying some more drugs for the two locations. It was a large raid and the woman who we bought from was well-known. The bust was on the news.

When Tony and Jerry got word that me and Black were caught in a big drug bust, they went to both the spots, took the money and the drugs, and opened up another drug house on the other side of town. We were arrested, but we got out about 4 hours later. We were not named in the indictment. The Feds were going after that particular woman who only did about nine months. We went to the dope houses looking for my brother and cousin. They played us. The people that worked in the crack house told us that they came and took everything. I was livid! I helped them get on their feet. They didn't have nothing, and they gonna rob me!

I searched for them for weeks, but they kept ducking and dodging me because they knew they owed me money. One day, I ran into my brother on the streets near our parents' home; he was with my cousin and some other guys. I confronted him about my money. Tony showed out again telling me that if I wanted it, I would have to take it. I lifted up my shirt and showed him I was packing. He continued to front on me. I handed the gun to my girl and said I'm about to beat his behind. She pleaded with me to stop before I went to jail. I listened to her and just got into the car and left.

The next time I saw Tony and Jerry, it was two or three months later and they had their own operation going with my money. I was still angry but I was also glad for them, too. Tony was buying dope from one of my best friends. I told my friend that the next time he bought some dope to take out the $2,500 because he and Jerry owed me. He said, *"Mike, I can't get into that; that's between y'all. Your brother is making money, why don't you squash your beef, and put y'all money together. Both of y'all are making way too much money for that foolishness."*

Eventually, I gave in and took my friend's advice. I called my friend and told him to call Tony so that we could sit down and talk about working together again. I realized that $2,500 wasn't going to make me or break me. I chose to keep the peace between us. Black, on the other hand, didn't want any part of their dealings anymore; he told me, "*Mike, I can't trust them as far as I can see them. If I was you, I wouldn't deal with them.*" When I didn't take his advice, he stopped working with us and decided to go his own separate way. What I didn't know is that I shouldn't have worked with *any* of them. They all knew that I was trustworthy and honest, yet not one of them was willing to give 100% in return. (When you deal with rejection, you are living for the acceptance of other people.)

I put in $20,000 cash and they put up a total of $20,000, which was $10,000 each. We started buying kilos of cocaine for about $38,000. In 1985, buying kilos gave you close to kingpin status in Detroit. We would put our money with my friend's money because he had a connection in Florida. We eventually started buying two kilos of cocaine at a time.

For some reason, I kept coming out of my pocket with more money to try to build our operation. I remember my girlfriend Mary had begged me not to go into business with my brother. She kept telling me that something wasn't sitting right about it in her spirit. I wish I had listened to her. My brother knew how to hustle and he was willing to hustle me and everyone around him. Tony and my cousins were money driven and were willing to do anything to make a dollar.

My brother and I lived in different apartments, and my cousin Jerry lived in a house. We kept the money we collected at Jerry's house. Tony's method was different from my method of selling. His method was always to grind to get more money. So every dollar we made, we would use to go and buy more drugs. My method was to get a certain amount and make a profit. Since I was coming out of my pocket to help us grow, a lot of my money was tied up and I really didn't see any money because we kept putting it back into the business.

Tony always tried to find ways to make extra money. He had his eye on another spot that belonged to someone else. We had no need to interfere in what they were doing because we were selling weight; and we clocked about $10,000 a day. Tony knew that the guy that was over the spot was getting high off of his own supply. Tony got with one of this guy's workers and planned to give him drugs to keep the joint going, but he intended to take over the spot. Tony's love of money got him set up and robbed, and all of this led to his demise!

On Sweetest Day 1985, we all went our separate ways to spend time with our girls. I was at a hotel with Mary. Tony was with a mystery lady because his regular girl's mother told her to stop seeing him because he was a drug dealer. Jerry was somewhere with his wife. I got a page around 9:30 that night. I called my pager back and a friend of mine, Rob, who worked for us, told me my brother was dead, and that there was money and drugs all over the place. Rob said he had been in there where Tony's body was and that his body was still in the room. My first mind was to tell Rob to get all of the drugs, guns, and money. But then I thought, *"Tony's not being truthful and he probably had Rob to call me and tell me that to get me over there for some reason"*. Furthermore, if he was telling the truth, drugs and no amount of money was more important than my brother's death.

I told Rob to stop lying. I hung up on him because I didn't believe him. He called me back a couple of times. I finally told him I was coming over there. Mary and I rode over to the apartment and when we pulled up, we saw three or four police cars, the medical examiner's van, my mother's car and people standing around. It was then that we knew it was true—Tony was dead. My father was standing near the entrance of the apartment building with everyone. Everyone was upset and came to me expressing their condolences.

My father threw his hands in the air. He yelled accusingly at me, *"I told you!"* He said it as if it was me who got Tony in the streets in the first place. In my heart I thought, *"if it wasn't for so much hell and condemnation in our home we would have never ended up in the streets anyway."* My mother was standing there in a daze, totally numb. I hugged her and then questioned my father, *"So I guess it's true, huh?"* "Yeah, yeah, yeah" he said in his argumentative voice. Suddenly, I ran into the apartment and down the hallway. The police tried to stop me, but I ran in anyway and I saw that his head was swollen and Rob was handcuffed. Tony had been shot seven times in the face at close range with a .45 caliber hand gun. Cordell looked at me and looked at Rob and asked, *"Did Rob do it?!"* I said, *"No, Rob is good."* Then I told Rob, *"Don't worry about nothing. I know you didn't do it."* I said that out loud to let everyone know that Rob didn't do it.

With Tony's death, our whole lives came to a standstill. Even though I still had connections, all I could think about was *"who killed my brother? How could this have happened? Who did this to my brother? I thought he was with some girl tonight? Who was he with? What was he doing?"* He was only 22 years old. He never got a chance to live his life. This is so unfair. I wished I was there with him because he needed my protection. All of these things raced through my mind, and at that moment, all I wanted to do was go somewhere, lie back for a little while, think things through, and get my life together.

CLOUD NINE

The day after my brother's death, a guy named Kane called me and told me that he saw my brother about 30 minutes before he was killed. Mary rode with me to meet him at the crack house he worked in. It was a two-family flat. At the time, I didn't know that he worked for the guy who had killed Tony. There was an old trick I learned, never park in front of where I was going, especially if someone was with me. I parked the car down the street and told Mary that I would be right back. I walked up to the flat and went in without a gun because I trusted Kane, but he thought I came to kill him. He thought I knew about everything that happened.

I walked into the flat and the joint was filled with dudes with guns. Kane took me into a bedroom and told me everything. He sang like a bird. He told me that the guy who ran the house we were in, J.R., killed my brother and that he didn't have nothing to do with it. He told me that J.R. was on his way. I thought to myself, *I don't have a gun and he's on his way.* I played it off like I thought Kane set him up, which was probably true. He thought I already knew what went down. I was nervous, but acted like I wanted to take him out. In truth, I was watching the windows and doors thinking about how I could get out of there. J.R. was on his way and if he caught me there, he could take me out. Not only that, I didn't have a gun. I told Kane that I would be back. He said, *"No, no you can stay here."* I told him again, *"I'll be back."*

I made it back to the car before J.R. got there and told Mary what had happened. I told her that the dude who killed my brother ran that joint I was just in. Mary said, *"This is exactly why I didn't want you and your brother to work together. I didn't think it was going to be a happy ending!"*

She cried saying, *"Michael, it could have been you."* I tried to cheer her up, telling her it wouldn't have been me and that I would have handled things differently. She was afraid because everything had hit so close to home. I took her home. Mary was my strength, she would build me up like always. She had my back, she saw the king in me. She saw my strength. That was why I kept her close to me; why I leaned on her for support because she always gave it to me.

The Bible says, *"If you live by the sword, you die by the sword".* A murderous spirit had taken over the streets of Detroit at that time and a lot of young black men were getting shot down in the streets like animals being hunted in the woods.

From 1985 until the summer of 1986, I was in a miserable state. Something that I only thought happened to other people, happened to me. I had lost my brother. I wanted revenge. I heard that the streets didn't play fair, and I saw it with my own eyes. I went back to God, but that didn't last longer than a week. I was trying to find myself. I was puzzled and searching for peace. I had so many unanswered questions.

"How will I ever be able to approach my mother and father again? How can I face my younger brother? Now, I'm the big brother. I wonder if Tony's death will bring my family back together again. I wonder if my father will have a change of heart. I wonder if my life will be short-lived. I wonder if I should go back home. Should I go and knock on the doors of the church?"

Two weeks later, the rumors in the street were that the guy who murdered my brother had been shot to death. After that I started drinking heavily; I believed that I had found my answers in drinking. My life mirrored the lyrics from Cloud Nine: *"You can be what you want to be, you ain't got no responsibilities, every man every woman is free. I ran into hard times.... needed something to ease my troubled mind."*

Indirectly, my friend, Deuce, turned me into an alcoholic. He was buying me a fifth of Remy Martin VSOP and a bottle of Moet every night. We would drink it together. He was trying to help me ease the pain of the loss of my brother. He would always bring me money to help with my expenses.

Mary's mother came and talked to me. She said if I continued to drink, I would be an alcoholic like Jimmy, her husband. Mary's father eventually died from cirrhosis of the liver. I told her that Jimmy drank Canada House and Smirnoff and I drank Remy Martin, so I'm a long way from being an alcoholic. In my mind, I thought being an alcoholic meant that you drank that cheap stuff. She said something powerful that day that stuck with me for the rest of my life. She said, *"When Jimmy first started drinking, he was drinking that expensive stuff, too; and Jimmy found out that the cheap liquor did the same job"*.

I looked up .- I was broke and broken. I suddenly remembered I had money in the credit union that I would give to my mom to put in my account. I went to get it and I only had $5.00 left in my account, just enough to keep the account open. I was supposed to have almost $10,000.00 in that account. I asked for a supervisor and said I wanted to see a printout of my account. They showed me my account. If I put $1,500.00 in my account on March 3rd, on March 4th, Tony would take it out. Most of the time, he would be there when I would give the money to my mom to deposit it for me. Not only that, the tellers couldn't tell us apart. They knew we were my mother's sons, and they trusted my mom so they thought everything was legit. I was mad. I told my mom that somebody was gonna give me my money. Mom begged me not to go to that credit union and embarrass her. Suddenly, I was really broke. Mary had to move back home because we lost our apartment. I wound up living on 24th and McGraw at Jerry's grandma's house. Once again, I was living at the bottom of the barrel. Jerry's grandmother's refrigerator had a lock on it because there were about 15 people living there. I had certifiably become an alcoholic and Mary was gone. The house stank and was infested with roaches. It reminded me of when I was living in the crack houses.

Mary would still come by occasionally to check on me. One of the most embarrassing moments was when Mary sent her daughter into the house to get me. She walked into the kitchen and let out a blood curdling yell! She was hollering and screaming at the top of her lungs saying, *"How can y'all live in this house with all of these bugs!"* She didn't even know that the insects were roaches. I grabbed her by the mouth and picked her up and said, *"Girl shut up, come on outside with me,"* just to save myself from some of the embarrassment.

I had been in that position before, so I could handle it. I had been broke, starving and on my knuckles and I had learned to master the loopholes of survival. I was well prepared for the next day and the next chapter of my life. I had stayed in the heart of the ghetto and also in the heart of the suburbs. It was time for my hustling game to be reborn.

Soon, I began selling weed on that side of town. Neighbors were growing their own weed. So me and my friend, Soda, would jump the fence and steal their weed. Soda was a big dog if I ever saw one. He was huge. He was 6'1' tall and weighed about 250 pounds. He was straight from the streets. He told me, *"Mike, if you can get over that fence and get that weed, I'll make the weed to do what it do."* He knew which houses to hit. I cleaned out the yards by stealing their weed. I tossed weed over the fences like garbage in a backyard. When people went to their yards, everything was gone. I knew how to get it; Soda knew how to operate on it. I was the thief and Soda was the doctor.

Soda would spray the weed with Raid roach spray and buy seeds from other people and sprinkle seeds in our concoction. City home-grown weed was naturally green. The good weed, like Gans, Black Russian, Chronic, Panama, or Columbian Gold was brown. So, in order to make it turn brown and look like the good stuff, we had to put it in the oven for four minutes to change the color. We had the best weed in town. It had two effects. The roach spray that Soda topped it off with made people drunk and high at the same time. They also had a headache afterwards, but they kept coming back for more.

It made us do good in a broke situation. I was a hustler and I knew how to take a bad situation and capitalize on it. I would make about $1,500.00 a week. I would buy my friends drinks and a couple boxes of chicken; then I'd go and spend about $200.00 at the after hour joints. Yes, I knew how to come out looking like I was the man in that little area during that time.

SECTION SIX:

BLOOD PACTS

1987-1989

LIVING FOR THE CITY

By 1987, everyone in the Detroit drug game was making money, except me. My friends were coming up. My cousins were making a killing. Black and his younger brother had reached a high mark. I didn't go around them because I was embarrassed. People who were once catching buses were now buying Benzs. I wasn't the only one broke; my cousin Jerry was broke; too. I decided to call Deuce. I could have called him at any time, but I was too proud to ask. I planned to help my cousin and myself; so it seemed like a good enough reason to make that call.

I called Deuce and explained to him that I really needed some help. He simply said, *"You need some money? You tired of being broke ain't cha?"* I told him, *"Yeah."* *"You ready? I got some room for you,"* he said without missing a beat. My man Deuce had come up and was selling kilos. He had become a real kingpin and made a killing in the game. He was so well known that he sold dope to the other kingpins. Deuce told me that he would give me enough room to make a $1,000.00 per kilo. I made more because the going rate was fluctuating and I sold to cats in Pontiac and Toledo for more. If I sold a kilo for $22,000.00, Deuce gave it to me for $20,000.00. If I would have taken the kilo, rolled it, and broke it down into crack cocaine, I could have made more than $100,000.00, but I preferred to sell it fast. My plan was to sell 15 to 20 of his keys throughout the week quick, and make $20,000.00 or more in profits. Selling crack was way too much work, but selling a kilo of cocaine was fast money. No houses to set up, no workers, no hassles, just a quick phone call and a drop off. That's how the big boys did it.

Because I was well respected on the streets, I would hand off the drugs and take the money without counting it. I could call later if the bag was short. Everybody in Detroit seemed to be selling drugs. Wherever you went, every club you entered, drugs were flowing. The lame guys in school were driving Corvettes. People who had no business in the street were getting money. It amazed me that for the six or seven months I was broke on my knuckles everybody had gotten a piece of the drug game. School teachers, attorneys, and police officers were all selling drugs in Detroit.

Still, with all that money changing hands, people were losing their lives. The funeral homes made a killing in 1987-88. Murders, robberies, and shoot outs were taking people out. They were using drugs at an alarming rate.

I got back on with Deuce, but Deuce didn't know my cousin Jerry. He had seen him around but didn't know him personally. When I would go to his house, he would tell me, "Don't bring Jerry to my house because I don't know that guy." I kept reminding him that Jerry was my first cousin, because I was trying get Jerry in; plus, Jerry was pressuring me to meet Deuce. He wanted to get to know Deuce.

I had been off the set for a while and didn't have a strong clientele. I only had a couple of people buying kilos because I had been missing in action for a little while. Jerry on the other hand, had seven or eight dudes buying. I needed Jerry just as much as he needed me. He needed me for the connection, and I needed him for his buyers.

The worse mistake I ever made was I physically and cordially introduced Jerry to Deuce. At that moment, Jerry had the connection and the buyers. The thanks I got from Jerry was that he was going behind my back to Deuce. In the beginning, Jerry and I split $20,000.00 up the middle, but after a time I was only making $2,000.00-$3,000.00 a week. My business took a nose dive and Jerry told me that his buyers weren't connecting with him anymore. Deuce on the other hand didn't care who came to pick up the kilos, he just wanted to sell them. He actually thought that Jerry was coming to transact business on my behalf. Deuce told me one day, *"Y'all doing pretty good huh?"* I caught it! I thought, *"My cousin Jerry has played me again"*. I couldn't believe that after I had pulled Jerry

96

in, he turned around a second time and bit the hand that fed him. Selling drugs is a dirty game. Every man is for himself and blood has nothing to do with it. In the streets, family don't mean nothing. I was making money but it wasn't a lot. I had to distance myself from Jerry. He didn't care because he was chasing money.

Mary and I separated in late 1987. I hung out every day and night at the topless bars, and at the clubs letting everyone know that I was back in the game. Even though Mary and I weren't together, I tried to get her attention and I gave her a couple thousand dollars to put down on a Honda Accord. Mary's dreams oftentimes came true. It seemed as if God spoke to her in her dreams. I always respected and honored what she dreamt. She called me on the phone and said she had a dream that I got into some trouble.

On October 29, 1987, me and my boys were going to the boxing match between Tommy Hearns and Martillo Roldan. We went to the Premiere Center in Sterling Heights to see it on the big screen T.V. There were about 25 of us hanging that night. I was driving a rental car, like I normally did. My other friends were driving Vettes and BMWs. At least ten of us had guns. At that time, carrying a pistol was legal because it only took three or four thousand dollars and a good attorney to beat a gun charge.

A friend of mine was riding with me when Mary called me and told me her dream. We were on our way to the Premiere Center and so we stopped by her mother's house on the way. I got my heater from her so I wouldn't get into any trouble. I didn't understand her dream and I didn't know that the gun was going to be the cause of the trouble.

My friend, Lightweight, who had been a kingpin had just gotten out of the penitentiary and was trying to get his status back. We all enjoyed ourselves at the fight and Hearns won. We left there and went to UBQ, a well-known club on Detroit's eastside.

They did body searches before entering the club so, we all left our guns in our cars. The club had two floors to party on. Lightweight, Jerry, and I were upstairs about to take some pictures.

We waited in line for about ten minutes. About that time, four huge linebacker looking guys pushed their way in front of us and said that they were taking their pictures next. Lightweight immediately tapped me and said, *"Let's go to the car to get the heaters."* I said, *"No. No, Lightweight."* I knew his track record and I wanted to talk those guys out of that foolishness. So, I respectfully tried to talk to them to help save their lives because I was standing next to a gangster who was itching for a scratch! He was trying to get his crown back. While I was explaining to those guys that we were next, one of them arrogantly sat in the wicker chair, totally disrespecting me and said, *"I will jump out of this chair and holler at you man!"* When he put both hands on the chair to get up, I grabbed the camera man's big, police-looking flashlight and bust him in the head with it. Batteries went everywhere. All I had left was my hands. I laid hands on him knowing that Lightweight didn't mind shooting. What I didn't know was that he could throw those hands, too, even though he was a little, skinny dude. I was knocked to the floor. They tried to stomp me, but the bouncer in the club saved my life and pulled them off of me. I was mad by that time. I ran to the car and got my heater. By the time I got back inside the club, my fellas were on the first floor fighting those guys!

I shot several bullets, but not at anyone in particular. It made everyone stop and I got my people out of there. I didn't let anyone else leave until my people were out. But, as we were leaving out, the police were coming in. I had on a red Mickey Mouse sweatshirt with some blue jeans on. I heard the owner of the club tell the officer, *"It's that guy in the red shirt, he got the gun."* I was walking fast with my crew trying to get away without running.

I could hear the police trying to sneak up behind me, so I took off and ran. I ran through the parking lot with the gun in my waist. I ran between parked cars, took the gun out and tried to slide it under the car. Then I kept running. I heard a noise and knew instinctively that the gun didn't go under the car. About 30 seconds later, I heard Deuce yell. *"Stop, Mike, stop, stopppppp!"* I looked back and the police were no longer chasing me they were taking aim. I stopped and turned around and held my hands up. They couldn't shoot me because a crowd had formed.

They threw me to the ground and started stomping me and beating me. One officer put his boot in my face and started grinding it. We found out that the guys we had the altercation with had to know the police. As the officers were taking me to the car handcuffed, one of the guys came up and punched me in the face. I saw the punch coming so I moved and the punch rolled off of me. If I hadn't moved he could have knocked me out. I said to the officer, so what are you going to do to him. He said, *"Shut the f*** up before I bust you in the face"*. There was nothing I could do. I said, *"Can you just put me in the car and take me to jail?"*

My attorney was expensive but he was also a beast. My charges were dropped from felonious assault to carrying a concealed weapon. My attorney got me out on a writ of Habeas Corpus, which meant the attorney was taking me into his custody and I would definitely be in court. I received some phone calls when I got out of jail. One of the calls was from Lightweight. He asked me to be on his team. For some crazy reason, he felt that what took place that night had proved me to him.

Deuce warned me not to get with Lightweight; he felt that I would get into trouble that I wouldn't be able to get out of. I took Deuce's advice and stayed away. A couple of months later, I caught another gun charge and was ordered to get a job. Somehow Mom convinced my father to let me come back home. I guess because I was willing to get a job, my father felt like I was on the right track. My cousin Phil helped me get a job at a boy's placement center for troubled teens. The boys there were between 12 and 17 years old. I was working there and could no longer afford to rent a car. I bought a 1988 Cutlass Supreme, with a first time buyer's choice and I was allowed to get it in my name. Mary and I were solidly separated. She was doing her own thing.

I'M A ROAD RUNNER

It was 1988 and I was getting back on my feet by trying to build my credit. One night, I got into my dad's house too late. When I got in that night Dad said, *"I thought you found some place to live."* My mother convinced him to let me stay one more night. I had a car and a job and I was trying to fly straight, but once again I was homeless. It had happened to me when I was 17, and it was happening again, only this time I was grown and without an excuse. I called Lightweight and told him, *"Man I ain't got nowhere to go."* Lightweight said, *"I wish you could wait for just a couple more weeks. I'm waiting on something real big."* I told him again with emphasis, *"Man I ain't got anywhere to live."* Then he said, *"Your step dad must be trippin' again."* (For some reason, he always thought that was my step dad.) *"Get your stuff, come on and stay with me"*, he continued. Lightweight liked me a lot because he had seen some of my work. He had a two-bedroom condo in Bloomfield Hills, Michigan.

When I moved in with Lightweight, I had no idea that my financial status would change. I still kept my job at the center for about two weeks. Lightweight was totally against working for the system. His philosophy was to make the system work for him. He told me to get some of the boys and strategically put them in spots to sell heroin while we were waiting on the cocaine. He wanted it like that because they were young and getting them out of jail was easier, because if they were caught they would go to juvenile. I refused to do that because I didn't want to mess up a young man's life who was already in trouble.

I got a call from my cousin, Jerry. When Jerry called me, he and Deuce were not seeing eye to eye. He'd heard that I had gotten with Lightweight and decided to give me a call. I was in the position where I couldn't keep my job and hustle at the same time. Truthfully, I didn't want to give up my job because I really felt good about working, but, I brought Jerry on. I didn't forget how he played me twice. I brought him on to help him, but I wasn't going to put him in a position to burn me again.

I was back hustling full time, making drops, and waiting on the big pay load. Lightweight let me know he was about to get 100 kilos a week. I couldn't have come in at a better time, plus he needed a right hand man. Lightweight and I lived together in his condo, but we always came in at different times during the night. Sometimes, he would be there with one of his women. He would be frustrated when I came in, because I interfered with his privacy. He quickly remedied that problem, because about a month later he told me to meet him at an apartment in Southfield. He had a fully furnished apartment for me in some chick's name that we both knew. I didn't know that he had told her to get the place for me. I never met a guy that was as free hearted as Lightweight was. If he was your friend, then he was your friend, but if he was your enemy, you wouldn't be an enemy of his for long. He had a special way of dealing with his enemies.

Overnight, it seemed that Lightweight began to pick up 100 bricks (kilos) a week. That changed my life completely. I was getting a $1,000.00 off each key I sold. Every now and then he'd give me two or three of them for what he was getting them for. That spoke volumes to his generosity. At first, I was trying to change my life around with a regular job, only now I was on the fast track to making lots of money and the temptation was too great to go back to being normal again.

Mary and I got back together again during that time. She confessed to me that she wanted me to go back to my original plan of working a regular job and going to school. Mary was tired of the ups and downs and the dangers in the drug game, but she was very aware, from the news on the street that her old church boyfriend had stepped into a whole different arena. She wasn't going to let another woman be by my side. I was making some real bread.

DON'T LEAVE ME THIS WAY

A typical day for me was to have lunch every afternoon at the topless bar with Lightweight. We would ride together. We were like two peas in a pod. Like twins, we would be together all day until it was time to go home. We would pick up the cocaine loads, drop off bricks, and pick up money, etc. and he never treated me like I was beneath him. We were in it together.

There was one negative with being around Lightweight. Some people that I had been cool with began staying away from me because they knew I hung with Lightweight. He had a great reputation for getting money but he was also known for being treacherous. Because of that one fact in particular, people thought the same about me. Remember the old adage, *"Birds of feather flock together."* I must admit Lightweight did have a treacherous side about him. Some of his close friends were also some of the most dangerous guys that ever walked the streets of Detroit. Here I am his right hand man. I was more than just a sergeant or a captain, I was a general or commander. My net worth had completely changed and so did my reputation in Detroit. I was known and respected as a guy who could hold his own. I was being respected on different levels, too. People who befriended me weren't genuine; they were just trying to keep a good rapport with Lightweight and his crew.

Lightweight had an old close friend of his that he knew from the juvenile system many years before. His friend carried the exact same reputation as Lightweight or even greater. They had a crew on the other side of town that was making money just like we were making money. When we were out of drugs, we would go to them and they would let us hold large quantities of drugs to keep us afloat, and we would do the same for them.

We had about seven people in our crew and they had about seven people in their crew. The difference between our crew and

102

their crew was that their crew was wanted by the police and FBI. Their pictures were constantly showing up on television and wanted posters. I'll never forget the day when I realized that I was out of my league.

I was driving around with some of the other crew. We had just grabbed some carryout and were riding down Seven Mile. I noticed the police riding behind us. Like I said before, these cats were wanted. The police had even gone so far as to say they wanted these cats off the street by any means necessary. The police car behind us was a black narcotics car. We called them "Narcos." (Narcos were police who were highly trained to take on any type of gangster situation in the city of Detroit. They were armed and ready to use deadly force at all times. Those cops weren't afraid to go after the deadliest people at any given time.)

I thought I would have a heart attack, not because I had any drugs on me, but it was the cargo that I was carrying. Those boys were the issue; they were considered dangerous and not to be played with. They were well known and they were no strangers to the Detroit Police Department.

It was the driver's responsibility to control the tempo, by looking in the rear view mirror. No one else in the car was supposed to turn around; that was a cardinal rule in the streets. Passengers turning around in the car signaled to the police that the driver had alerted the passengers and that something was wrong. I told them that the police were behind us, trying to give them a heads up. Suddenly, they all pulled out their guns, turn around, and checked for themselves. I guess when you're at the particular level that they were in the drug game, and wanted by the police; the street rules that I followed didn't apply to them. They didn't listen to me. They were literally turned around looking out the back window eyeball to eyeball with the police. What blew my mind even more was the passenger who was sitting next to me, looked at me and said, "*You know how we going out, right, Killer?*" When the guy said what he said, I couldn't believe it. I thought to myself, "*I ain't no killer. I mean, I can hold my own, but I need a reason to retaliate, and killing the police was not in my repertoire."*

Before I knew it, I was praying to God that we didn't get pulled over. I was sweating bullets because I knew I was locked into a situation that I could not get out of. I knew that I couldn't renege on my loyalty, and if we got into a gun fight, I was going to spend a long time in jail because the car was in my name.

In my generation, loyalty meant something. You didn't snitch, and you remained true to your friends even in life threatening situations. Friends were really friends in my era. Although I knew that I was in danger and traveling unchartered territory, because these guys were my friends, I would not break the bond of loyalty. It was the law of loyalty. It was as if we had made a blood covenant. When the guy sitting next to me said what he did about going out, that was an unspoken agreement that I signed when I said yes, because I was loyal.

My throat got dry and I couldn't even swallow. I had to grip the steering wheel tightly to keep my hands from shaking. For five more blocks, I called on Jesus under my breath. Sure enough, Detroit's finest turned and headed in the other direction. They just didn't know how close they came to an all-out gun fight in the middle of Seven Mile. Because of His grace, God heard my prayer. Thank You God for answering a sinner's prayers!

When the police took a sharp right turn and pulled off, one of the guys in the car with me said that they probably recognized who was in the car and they didn't want any real drama. After that I grabbed my phone and called Mary. I cussed her out from the rooter to the tooter. I called her every name but a child of God. I used that argument as a strategy pretending that I had to go to my place to check on my girl about some stuff that she had no business doing. I had to hurry and drop them off to get out of that situation. The next police car just might not turn off.

In hindsight, I realized our mentalities were totally different. While I viewed the police as an authority that I would have to submit to, these guys viewed them as just another crew that they would have to take out first. As I drove them to their car, I kept wondering, *how did I connect to people that seemed so loyal when we were together, but they were so misguided. They had a crazy direction.*

One of them began to talk about some of the things he did while incarcerated. He was reminiscing and the rest chimed in telling similar stories. One of them asked me, *"Mike where were you locked up at?"* I told them, *"I never did no time and I ain't planning on doing none."* He simply said, *"We all going to be dead one day or we're going to spend the rest of our lives in the penitentiary."* I was baffled by that because that wasn't my plan for my destiny. I still believed that God at some point in time had an expected end for me.

IF THE TRUTH BE TOLD

Judges 11:1-3 (WEB), Now Jephthah the Gileadite was a mighty man of valor, and he was the son of a prostitute. Gilead became the father of Jephthah. Gilead's wife bore him sons. When his wife's sons grew up, they drove Jephthah out, and said to him, "You will not inherit in our father's house, for you are the son of another woman." Then Jephthah fled from his brothers, and lived in the land of Tob. Outlaws joined up with Jephthah, and they went out with him.

It wasn't that my mother was a prostitute, but just like Jephthah, I was put out of my father's house and I could not inherit the things that seemed to come so easily to my brothers. My father, for some reason, did not accept me and I chose to befriend and identify with people who were outlaws. Outlaws are lawless people and habitual criminals, especially ones who are fugitives. It was unfortunate that I was with them, when all I wanted was to be accepted by my family. Those outlaws were friends who stuck closer than brothers. If they went to jail, I was willing to go to jail. If they lost their lives, I was willing to put my life on the line, too.

Those were the type of people I found myself connected to. That's what the spirit of rejection does; it leads you to connect to someone who will embrace you and accept you, no matter who that someone is. I was looking for love and acceptance in all the wrong places. At the time, I didn't realize that those same outlaws I hung with were dealing with the same spirit of rejection that I was. They needed me just as much as I needed them.

It's the enemy's plan to get you to look for acceptance and approval at all costs from whoever is willing to give it, no matter what their background and regardless if it puts you in danger. I was always trying to get my dad's approval. I tried to buy my brothers, and relatives' love. I felt that if I could show each of them how much I cared for them, they would reciprocate. That didn't happen.

That wicked spirit of rejection will make you a prostitute, a killer, or any other criminal just to be accepted. Many people in prison didn't have thoughts of prostitution or murder in them, but in their search for acceptance they were influenced by unsavory people. They joined cults, endured harsh and endangering initiations in fraternities and other dark organizations just to be accepted.

The guys I hung with had "daddy issues, too. Some never even knew their fathers; others had fathers in prison, and some of their fathers were strung out on drugs, too. Sadly, those who did know their fathers didn't have good relationships with them. When their fathers were present in the home, they never spent much time with their sons, and eventually the young men were put out on the streets. We all had that in common.

"Or again, how can anyone enter a strong man's house and carry off his possessions unless he first ties up the strong man? Then he can plunder his house." (Matthew 12:29 NIV)

In urban areas of the country and the world, the enemy's objective is to destroy the strong man. The strong men have been incarcerated, some are sitting on milk crates outside of the corner liquor stores, some being strung out on drugs, and some dabbling in the homosexual lifestyle. We will never find out who we really are until we experience real agape love in Jesus! Yes, that was what was missing, the love of Jesus. When we surrender to Jesus' love, immediately the shackles of bondage, rejection, abandonment, and bitterness fall off.

I CAN'T HELP MYSELF

In 1988 and 1989, I made the most money of my life; life was good for me. There were no breaks in what I was doing and I wasn't homeless as I had been before. Foolishly, I thought I was on the road to success; not realizing that Satan was out to destroy me.

My girl and I traveled and stayed in five-star hotels living the good life. At the clubs and bars, it was easy to spend thousands of dollars a night. I bought everyone drinks, and my boys who were with me each had $300.00 to $400.00 that I gave to them. I gave large tips to the waitresses, and gave the topless dancers at lot of money, too. I was full of pride because I was making so much money, up to $35,000.00 on a good week. We all had shopping addictions, spending habits, and competitive spending practices. Fast money spends fast. I can see how so many wealthy athletes and entertainers become broke overnight.

That money-making year of 1989 became a year of nightmares for me. I was so full of pride that no one could tell me anything. I got to a point where I became my own god. I fell in love with money. I lived where I wanted, drove what I wanted, and I did it all without an education. Who needed an education? I had money. The scriptures say that pride goes before destruction.

In March of 1989, my cousin, Jerry was found dead in a hotel room with a half kilo of cocaine and $30,000.00 in cash. They said his heart burst from smoking crack. Lightweight didn't believe he died from smoking. He thought that someone killed him, and he wanted to find out who did it. I knew it was true, because five months before Jerry died, he was free-basing and I was smoking 51's. I'd take a cigarette, roll it between my fingers to get some of the tobacco out, scoop up some cocaine into the cigarette, and light it up. I thought it wasn't as bad as free-basing with a pipe. I fooled myself into thinking that I didn't have a crack habit because I wasn't using a pipe.

I would leave the club, go get a room at 2:30 in the morning, buy 3 packs of cigarettes, lace them with cocaine, and smoke all of it back to back until 7:00 in the morning. Crack cocaine keeps you high only while you're doing it. So, in order to stay high you have to keep smoking it.

There were three or four different seasons in my life when I was getting high. I knew I was in trouble and putting my life on the line. Believe it or not, I was ashamed of my behavior. No one ever knew that I was getting high. I kept it a secret. No one could even tell I was smoking, because I was getting money. I had access to as much cocaine as I wanted.

When I finished smoking that cocaine at about 7:00 in the morning, I would go to the liquor store and buy a fifth of Remy Martin V.S.O.P. I'd drink it down like water to make me drunk enough to fall asleep. If I didn't do that, I would keep getting high. That was the only way I could stop myself. I did that three to four times a week. Jerry was my getting high partner during that time. When I would get high, my heart would race; I knew if I didn't stop I would die. I had access to too much drugs. A crack head has to stop when he runs out of money. Women who smoke sell their bodies to get high, but a person with money has no limits. Death is the only thing that stops him or her from getting high. Jerry always invited me to smoke the pipe with him. I never did because I thought if I did that I would get to the point of no return. I was deceived because I was doing the same thing as Jerry, just a different way.

One day when Jerry and I left the club he said, *"When you leave the club, meet me at my house"*. I told him these exact words, *"I quit, because someone is going to end up dying."* I had tears in my eyes when I told him that. I didn't know I was prophetic at that time. Jerry went his own way, he couldn't stop. I quit cold turkey and never looked back.

MAKE ME WANNA HOLLER

My life took a nose dive in June of 1989. I was arrested at my apartment in Southfield on a murder charge. I wanted to hire a good attorney since I had seen so many people behind bars only because they didn't have competent representation. While I was going back and forth on the murder case, in September of that same year, I was charged with selling a kilo of cocaine to the federal government. They had confiscated my car and I was under surveillance by the Feds. They were trying to build a case against me. It happened like this:

It was springtime. Mary and I were kicking it strong and talking about marriage again. From time to time, I'd take Mary to work and pick her up. She had a friend and I'd do the same for her friend. Sometimes, we would stop at the mall or go and get something to eat. I always offered to treat her friend, too. Mary's friend would make hints about her boyfriend, telling me that he and I should hook up and do some business together. At that time, I was a mover and shaker at the highest level and was offended by the comparison. *I was making more money than I ever made in my life and I had access to over 100 kilos a week. I could almost supply the entire city of Detroit!* I was so bold and arrogant that I would ask the girls at the club, "Are you a sack chaser?" They would be offended and say, "What?" I said, I just wanted to know because I got a sack!" I let them know straight out, they were not going to work me. It was a fair exchange and I would throw them some money to go shopping after I got the cookie. I was full of myself.

I denied doing anything illegal and told Mary's friend that I worked at the factory. Anyone looking could tell by my "iced out paraphernalia" and the way I dressed that I was a drug dealer. Whenever she brought the subject up, I would always play her off and ignore her. But one day, she made a remark that made me take the bait. She said, "You and my boyfriend ought to hook up, but he be doing that big stuff!" That was it. I thought to myself, "*we buying 100 kilos a week. What could he possibly be getting that I didn't have?*" I said to her, tell him to give me a call. I was irritated, agitated, and frustrated.

Time went by and the man still hadn't called me. One day in September, Mary called and told me that her friend's boyfriend was going to call me. Then she said, "*Whatever you do don't take your crazy friends to meet him, because he's older than us and he's a very nice guy.*" She knew that I was laid back, but my friends were ruthless. The guy called me not three minutes later. I told him I had already talked to my girl; I knew what he wanted and I knew what was going on.

He surprised me when he said, "*Mike, I want to buy a kilo of cocaine.*" I hung up immediately and called my girl back. I asked her, "*What's wrong with that dude? Is he working for the police?*" I had never met him; I was going on the strength and trust in my girl. I knew she wouldn't lead me down a dead end street.

She convinced me that he was alright, just very naïve. She assured me that he was on the up and up, so I called him back and said, "*I already know what's going on. My daughter is 19 years old.*" (I was talking in code letting him know the cost.) That dude repeated back, "*$19,000.00?*" When he said that I got angry and frustrated. I said, "*Yeah man, I'll be there, I already know where to go.*" He told me the color of the car that would be in the driveway. I drove from my other apartment in Madison Heights to Detroit's west side in the Six Mile and Southfield Road area with a kilo of cocaine in a brown paper bag on my front seat. I was wearing shorts. I knew the law, too. Throwing anything in the glovebox meant they could not search the car without a search warrant. If they did open the glove box illegally without a warrant, I could beat the charge. I was still taking a chance because my Cutlass didn't have a key to the glove box.

Over the phone before I left, I told the guy that I was not dealing with any second or third party. I told him I don't even know you. He said everything was cool and that I wouldn't be dealing with nobody but him, but, I felt something was wrong. I was breaking all of my own rules. I went against everything that I was taught in the game not to do. I had butterflies in my stomach when I got in the car. In the past, whenever I had gotten that feeling, things went sour.

I got to the man's house, got out of the car with the bag in my hand, walked up to the porch and he was standing at the screen door. He casually said, *"Hey Mike, come on in."* We greeted each other with some dap on that beautiful, hot summer day. I had already made up my mind that after I dealt with this guy I was going to spend some quality time with Mary.

Pete escorted me into his house and into the kitchen. I saw two guys sitting in the living room out of the side of my eye. I immediately became paranoid. *"Who are those two guys in there,"* I asked him. Without answering my question Pete said, *"Let them take the package around the corner and get the money and come back."* I thought to myself, *"this could be a setup and I don't have my gun with me. What did Mary get me into?"* I took the bag and walked to the door. I said, *"I'm gone man. I ain't got time for this mess."* He followed me outside trying to convince me that it's alright and to make the sell. I knew that desperation could get you in trouble.

I sat in the car trying to figure out my next move. My windows were down and I called Pete over to the car. I told him to get in. I looked at him and said, *"I'm going to blow the horn and let your boys take this around the corner and I'm going to follow them. If something happens to my stuff then something is going to happen to you."* I was using him as collateral. I blew the horn twice and they came out. We followed them about three or four blocks over. They pulled up behind a candy apple red Corvette with two white guys in it. Detroit was 85 percent black; so when I saw those white guys in the Corvette, it spelled the police. I thought, *"I mean how do you get white clientele in Detroit to buy drugs?"* Pete told me to pull up behind the guys, but I kept driving. I told him that we would catch up with them later. I drove about two more blocks and suddenly unmarked police cars came from everywhere cutting me off. They jumped out of moving cars with the doors wide open, wearing bullet proof vests and pointing guns at us yelling, *"DEA, get out of the car!"* I could have sped up and maneuvered around them, but I didn't. I knew that I didn't have any drugs or money on me. Looking back, had I known the federal laws like I knew the local law, I would have floored it and sailed through that blockade!

I got out of jail about four or five hours later on an $80,000.00 unsecured bond. I thought my life was over. I was already facing a murder charge that I didn't commit and now the DEA was trying to convict me for the sale of cocaine. Not only that, but none of my friends wanted anything to do with me once I'd had contact with the Feds. They were all paranoid that the Feds were following me and taking pictures.

IF THE TRUTH BE TOLD

Pride goeth before destruction, and a haughty spirit before a fall. (Proverbs 16:18 KJV)

Pride is why men are packed into the penitentiary and some of them are buried six feet under. When pride is present, an individual won't listen to sound judgment. At that point in my life, there wasn't anyone who could tell me anything. I was even getting signs from God, but I ignored them.

For the love of money is the root of all evil: which while some coveted after, they have erred from the faith, and pierced themselves through with many sorrows. (I Timothy 6:10 KJV)

It's amazing and shocking what I've seen money do, and how people seem to worship it. I've seen people take risks with their lives by selling drugs, prostituting their bodies, and even robbing or stealing from their own family members for that almighty dollar. I lived in a generation where mothers would prostitute their own sons and daughters just so they would give them some of their profits. Preachers learned how to preach just to rob their congregations through large church offerings. People have gotten married for money, and not for love. Many are willing to sell their souls to the devil for the love of money. Women have tried to get pregnant by the guy with the biggest bankroll.

Jesus said, "You can't love God and mammon. You will hate one and love the other." What Jesus was really saying is, "God is a Spirit" and mammon is not money, but the spirit of money. You cannot worship two spirits. You will either love or chase after one of them all the time.

MICHAEL C. ROBINSON

SECTION SEVEN:

BLOOD LUST

1989-1994

SOMEBODY IS WATCHING ME

After my encounter with the authorities, people were avoiding me like the plague. My car had been impounded. I was paying two car notes, rent on two apartments, plus I was paying attorney fees. Even though my friends called and checked on me, they didn't give me any drugs to sell. I was sitting on a nice sum of money, but I still had to try to make things happen. Not only that, but I was accustomed to living large, so I didn't change my spending habits. I didn't try to look for an alternate plan. I was highly frustrated. Holes were forming in my pockets and I didn't have any dope to sell. I was getting calls from people who thought I had access to what I didn't have.

I was desperate. So, when a guy called me one day and wanted to buy a half key of cocaine, I said okay even though I didn't have it to sell. A half a key of cocaine was going for about $12,000.00. I decided I was just going to rob this guy of his money. A couple of days before I had been in a bar fight and had been cut on my right hand, which has been stitched and wrapped up. I pulled up to meet the guy. I pointed my 9mm in his face, with my left hand and I told him to give me the money. When I reached to grab the money with my bandaged right hand the guy grabbed the gun with both his hands. We tussled and I fired a few shots thinking I hit him, but I didn't; he was ducking while I was shooting at him. He overpowered me and took my gun. I took off running down the street and he was running behind me yelling, *"Give me my money, n***er you tried to kill me! You tried to kill me!"* The car was in the middle of the street, running with the door wide open. I was a fast runner, but he was on my heels. I was running low, with my head down knowing he was going to shoot at me.

The guy threw something at me and it hit me on the side of my left hip. He finally stopped chasing me. I was so tired and ended up sitting on somebody's porch trying to catch my breath. I hoped that no one in the house came out and saw me sitting there. Finally, I walked away. When I looked up I saw the police down the street. I had on a blue Nautica jacket, Nike tennis shoes, and some Damage jeans walking toward Fenkell Avenue to catch a cab back home. I flagged down a cab and jumped in. The police pulled up next to the cab. I hit that bulletproof window between me and the cab driver. I gave him $50.00 and told him to let them know he picked me up on Grand River. He took the money and said, "Okay." The police gave the cab driver the description of who they were looking for. That cab driver had the nerve to say, "It's probably him in the back." I quickly stuck the bag of money deep into the back seat of the cab. The police snatched me out of the cab and started beating me. Afterwards, they handcuffed me and took me to the precinct.

At the precinct, a detective asked me if I was driving a grey car. I said, *"No, I was driving a gold car."* I could barely walk to the cell because I was injured when that man who chased me threw something like a brick and hit me in my hip. The police put me in a cell, but when they closed the cell door, it didn't lock. I sat there for about 20 minutes before I opened it up and checked out the scene. I walked out and saw a policeman sitting at the desk. I really wanted to run, jump over the desk and run out of the police station, but I couldn't because my hip hurt too badly. Honestly, I was so upset because I knew I could have made it out the door if I wasn't injured. They didn't know that the cell door didn't lock, that I opened it up and checked out the scene. It would have only taken me about three or four seconds to get out of there, but, I couldn't do it. Looking back on that instance, I knew it had to be God who held me there keeping me from something worse.

Along with everything else going on in my life, I was facing armed robbery charges because the dude I robbed pointed me out in a line up the following day. I was already on bond for a murder case and selling a kilo of cocaine to the Feds. Adding to those charges, I was in a bullpen waiting to go to court.

I didn't know the consequences of armed robbery. I thought it was a lightweight case. I asked other people in the bullpen with me, "How long do you get for armed robbery?" One guy said, "It's a floater man." I asked, "What's a floater?" He said, "The sentence just floats, you can get 10 to 20, 20 to 40 or 40 to life."

The sentence just floats! *"What the heck?! What did I get myself into?"* I was supposed to go to court at 9:00 a.m. that morning. Everyone except five of us was called into court. The officer came and told us, *"You guys are going to court at 11:00."* I called my attorney and he sounded frustrated on the phone. He said, *"What did you get yourself into this time man? I don't know what all I can do!"* I knew then that I had blown it.

The bullpen filled up again at 11:00 and I was still left behind. I had really messed up that time. I sat in deep anguish with my head in my hands. *"What keeps making me make these dumb stupid decisions?"* The deputy came to the bullpen and said three names; we had to say our date of birth to identify ourselves. Then, he shocked me with his next words. He said, *"The judge threw your cases out."* Addressing me personally, he said, *"They're holding you Robinson because you owe $500.00 to Madison Heights."* I found out the Madison Heights police were on their way to come get me, and then I was home free. I didn't need an attorney or an alibi. To this very day I don't know what happened. I do know that God is good!

IF THE TRUTH BE TOLD

There were times in my life such as these that God was showing me how strong and rich His mercy was. In the midst of my crazy choices and stupid mistakes, God was still letting me know that His hand was not too short to reach me in the time of trouble.

MIRACLE

At the end of 1989, I went to court for the murder case and was acquitted. By 1990, I was trying to find a hustle because I kept spending money on attorneys trying to keep up with the lavish lifestyle that I had become accustomed to. I hooked up with an old friend of mine that I used to play ball with, Big Rick. He had a girl over in Canada who stayed in the projects. The projects in Windsor are not like living in the projects of Detroit. It was more like living in the suburbs.

We could take an eighth of a kilo of cocaine to Canada and make about $20,000.00. The problem was everyone was afraid to take it over there because they didn't know the consequences of being caught with drugs in another country. Rick and I would put the drugs inside our underwear. We did that because during random car searches, the police would tell us to get out of the car. Our game plan was to pour the cocaine into the river if push came to shove. There were times when we would hide drugs in girls' cars and tell them to meet us over in Canada so we could take them shopping. It was wrong and it wasn't fair to them, because they didn't even know they had the drugs in their cars. Thank God they never got stopped and searched at the Canadian border.

One particular ride to Canada was short lived because Big Rick was charged with a murder he didn't commit. I knew personally that he didn't commit the crime that he was charged with because he was selling drugs in Canada. I couldn't testify on his behalf because I was in trouble with the law myself.

In the summer of 1990, I reconnected with my old childhood friends. My other friends were still not hanging with me for fear of the Feds. Back in the old neighborhood, I was cool with the owners of the liquor store and I would run tabs at the local stores because I was always in the neighborhood. I used the liquor store to make me look good. If I would bring a girl up there, she would think I was part owner of the store. I would go behind the counter, use the phone, etc. I would even grab a bottle of Moet, Remy Martin V.S.O.P., a 6-pack of Corona and tell the owner to put everything on my tab without pulling a dime out of my pocket.

Most Middle Eastern store owners believe they are smarter than black people; at least this is what one of them told me. They always tried to prove their superiority and make black people feel inferior. However, my boys and I had influence in that area, so the owners pretended to want our business. In truth, they really wanted our protection in the black community. We were well-known and well-respected, which meant we would make sure that no unnecessary drama went down in the stores. We were the voice in that community because of our image and notoriety.

A friend of mine, B.T. was about to go to jail, so his girl was giving him a "going away party." He was ordered to turn himself in the next day after the party. That would be the last time that Rick and our friends hung out. We were all living on a wing and a prayer. The ship was slowly sinking, but I was still too blind to see.

There were about 25 to 30 people in the house playing spades, drinking, and dancing. A friend of mine was on the phone arguing with somebody. When he got off of the phone, he told me and Rick, *"Let's go and get some heat because this dude is on his way over here and I got a beef with him."* I told him, *"We don't have to go get no heat, we good already!"* So, the party continued and I forgot all about the beef. I was just having a few drinks and enjoying myself.

Twenty more minutes had gone by when there was a hard knock at the door. I told the lady that someone was at her door. She told me to go ahead and open it. Before opening the door, I looked through the peep hole. What I saw scared me a little. I saw a man standing on the porch wearing all black with a hood over his head. I knew that trouble had arrived. I opened the door. The guy didn't see me as I was behind the door. He ran into the house and started arguing with B.T. and of course a fight broke out. Suddenly, several shots rang out from somewhere and the guy in the hood fell to the floor. Big Rick ran from the back and picked him up. The guy was screaming that he couldn't walk. When the guy stood up, shots were fired again. I don't think the shooter wanted to kill him, but he went down again. I didn't want to be a witness to a murder so I got in my car and left. I found out later that the EMS took the guy who got shot to the hospital and he was alright.

Months later, Big Rick went to jail for that murder he didn't commit. B.T. was already in jail. I was still out on the streets running a tab at the liquor store.

One particular day as I was taking my mom out to dinner, I decided to stop at the liquor store and pay the tab that I owed. My mom wanted to grab something out of the store, too, so we went in together. Just as we were leaving the store a guy walked in and said, *"Hey what's up man, you remember me?"* I didn't remember him, but in my heart, I knew what was going on. I tried to play it off and gave him some dap and said, *"What's up man?"* He told me that he was the brother of the guy who had gotten shot at the party that night about three months prior. He accused me as the culprit. Then about five or six other guys ran into the store. I didn't have a gun or a slingshot on me and my mom was in the store with me. I tried hard to defend myself against six guys, but they got the best of me and I was on the floor of the party store getting beat. I looked straight into the eyes of the store owner and shouted, *"You going to let them do this to me?"* He said these exact words, *"Drag him out of my store, man!"* When he said that I knew my security services had been replaced by a new posse in the neighborhood.

They drug me out and start stomping me and kicking me in the mouth and busting me in the back of the head. I kept fighting as best I could from the ground. A crowd had gathered and my mom was in that crowd. I heard her say, *"Y'all killed one of my sons and now y'all about to kill the other one!"* I was helpless to defend her or myself. I disguised my voice, *"Aye man the police coming!"* Everything stopped. I was able to get on my feet. I immediately checked on my mom. At that very moment, someone came around with a gun. I could see the fire coming out of the gun and the gun pointed in my direction. I ran toward my mother and like a football lineman tackled her to the ground. I laid over her in order to keep her protected from the gun shots. I started breathing and gasping as if I was taking my last breath. I began to yell, *"I can't breathe, I can't move!"* I saw two feet walking towards me and I heard a voice say, *"That's enough, leave him alone!"* I didn't know who he was. I didn't know if he was a well-respected person in the neighborhood. I didn't know if he was somebody's brother or if he was an angel. All I know was that everything stopped.

Afterwards, I told my mother, *"Let's go!"* She asked, *"Can you move, can you breathe?"* I said, *"Yeah, mom, I just wanted them to think that I couldn't move."* I knew that I had to go to the hospital because I was badly injured from the fight. When I walked into the hospital emergency room I collapsed. I was rushed into the ER. There were at least eight nurses and doctors working on me. I was hooked up to about four machines and nurses and doctors were sticking me with needles and talking to me. I could tell from all the activity and attention I was getting that I was in trouble, but I didn't know I had been hit by one of the bullets. They finally allowed my mother into the room to see me. When she got to me she told me, *"They said you got shot five times, once in the head. The bullet that went into your chest fell out on the floor as they were working on you. Two bullets are in your arm and one is in your foot."* Then she said, *"I need you to do me a favor. Will you promise me, Mike, that you will fight your way through this? I ain't strong enough to go through another funeral."* I said, *"I promise"*. My mother knew that I was a man of my word and if I promised her then I would do it.

My father had a lot of people from our church to come to see me and pray for me. He started preaching to me and I knew that he was doing it to make himself look good. He addressed me from a spirit of condemnation telling me how much I needed to be saved and if I didn't change my ways the wrath of God would continue to fall on me. Religious people will use any situation to make themselves look good. He preached to me as if he had been a good father, as if he were trying to help me all along. He was no doubt trying to prove to everyone why he didn't want me in his home — because I was too busy living in the streets.

Mary came back and forth to see me at the hospital along with some of my other female friends. I made sure that my female friends came during the day so they would not run into Mary, who came after work. She was free to come and stay all evening, without running into anyone.

One day, Mary decided to work a half day and spend the rest of the day with me at the hospital. That was the day that all hell broke loose in our relationship. She had been in the hospital for over an hour and couldn't get in to see me because there were other people visiting me. My cousin came up and told me that Mary was there. I hurried and cleared my room but it was too late. Mary was furious when she got to my room! I was hooked up to a lot of machines, so I began to play one of my Oscar-nominated, academy winning acting roles. I played like I was dying all over again, but, she wasn't buying it. Not only that she had come to share some news with me that a mutual friend of ours was killed the same day I had gotten shot. She told me that while she was at lunch on her job, some of them were talking about the murder. Then, one of my other girlfriend's mother who worked with Mary, told her that her daughter's boyfriend was shot the other day and almost died. Mary asked her, "*What is his name?*" That lady gave her my name. At the hospital, Mary came and told me about her conversation with that woman. Then she told me that she was going to remain with me while I was at the hospital, but when it was over "*Your behind is grass and I'm going to be lawn mower.*" I was too sick to talk. Even though she kept comforting me, she also reminded me that she was through. I knew that it was a wrap.

IF THE TRUTH BE TOLD

As a teenager I read the scriptures and I thoroughly studied King David. I always wondered why God never destroyed King David for the horrific sins he had committed. David was guilty of adultery and murder, and those sins carried the death penalty in the Old Testament, but God still spared his life. I came to believe that God had made an irrevocable covenant with King David. He needed David around to fulfill the covenant.

I knew as a teenager that I had a call on my life to preach the Gospel. I would get drunk sometimes and preach to my friends, playing around. They would be completely amazed and say, "*Man you are called to preach and just don't know it.*" What *they* didn't know is that I *did* know it. They just didn't know that I knew it. During the most challenging times in my life, I wondered if God spared me because he had a covenant with me.

NOWHERE TO RUN

I was ordered to do community service for a previous gun charge because I had violated my probation. My community service was working as a cook in the county jail. My friend, Big Rick, was in jail awaiting trial on a murder case. The police knew that he didn't commit the murder; however, they were trying to convict him because of his numerous run-ins with the law. They felt he was a menace to society. These are normal procedures when you're a black man.

I always had some kind of hustle going on, but I knew that the Feds had a conspiracy and distribution charge pinned on me so my days were numbered. I was also aware that I could go to jail for many years if I didn't win my case. Since Big Rick was in the county jail, I was able to smuggle weed into the jail to help him out. I would bring a $20.00 bag of weed to give to him to sell to help his hustle since I was doing community service there.

I gave the weed to the trustees who worked in the cafeteria. I told them to put it on the tray of the diabetic guy who was in the same unit with Big Rick. I worked in close proximity so I knew the diabetic trays were marked. I told Rick whose tray the weed would be on. The trustees played me over and over again. Each time I tried the trustee didn't put it on the tray and I would never see him again. There was always a different trustee. Rick complained each day that he never got the weed. There was nothing I could do. I couldn't fight or give myself away or I would no longer be doing community service; I would be a resident.

While I was doing community service, I was indicted on a conspiracy drug charge and I had to pay $25,000.00 to my attorney for representation. My attorney made an appointment for me to turn myself in at the federal courthouse in downtown Detroit. He said, *"Don't worry, they won't lock you up, but will probably just set you up with a court date."* My attorney met me there shortly after I turned myself in. The officer asked me if I was three different Michael Robinsons. When I heard the charges of those *other* Michael Robinsons, I was in a better position than those three, because I was only being charged with a kilo of cocaine. The Feds eventually offered me a plea bargain of 4 ½ years and gave me time to decide. My attorney said it was my decision and of course he would represent me if I wanted to go to court.

I still kept in touch with Pete, the one who had set up the whole drug deal. I told Pete that although I didn't know that much about federal law, all he needed to say was that I didn't know any of his friends, which was the truth. They were the ones caught with the drugs and the money. Those guys didn't serve a day in jail. I told him to tell his friends to say that they didn't know us either. Pete said okay to that plan. Then he asked me, *"What are you going to do?"* I told him, *"I'm taking the plea bargain."* He told me that he was taking a plea, too, but in reality, he and his lawyer wanted me to plead guilty, so that everything would fall on me. The two snitches had already put everything on me, and Pete was going to play the same role with them and pretend he had nothing to do with the deal either. I had caught a case and was out of $19,000.00 because of my own ignorance. I couldn't explain how upset I was. All the people who set the entire thing up looked like they were about to go free. That was federal court. I thought that those guys should have suffered the consequences.

It was my lawyer who found out that Pete and his attorney were lying and trying to pin everything on me, if I pleaded guilty. He gave me a few words of wisdom: *"I've never been to prison before, but if you go to trial and are found guilty, you may get about seven years. Since I've never been to prison before, you have to make this call. Is there a difference between serving four years or seven years? I don't know, but what I do know is that if you go to trial and you get off you won't serve a day. If you take the plea you will have to do four years for sure."*

I decided to go to trial. I didn't mind taking the rap because I was guilty. The problem was that Pete and his boys set everything up. I was at home minding my own business. I didn't even know them! I wasn't going to plead guilty and let that cat go free and put all of the blame on me. People had come up missing for what they were trying to pull. Pete rejected the plea. He and his attorney were flabbergasted that I rejected the plea, too.

Going to trial is a monster. I was going to make the court do its job and find me guilty before I took a plea for anything. Pete decided to go to trial, too. We were tried together. Indirectly, both attorneys had to work together since we were in the car together. When the jury selection process began, it was clear that racism had a big hand in it. There were 12 people seated in the jury box with about 50 more people sitting in the courtroom. Ninety-five percent of all those people were white. Not only that, but we were in the Ann Arbor federal court, which didn't make sense to me since the crime took place in Detroit. During jury selection, we made sure to replace the 60 and 70 year olds because we were sure they would stereotype us. Of course, they were replaced by another 60 or 70 year old white male or female juror. We only got a certain number of picks and only five blacks were there. All of the jurors were from white suburbia. None of them were from Detroit. I was not tried by a jury of my peers. Most of those people had never stepped foot in a Detroit neighborhood. It was racial profiling at its best.

There was a kilo of cocaine on the table and two young black guys from Detroit. I was sure the only thing running through those jurors' minds was cocaine, blacks, and guilty. I could have been a Harvard graduate and they still would have found me guilty. I was in that courtroom with my Black mother, my Black brother, and my three Black cousins, Linda, Glenda, and Michelle. They were there with me for every session. I still had hope, and I thought I had this case in the bag. I wasn't caught with the drugs or the money, but the fear of being found guilty began to rise higher than me being found innocent. The reason I felt that way was because the Feds were the ones buying the drugs; they had the money. I never left with it. I didn't know if I disobeyed my gut or disobeyed God, but I did know that I was in a world of trouble. I could hear the sound of *"guilty"* in the atmosphere.

My original attorney removed himself from the case because the judge that was hearing my case didn't treat his previous clients fairly. He thought it would be in my best interest to allow another attorney to represent me in the courtroom and he would still assist. I was out on bond going back and forth to court. I knew that if I was found guilty, they wouldn't cancel my bond, but they would give me a date to come back for sentencing. Honestly, it didn't make a difference at the time if I was found guilty or not because I had already planned to run.

My trial lasted about a week. It blew my mind when I found out that the guys who were involved with the drug deal had become Federal informants! They were the ones who actually gave the drugs to the Federal agents. Yet, they were not even going to trial, they were snitching on us.

My attorney asked the snitches questions like, *"Are you willing to do anything that the Feds ask you to do so that your deal will go through?"* Their deal was that they would not spend a day in prison. They said, *"Yes."* Then she asked *"how long have you known Michael Robinson?"* They said they didn't know Michael Robinson. She asked, *"When did you meet Michael Robinson?"* They replied, *"On the day of the offense."* She said, *"That sounds kind of stupid to me; for someone to give you a kilo of cocaine and ask you to sell it and bring them $19.000.00 and you never met them before a day in your life?"* When asked how long they had known Pete, they said that they had known him since they were young kids. I remember my attorney's closing remarks to the jury, *"Don't look at this young man as just some stereotypical drug dealer, because he's black, from Detroit and you see drugs on this table."*

After jury deliberation and I entered the courtroom, I was charged with both conspiracy to sell and distribution. It only took a few hours. I had thought that I would be found guilty on one of the charges, but not both. Technically, it didn't matter because I was still going to do the same time and this system was out for my blood.

Sitting in the courtroom, I felt helpless and out of control. They read the verdict, and we were both found guilty on both counts. It was the Monday right after my cousin Black's funeral. Black had been shot and killed at Clubland in downtown Detroit. He had gotten all the way on his feet and had gotten a well-known and respected name for himself on the streets of Detroit for making money. Then he got shot one time and lost his life. I thought to myself, *"When it rains it pours. My life is falling apart. I was living high on the hog just a few months ago. Something is happening to me that only happens to other people."* I just knew that I was going home on bond. I had a pocket full of money. Little did I know that my entire life was about to change drastically. After the sentencing, the judge revoked my bond. I was the newest resident in the system. I had new living quarters and a new home. I felt like a failure. I felt powerless to help myself. I looked at the prosecuting attorney, I looked at the deputies and I felt like I could run out of the courtroom and fight for my life.

My attorney said to the judge, "*You snatch the bond, they have been here every day!*" The judge answered back and said, "*This is my courtroom and I can do what I want to do.*" I was immediately escorted to the holding cell from the courtroom. I was doomed and I had no way out. Pete and I had to wait on the van to come and pick us up and take us to Washtenaw County Jail. In the cell Pete said, "*For real, Mike, our girls set this whole deal up. If we try to work a deal with the government and let them know that they set us up, they might take some time off our sentence.*" I was pissed with this coward. I said, "*Naw man, I knew I was selling drugs. You set me up. And since we talking about it you're gonna pay me my $19,000.00 back for that kilo or I'm going be dealing with you.*"

I WISH IT WOULD RAIN

The van came and picked us up. We were supposed to go to the Washtenaw County jail, and then on to Wayne County. Washtenaw County was located on the outskirts of Detroit. I wanted to go to the Wayne County Jail, which was located in downtown Detroit where all the happenings were. Since I was locked up, I might as well go on over to Wayne County and get accustomed to my new living arrangements. I was frustrated and I needed to take it out on somebody. Pete could very easily become a victim because I wasn't going to hold it in.

We stayed in Washtenaw County Jail for about ten days. I kept bugging the officers to take us to Wayne County. Wayne County in Detroit was like Cooke County in Chicago or Rikers Island in New York. I was angry and hotheaded and I wanted to be around a much wilder bunch. Pete was afraid and kept saying let's stay here because Wayne County is like a rat race. We were eventually transferred to Wayne County and I stayed there for about 79 days.

Once in Detroit, they put me and Pete on the same floor. There was an entire floor for federal inmates, which was separate from the state inmates.

My attitude and disposition changed and I became a madman. I knew I was guilty for selling drugs, but I felt like I was mistreated in the courtroom. I felt it was a purely racist justice system designed to enslave the black man. I should have been found not guilty. They didn't have a good case. Nevertheless, I was in jail for a crime that I did commit. They got their man. They needed me off the streets for a while.

I had been to the county before and I have butterflies wondering how real prison life was going to be. I was getting regular visits from my mom. She was concerned about me and asking how I was doing. I told her that when I was living in the hit houses the conditions on the street was worse than in jail. The only difference was going to prison was a mental battle. For some people, it was a physical battle. I could hold my own and I wasn't afraid of that. It was mental for me because I felt like Satan was tormenting me.

I would talk to my brother and other family members, but in the late night hours tears would roll down my cheeks as I thought *"I'm not going to see them again until I'm in my thirties."* I was 26 years old at the time. Don't do the crime, if you can't do the time.

I was already a card shark, because I learned the game from my father. So my roommate and I became the poker and card sharks on our floor. It wasn't bad because we would win potato chips, candy bars, honey buns, etc. Our room was stacked with goodies. Every night, I would go in my room and show my roommate more card schemes and hustles that I learned years ago from my father. I taught him how to shoot a hand. All of those old skills came in handy. One time, I had the Ace, King, Queen, and Jack of spades in my lap while dealing the hand. That meant I had to miss myself four times during the deal. It wasn't hard because I could deal cards real fast. While playing one day, this young white boy stood over me refereeing the game. He saw the card in my lap and said, "Hey, you got cards in your lap." I had to talk over him several times. I told him to go to my cell and grab some chips. He kept trying to talk and I kept talking over him. Had those guys heard what he was trying to say there would have been a big commotion because me and my cellie were beating everyone out of their snacks. We would have had to defend ourselves from the entire block. Thankfully, the guards said that it was time to lock down for the count. As I got up, I walked by that white guy and I elbowed him in the eye real hard. I tried to do it smoothly but then the guard caught me and yelled, *"Robinson, pack up your stuff!"* I wasn't going to the hole, but I was sent to a different floor. I was glad to get out of there anyway because eventually that white boy would have told on us and there would have been hell to pay. I was transferred to a disciplinary floor. Everyone there had been in trouble. There were a bunch of young, wild guys. They busted water pipes, tried to escape and more. Everyone on that floor had done a bunch of dumb stuff. They were between the ages of 18 and 23 and they got on my last nerves. They played too much; they would fight and just keep up a lot of foolishness. Anything stupid, they were for it. One guy named Big Fella, would do pushups with his roommate standing on his back. He was huge. He would turn the television channel at will. We would all be in the middle of a movie and he would just change the channel. That dude acted like he was the president. Everybody would just walk away, intimidated.

I tried to play a game like it didn't bother me although it did. One day I had an altercation with a guy. The rooms we were in would be locked during the midnight shift change and we were unattended for 20 to 25 minutes. We knew how to jiggle the door handles until they unlocked and we were free to hang out in the common area before the guards came in. We had a lookout for the guards while we were free. That was also the time when guys who had a beef with each other could get into it before the guards came on shift. They had plenty of time to handle their business.

One particular night one of the young guys had a beef going on with my roommate. My roommate, who normally went out to the common area at other times, didn't go this time. He said that he couldn't open the cell. I told him I would open it for him. Well, the guy was on the outside called my roommate all kind of names and then he started calling me all kinds of names, too.

I said, *"That's between y'all two."* He said *"I'm gonna holler at you too!"* I didn't know why he wanted to put himself in that situation. So I put a bar of county jail soap in a sock. Back then, the soap was so hard that if a person got hit with it, it felt like a brick. I unlocked my cell and flew out of the door like a madman and I just started swinging. I knew that the soap in the sock trick was very effective. The way he was acting reminded me of how we reacted when my father used to whip us with an extension cord.

He would cringe every time I hit him. He was jerking, hollering and screaming. His reaction only gave me an adrenaline rush and I started hitting him even harder. The other inmates pulled me off of him and somebody yelled that the guards were coming. There was blood on the sock that I hit him with. So I crunched up the soap and flushed it along with the sock down the toilet.

The next morning, they rushed him out on a stretcher; and at 5:30 a.m. they raided our rock. They made everyone line up naked and the guards searched the rooms, asking, *"Where is the pipe?"* Obviously, he told the guards that he got hit with a pipe, but he never snitched on who hit him. I'll give that to him. Later on, I was watching TV and Big Fella's attitude had changed. Before he would just change the channel not caring what anyone was watching. After my altercation with the other inmate he asked me *"Hey man are you watching this?"* I said, *"Naw, go ahead and change it."* Then he went to his room and offered me a cigarette. Yep, things were different, but the difference between me and him was that he was a bully. I was just a man who was willing and ready to protect myself.

IF THE TRUTH BE TOLD

For everything that is hidden, will eventually be brought into the open, and every secret will be brought to light. (Mark 4:22 NLT)

It's amazing how upset I was because the two informants snitched on me. Truthfully, God allowed it to happen. If I hadn't gotten caught, I would have continued destroying people's lives by selling them narcotics. Racism or no racism, God was shutting that madness down. He did so by bringing everything to the light. The enemy uses the cover of darkness to do most of his evil work. More wickedness is done at midnight than in the middle of the day.

When I lived in houses infested with roaches, in the dark those roaches would be running around in the kitchen. As soon as the lights came on, they would go into hiding as if they never existed. That's how the enemy works. Jesus came to dispel the darkness that's in this world. When the light comes it exposes what was done in the dark. God can't bless you until the darkness has been removed.

I'M ENCOURAGED

We stayed in the Wayne County Jail for a few more days, until it was time for our sentencing. On the day of sentencing, the judge asked if I had anything to say. I stood up and said, *"Your honor, I'm 26 years old, and I'm in the prime of my life. I don't have any children and I have never been married. I understand that the courts have found me to be guilty, which was the right decision. I am just asking that you be lenient with the sentence. I don't want this case to be the destruction of my life. I do want a future. Thank you."* Without hesitating the judge sentenced me to 87 months.

All of my family who was there that day was so surprised at my sentence. I was, too. We all expected that I would get a lighter sentence since it was my first time going to prison. I had to hide my pain and hurt because my mom was there in the courtroom. I could see the sadness written all over her face. Eighty-seven months! I tried to add up the years in my head, but I couldn't. All I knew was that I wouldn't see Detroit for some years. Everything became a blur. I told my attorneys that they did an excellent job, and they did. But the fact remained that I was in a bad situation. I was guilty and I was never in a position to be proven innocent. It's a well-known fact that 95 percent of federal cases are won. I didn't know that at the time; my experience was daunting. I was in an arena I'd never been in before and didn't know what to expect. Yes, I had been in jail before, but this was different. I was going to prison.

The officers escorted me out of the courtroom and immediately into a van going to Milan Federal Correctional Institution. When we pulled up to the prison, I saw inmates on the other side of the double barbed wire fence and a correctional officer in the gun tower. I was terrified. Right then, I knew that place was my reality. Fear of the unknown made my palms sweat and my heart race. I had finally figured out that 87 months was 7 years and 3 months. I made up in my mind that I was going to go into this prison with the attitude that the first hint of someone disrespecting me would definitely be the last time for them.

In prison, I met men who were serving 30 or 40 years. To me, seven years was the same as a life sentence. I was dealing with dueling emotions. I was afraid, anxious, and in suspense about what my future was going to be. They took me to R&D – Receiving and Delivery. They did the strip search; gave me socks, underwear, the beige prison gear and sent me up to the unit. Walking to my unit, I saw at least 20 guys I knew from Detroit. I hadn't seen them in a long time. I knew why. They had been locked up.

My first stop was E-unit. E-unit was the unit where all the new inmates were placed. There were about 100 people in that unit; only about 50 of the guys actually lived there. The rest were shuffled out because E-unit was like a holding place until you were assigned to your permanent unit. My roommate gave me the bottom bunk. He had been in prison for 26 years and he was about to go home. He was an older white guy around 52 years old (which was old to me at that time). So I asked him in amazement, "*So you been in prison for 26 years?!*" He replied, "*I'm about to go home.*" I said, "*You probably don't want to go home.*" I was thinking that he had been there for so long that he wanted to remain institutionalized. He said, "*The hell if I don't!*"

I was new to this life and I was totally disrespecting my roommate without even knowing it. The light in the room was over his bed. He would go to bed early, I would stay up late and come in the cell and turn on the light. He would be grumpy and pull the covers over his head, but he never said anything about it. I didn't know that I was being inconsiderate, I was new and naïve.

Milan prison was infested with roaches. I washed down my locker. The lockers were about the size of a college refrigerator and they were stacked on top of each other. Roaches were in the locker, under the mattresses, they were crawling on the walls, on the desk and everywhere. I fumigated the entire cell with Lysol. I sprayed and washed everything down and the next day it was like I hadn't done anything.

I had to learn to adapt quickly. One of the white guys who came in with us walked through the unit and spit into the water fountain. Another Black guy hit him in the mouth and said, "*Look man, we live here. You ain't going to be spitting in the water fountain, we gotta use that!*" What he said was like a revelation. We did live there and I had to treat it like home.

People that I knew from the streets looked out for me, asking me if I needed anything knowing that I didn't have any money on my books yet. They brought me noodles, packs of cigarettes, candy, you name it, I had it. We didn't have paper money, but we were allowed to have $20.00 worth of silver money in our possession. If someone was caught with anything, he'd be put in the hole because they thought that man had been gambling or selling drugs. When I first got to Milan, it was extremely wild. In fact, it was off the hook. Every fifteen minutes, someone was getting his head busted, getting stabbed, beat up, and kicked. Everything went down in Milan.

Federal prison was different from going to jail or being in a state prison. In state prison, you could go in and fall in with the boys from your area easily. Federal prison was different; a reputation didn't mean a thing. My name was only strong in Detroit. Everyone had a reputation in their own city. For the most part the dudes from Washington D.C. ran the federal institutions, because in Washington D.C. every crime was a federal crime. The crimes that the D.C. dudes committed would have landed them in state prison if the crime had taken place anywhere else. The D.C. guys really stuck together and took advantage of everyone else in prison. If you held your own in the federal institution against the D.C. dudes, then your name rang in the system. However, a lot of people did not want to go against them. In prison, either the man came out of you or the punk came out of you. What a guy really was about was revealed in prison.

From my experience, only about two out of ten men could hold their own, and of the two only one of them could really fight. You find out who the real men are in prison. You find out who is jiving, who is lying, who is under pressure, and everything else about a brother. Also, you live with the Mexican mob, the Italian mob, the Chinese mob, money launderers, drug dealers, killers, rapists, etc. Living in a federal institution actually teaches you how to professionally run a criminal enterprise in whatever crime you major in. I served time with the best of the best. I realized what an amateur I was while in the federal pen. In the pen, I met the highest level of criminals ever. They were masters who really never got caught for their crimes. They were only there because of snitches, tax evasion, etc.

I wanted to get in with these guys, even though I wasn't a big player to them. I was from a major crime city and they trusted me. I was so blind. I thought that God had sent me there to meet the right hookup. I was turning reprobate. My stay at Milan was very short. The people that I knew in the streets who were there in Milan with me told me that Pete, my co-defendant was blabbing that he was making major money in Detroit and how he was still getting it while in prison. Later that day, I saw Pete and said, *"Hey Pete. I didn't know you was getting money like that in the street?"* He started bragging saying, *"Yeah I'm getting a couple hundred pounds of weed a week."* I scowled at him and said, *"Good, you're going to pay me my money. I want that $19,000.00 that you owe me. I have a brother out there in the streets. You saw my brother in the courtroom. I want your people to meet my brother on a certain day at a certain time every week until you pay off that $19,000.00"*. Then I said, *"If something happens to my brother, then something is going to happen to you."*

An hour later, I was in the hole. Two officers came to my unit with my picture asking for me. They handcuffed me and took me to the hole. I asked them why was I going to the hole, and they told me that I was under investigation.

The people in the hole could hear people coming in, but they couldn't see anything next to them or across from each other. A guy can reach out for cigarettes and pass things down but can't see anyone. When I got there, the other inmates asked, *"Hey man, where are you from? Why are you in here?"* I told them I was from Detroit and I didn't know why I was sent to the hole. They asked if I had a co-defendant. I said, *"Yes."* Then one guy said, *"You know why you're here? You a snitch."* Everybody else started chiming in and calling me a snitch.

The only thing I knew is that I was under investigation. For ten days, they called me a snitch. I literally didn't know why I was in the hole or how to respond, but I was highly pissed off for being disrespected and called a snitch. I hated that. I was in jail myself because somebody snitched on me. I was raised on the phrase, *"Snitches are found in ditches!"* To be called a snitch was the worst thing you could be labeled in prison. I was full of rage! Those were the most frustrating ten days I had to endure. I was on lockdown and couldn't do nothing about it.

Finally, one of the guys said, *"Hey Detroit - let me holler at you."* He said, *"You said you got a co-defendant on the compound?"* I said, *"Yeah!"* He said, *"Y'all got the same amount of time?"* *"Yeah."* *"He didn't get put in the hole?"* I said, *"No."* He asked, *"Did y'all have a beef or something?"* I said, *"Naw! I just told him he got to pay my money back he owes me."* The dude says, *"That's why you in here Detroit, because you threatened your co-defendant."* Then he yells out, *"Hey y'all! This dude ain't no snitch, he a soldier."*

"What's his name man? I'm getting ready to get out the hole and I'm gonna holler at him for you, but they are transferring you." I was in shock, *"What? "Yeah man, they transferring you."* I said, *"Where?"* He said, *"It ain't no other federal prisons in Michigan."* I said, *"Where they gonna transfer me to?"* He said, *"They could transfer you anywhere in the country... they could send you as far as California!"* I was pissed! Here I am 60 miles from Detroit and they getting ready to move me. I vowed that whenever I saw Pete again, it wasn't going to be nice. I was so mad I could have spit fire! That dirty, conniving, low down snake in the grass. First, he got me imprisoned, then he wanted to snitch on my girl, and next he got me transferred out of Michigan.

I was discouraged and frustrated, but thank God I could have visits while in the hole. I could only use the phone every other day for about five minutes. I found out that they were going to transfer me to Ashland, Kentucky. I asked when and they said that I might leave the next day. The phone was down stairs, so I yelled down to one of the guys to make a collect call to my mother. I wanted her to come and visit me because I may not be able to see her again for a long time.

The dude called and my father answered the phone. I told him to tell whoever answered the phone, to tell my mother to come and see me, because they might transfer me the next day. My father said, *"He's lying! He just wants someone to come and see him."* I could hear the dude going back and forth with my father saying, *"Sir, sir he's serious. They getting ready to transfer him."*
The dude yells to me, *"Mike, you be lying to this guy."* He says, *"You're trying to trick your mother to come and see you."* I said, *"Just tell my mother to come and see me!"* I was so frustrated. He did get the message to her and she came and sat up there with me until visiting hours were over. That was the last time I would see her for a while. The next day they transferred me to Ashland, Kentucky.

They put about 30 of us on what looked like a greyhound bus. We were caged off from the bus driver. An officer sat up front next to the bus driver with a 12 gage shot gun and another officer sat in the back next to the bathroom inside a cage with a 12 gage shot gun, too. All of the prisoners were shackled and handcuffed. We were taken to the airport. When we arrived, there were about 30 officers surrounding us with guns and shotguns. I wondered who was on the bus with me. I was afraid someone was going to start shooting. I had never been in that situation before.

The plane flew all over the country. We stopped in Virginia, Georgia, and Dakota. They dropped me off in El Reno, Oklahoma. I was in the air cuffed and shackled for over eight hours. A bus was waiting on us at the airport and drove us to El Reno Federal Correctional Institution (FCI). I was totally confused because I was told that I was going to Kentucky. I found out, El Reno was just a holding spot for me, because ten days later, they called my name and told me to pack my stuff. They put me on the plane and I did the all-day plane ride all over again. I wound up in the Atlanta United States Penitentiary (USP).

Most of the guys there had life sentences. The entire penitentiary was surrounded by a wall and you couldn't see outside. I was there in a holding area that had about five or six tiers. I could feel that I was in a different atmosphere. The unit I was on held about 300 inmates. We were isolated from the general population, as we were on a transfer unit.

About 50 percent of the correctional officers were pretty Black women. If they were respected, they would respect us. It made you feel human again. In Atlanta, there was a guy breathing down my neck as we watched TV. I was angry and I turned around to back him up. When I looked at him, I recognized Pony Down - Lil Dogg from Detroit, and he was going to Ashland, Kentucky, too. I had somebody that I knew would be loyal to me and I would be loyal to him. Loyalty is like currency in the joint, like precious jewels. It's the most valuable thing there is in prison. I was in Atlanta for about two weeks and they made sure to keep us moving.

I finally arrived in Ashland, Kentucky. At the time, that facility was a medium to high security institution. Lifers were kept there, but they were pretty laid back. When I was sentenced, my level was medium security, which meant I would never qualify to be sent to a camp. It was due to the fact that I had those two gun charges while on probation. It was a good thing; I had already made up my mind, that if I ever got to a prison camp, I wouldn't be hanging around long. I would walk away, because the camps didn't have any fences. Ashland, Kentucky was my new home. After I was there for about a week, they put me in J unit. My street reputation in Detroit didn't follow me into the federal institution. So I felt like I was nobody and I would have to prove myself. There were only seven people from Detroit, Michigan in Ashland, Kentucky and I didn't know any of them, except Lil Dogg. We did hook up with the other Detroit guys and got to know each other. When I was in the Milan prison, there were at least 400 people from Detroit. At Ashland, it was different.

Big Al was a big fella from Detroit who stood about 6'5 and weighed about 280 pounds. He had 20 plus years and he was young… only about 19 years old. One day, Big Al got into it with one of the D.C. dudes. The D.C. dudes were known for violent acts. They ran the whole federal penitentiary system on the east coast. Big Al walked away from the fight to go and get a weapon. Lil Dogg and I thought he walked away from the fight because he didn't want no beef. Everyone else scattered. Me and Lil Dogg went into the gym and watched some guys play a basketball game.

We overheard the D.C. dudes say that the Detroit guys better not come out on the yard. We heard them clearly, and it was obvious that they wanted us to hear them. I asked Lil Dogg, *"What do you want to do on the next move?"* Move is when a bell or whistle rings that allows the prisoners to move to other areas of the prison; you only have ten minutes to do so. Lil Dogg looked me straight in the eye and said *"I'm going to the yard"*. I knew then that I had a soldier with me.

Ashland, Kentucky was the only prison that gave us fruit of the loom bikini underwear. I told him, *"When the whistle blows, we're going to be the first ones out on the yard. We are going to go to the weight area and put the 2½ pound weights in our underwear. When they come at us, we are going to pull the weights out of our underwear and start swinging."* Somebody was going to die, but all we were doing was defending ourselves. Detroit was going to show up. There were about 80 D.C. dudes on the yard and only two of us. The penal system didn't realize that they had just created a monster in me by sending me to Ashland, Kentucky. I felt betrayed, and every time I got a chance somebody was going to pay for my frustrations. I was an inmate with a chip on my shoulder. I wasn't starting any problems, although I was praying that some would come my way.

There were two reasons we decided to go on the yard. The first is that I had to represent my city. I believed that we came from a stand up town and I grew up in a tough era in Detroit, and I was a standup guy. The second reason was that I believed we had to make a showing and stand up for ourselves. If we didn't, we would be labeled as punks, which would give those cats permission to dog us for the rest of our prison sentences. Martin Luther King Jr. said, "*If you don't stand for something, you will fall for anything.*" I was always one who was willing to die for my rights.

About 80 dudes from D.C. were standing around in patches. Lil Dogg and I walked proudly around the yard like we didn't have a care in the world. I was sure they thought we had to have some type of weapon. The D.C. dudes didn't confront us and of course quite naturally, we didn't pick a fight with them. We gained their respect from that point on.

After that incident, I went buck wild. I stayed in trouble when I was incarcerated. I had surgery for a hernia in my groin area. I was confined to a wheelchair for about ten days. Sad to say, my homeboy Q from Inkster got into a beef and I told the fellas he was beefing with and that if anybody was thinking about doing something to him, that guy was going home in a pine box. None of them knew I had a knife under each of my thighs. I was ready for war. I became a regular in the hole. It was one thing after the other with me. I just couldn't adapt to the prison system.

I hated the feeling of being outnumbered. I always knew that God was a prayer answering God; I could only pray to God on the level that I was on with Him. So, I prayed, "*God, please even the number of Detroit inmates to D.C. inmates so that the playing field would be level, in Jesus' name.*" Within two weeks, God started answering my prayer. In Virginia, there is a state prison called Lorton. When the federal institutions are overcrowded with D.C. inmates they were sent to Lorton. That was one of those times when they started bussing the D.C. dudes to Lorton, in Virginia. Then Milan was restructured as a low level prison and the Feds began to bus the medium level prisoners from Milan to Ashland, Kentucky. God was evening the playing field. Soon there were only 200 D.C. prisoners left and about 200 prisoners from Detroit had been transferred in.

I met a dude through Lil Dogg from North Carolina named Hairio. Both Hairio and Lil Dogg would always go to the law library. Hairio was considered a jailhouse lawyer on my unit. He was very intelligent. He seemed like a college boy who attended seminary and he looked out of place in jail. He stayed in his lane and didn't try to be anything that he wasn't. He was a good-looking guy, and kind of nerdy, so I knew he was probably in for some type of white collar crime. He could have easily been studying for his doctorate.

Hairio was very articulate and he studied my case. He told me that he thought he could shave some time off my sentence. He charged me $225.00 to work on my case and his efforts got me back in the courtroom for resentencing. He knew how to type up affidavits, motions, everything. They granted all of my motions and approved my appeals. We were both excited about him helping me with my case. It got him more clients from the other inmates. He also wrote the district court of Detroit. He filed a guilty plea on all of my traffic tickets, fleeing and eluding, drunk driving and other misdemeanors and the verdict came back time served, which fulfilled my obligation and I didn't owe anything.

My brother, Cordell left the University of Southern California and started attending Liberty University in Virginia on another full ride scholarship. My parents would go and visit Cordell and then would stop by Ashland to see me on the way back home. Usually, if I knew I was getting a visit I would get a haircut, have my clothes ironed and my shoes shined. I wanted to look good for my visitors. On one particular day, I knew that my parents were coming to see me. I waited and waited. I didn't even play basketball, I was cleaned up and waiting. I kept checking with the guard every hour to see if they had arrived. I called home, the phone was busy, which was usually what they did when they went out of town; they would leave the phone off the hook. I called my Auntie and she said that they were coming to see me. After a time I was scared to death that something had happened. That's the scariest thing about being in prison, the fear that something would happen to your loved ones and the thought that you could be the cause of it, because they were coming to see you. Later on, I found out that they were, in fact, all right and had decided to go straight home from visiting my brother.

I was getting acclimated to prison life. I met a guy from Detroit named D.D. Coles. He was what Jonathan in the Bible was to David. He showed me how to do time. I felt like a little brother to him and he took me on as his responsibility. He came from Terra Haute, Indiana. Usually, when a homeboy came into the prison from another institution, we always looked out for him until he got his property. We would supply cigarettes, candy, food etc. I looked out for him when he first got there. He took a liking to me. We both played football, basketball and baseball. He was about seven years older than me and had spent ten years in Jackson State Prison. He got out for six months and the Feds gave him 15 more years. So, by the time I met him, he had already done 15 years.

D.D. was like an overprotective big brother. Once he told me, "*let's walk the yard*", and he gave me the laws to live by while in prison.

The Prison Commandments:
1. We gonna sleep comfortable every night. That meant that if we ever got into a beef or altercation, we must handle it at that particular time. We are not going to wait until the next day because we are going to sleep in peace every night.
2. Don't ever get into any gambling debt. It's alright to gamble, but don't get into owing anybody. It's an unnecessary beef.
3. You don't speak to homosexuals. You don't hang out with them. You don't argue with them, and you don't fight them. I said, "*Why not? What if I have to check one of them?*" His response was, "*Why would you get into it with them? Why would you have to check one of them? Why would you be arguing with one of them, unless you **are** one of them?*" Ten percent of

the population at Ashland was openly homosexual. That was a lot.

4. We must always stick together. I got your back, and you got mine.

My cellmate's nickname was C. He was from the eastside of Detroit and he was about to go home. C had to go to a state institution for about six months and afterwards, he was going home.

I had gotten real cool with my caseworker. She was laid back and she had a nice shape. Honestly, I thought that I could have sex with her, but I was afraid to go to the next step. The rumor was that she was a lesbian. She always drank Squirt soda. I got up enough nerve to buy her a Squirt and I put it on her desk. She told me that inmates can't buy officers anything, I told her to throw it away then. I walked out and watched through the blinds if she was going to drink it. She did. From that point on, I would take her a Squirt to her office, daily.

There were times she would come to my cell and wake me up and tell me, *"Robinson, I need two quarters."* I felt like she owed me, but at the same time I was afraid to cross the line because she was a white woman. I didn't want the system to punish me for enticing a correctional officer. I was able to put in a transfer, because I didn't get into any major trouble for six months. So, I asked my caseworker if she could send me to Pennsylvania. By that time, Lightweight had been indicted and he was in Pennsylvania at McKean (FCI). To my surprise, my caseworker said that she could get me in Milan. She asked me, *"Do you want to go back to Milan?"* I said, *"Yes, that's only 60 minutes from my mom's house."* Then I told her that I could never go back to Milan because I had to be separated from my co-defendant—He and I could never be in the same institution together again. She asked me to sit down for a minute and said, *"If I can get you in Milan, will you go?"* I said, *"Yes!"*

144

She said, "*Let me work my magic.*" At that point, I knew that she liked me and wanted me to get with her. I was scared, though. If something went wrong I could forfeit my opportunity to go back to Milan.

Cordell reached out to an old friend of mine named Linda and she began writing me in prison. She started writing me about twice a week. I fell in love with her, because she was the only one that I knew who was there for me 100 percent of the time. Mary was long gone. After the daily count of prisoners, there would be a mail call. The mail would be poured out on the pool table and they would call names to get the mail. Usually there was about 50 people waiting for their names to be called. It felt so good to get mail. My girl, Linda, was writing me like a secretary. She would send pictures and letters. She begged to come to Kentucky to see me. I told her to wait because I had already put in a transfer to Milan, and I would be closer to her then.

The atmosphere at Ashland was an extremely racist, but we found out that they were in the process of getting a dental program. College students would be the ones working on the inmates' mouths because there were interning. We were excited about getting dental treatment and everyone signed up. I had two chipped teeth in the front of my mouth, and I wanted to get them fixed. Before I could get them fixed, I was transferred. A couple years later, rumors circulated that one of the dentists at Ashland had injected some black inmates with the H.I.V. virus and a lawsuit had been filed.

My caseworker worked her magic and I was getting transferred to Milan; however, my roommate C and I got into a beef with the North Carolina boys. I was waiting on a transfer and he was about to go home. D.D. Coles came to our unit and told some of the guys to get me and C out there right away! We went out like we were talking to our father. He said, "*Y'all had a beef with the North Carolina dudes?*" We were denying it so he wouldn't know and wouldn't get involved. D.D. Coles said, in no uncertain terms, "*I squashed the beef!"* Then he looked at me and said, *"Aren't you going home? You are only going to be about 45 minutes away from your mom? Go home and see your mama."* He looked at C and says, *"Ain't you about to get out? Why are y'all around here beefing with these dudes? THE BEEF IS SQUASHED! I squashed the beef!"* At that moment, I knew he had real love for us when he said that. He didn't have to do a thing, but he did it to get me closer to home.

He was loyal and he really took the time out to take me under his wing and taught me how to survive in the system. I was so wild and cocky at the time. I really needed him. He tried his best to mentor me and slow me down. He taught me how to do the time and not let the time do me. Because of his help I was on my way back to Milan, Michigan.

IF THE TRUTH BE TOLD

I had to live my life based on a certain reputation. Reputation is defined as a standard which people set for others to live by. Trying to protect a reputation causes one to do things that he or she doesn't want to do. Protecting your reputation means you are binding yourself to that reputation others have set for you. It's a very strong form of demonic bondage. I've seen people pistol whip others and even heard of people killing others just to live up to a reputation. Living up to reputation doesn't always mean you are a bad person. Sometimes it means that you are willing to do bad things to uphold the standard other people have set for you to live by. It is bondage at its best.

People saw me as being "tough". That put me in a position to live up to their expectations. The truth of the matter is there were times when my heart wasn't aligned with the standard my reputation forced me to live by. There were times in the streets when I did things that forced me to call my mother and ask her to pray for me because I felt guilty. Like Jesus said, *"My spirit/heart was*

146

willing to endure the cross, but my flesh was weak." Often times, it forced me to do the wrong thing. It wasn't the real me who did it. It was the guy with the big reputation that he had to live up to. Reputation is influenced by the flesh and the spirit is always influenced by God. I was more attentive to my flesh, which was driven by my reputation and I neglected to hear God speaking to my spirit.

WAR

As soon as I got back to Milan, I purposely went looking for Pete. I checked him hard and told him how pissed off I was at him for snitching and having me transferred to Kentucky. I let him know in no uncertain terms that he owed me and I expected him to pay me. A friend of mine was standing behind Pete motioning me to leave him alone. In the middle of the conversation my friend grabbed me and walked me away from Pete. He told Pete, *"Stay right there. We will be right back."* When we were alone he said, *"Mike, you're going to have to wear that!"* (That meant you need to leave the situation alone.) *"What"* I blurted out. I didn't understand why he said that to me. *"Mike, what do you think you got kicked out of here for the first time? If you keep it up they are going to transfer you out of here again. I'm telling you that you gonna have to wear that. Leave him alone."* I listened to my friend and agreed that he was right. There were times when I couldn't seem to let things go. But this time I did. I didn't want to be transferred back out of Milan. I walked back over to Pete and apologized. *"Man, I was just letting you know that I was angry at how everything went down, but since I am back at Milan, I will be man enough to let it go."* Yes, I did leave Pete alone that day, but I was like a living terror in that institution. I probably spent more time in the hole than I did in the compound.

I ran into another big brother figure named Wyman. He was also called Gorilla Green. He became my mentor. I believe God placed him in my life to help save my life because I was accused of stabbing and hitting a guy with some frozen cans of juices in a pillow case. I was being accused of all kinds of things, but Big Wyman always had long talks with me to try to slow me down. I guess they worked because I could have gotten into so much trouble; he would get the word and he would talk me out of that trouble. There were times at Milan when guys would settle their differences one on one in the laundry room. The laundry room was a place where there would be no one to interfere with what was going on. Not only that, but when two guys fought in the laundry the one who came out was the victor, while the other one would most probably be laid out on the floor in the laundry. I can thank my father for teaching me how to box because whenever I went into the laundry room, I came out walking on my own two feet.

Linda started coming to see me once a week. She was my girl. I even had to tell my mother to slow down so that Linda could use some of the visits. I think my mom was coming to see me at times just to get away from my dad. I was sad when I returned from Ashland, because I had been missing in action from Milan and people who were visiting me before stopped when I was transferred and they didn't come to see me when I returned to Milan. Linda took all that pain away. There was lots of competition in Milan and the photo album was used to brag and show that you were getting money when you were out on the streets.

We would have a separate photo album of women sending pictures of themselves in fur coats, short dresses, shorts, bikinis and all types of gear. Having the photo albums of different women helped us men to get through the miserable moments of some of our days and nights.

I was so excited to be able to see my family and friends without them having to travel to another state just to visit me. I was in prison, but I was still close to home. There are perks that come along with an institution that is close to a major city. From time to time, the inmates could get real liquor, heroin, and cocaine on the inside. There were times when even the guard didn't stop the action that was coursing through the prison. At Milan, there were two guards I knew personally. When they saw me doing something I wasn't supposed to do, they never snitched on me. Everything went on at Milan. People were even having sex in the visiting rooms, selling weed, cocaine, heroin, and getting drunk. It was a world inside of another world.

Mom came to visit me just as much as Linda. She was there so much that a lot of my friends knew her. The inmates would tell me when she was there. They even teased me saying, "*Mrs. Robinson loves her son.*" Mary was long gone by this time. Yes, she broke it off between us before I was sentenced, but I thought she could have come to visit me at least once while I was incarcerated. She did play a major role in me being here! Inmates need visits to encourage them and make them want to go home at some point. Some of them never got visits from family or friends. Those guys gave up because they felt as if no one cared about them.

———————————

When people deal with a spirit of rejection, others on the outside notice it, as well. The very ones who are closest to you oftentimes believe that you've taken so much from them that they can hurt you at any time since you're strong enough to bear the pain.

Prison actually made me feel free. Although I was physically locked up, I was mentally free. I didn't have to get close to people like I did when I was in the streets. It was a place where I could be myself, protect myself, love myself, and say "no" to whomever I felt like saying "no" to. In the world, I constantly tried to make everyone happy. I sought their approval, tried to please them, and even spoil them through buying their friendship and love. I suffered their pain, as well, since I thought I could handle anything.

In my six years of being incarcerated, my homie, my girl, my 'ride or die' wrote me one letter, which said:

"I hate to share this with you, but I'm about to get married...I would come and visit you, but you know I never like going to places like that."
I didn't respond, but I felt as if coming here was the epitome of life when you're marked as "the rejected one".

I sold a lot of weed in Milan; and Pete was the person I got most of it from. He was able to get a lot of it smuggled into the prison. He may have felt that was his way of paying me back. When an inmate sold drugs in prison, it wasn't really necessary for people to send money. I was selling drugs, and making money; however, my cousin, Pam, reached out to me and started sending me a hundred dollars every month, faithfully. It was a blessing. She sent it so regularly that I took it for granted that I got some money from her. I really appreciated her.

I had a friend who was cool with someone on the recreational staff at Milan. One summer, we worked some magic and got a team from the outside to come and play against us. I told Cordell to get a team together and we would get them into the prison to play our team. Cordell was on the team, himself. Actually, he shouldn't have been because he was on my visitor's list. When the outside team came in to play ball, the prison would lock down the bathroom because that was the one the outside team would use to change into their clothes. The bathroom stayed locked until the visiting team left because their street clothes and personal items were in there. Whenever Cordell left, he would leave an old gym bag in the ceiling of the bathroom with sweat suits, tennis shoes, and all of the latest styles for me to wear. A few of the other visiting guys did the same for their friends. We didn't allow anyone to use that bathroom until we had secured our stuff.

On different occasions people would ask me if I could get Cordell to bring some weed and stuff from the outside but there was no way in the world I would put my brother in a position that could get him caught doing something for another joker. I tended to get away with more since I was close to home, and because I knew some of the officers. They didn't jeopardize their jobs, but they would overlook certain things for people that they knew. Cordell was there for me. He was my little brother, but when I was incarcerated, he became a big brother to me. I needed him and he was there. Every now and then, he would see my friends from the streets and they would give him anywhere from $500.00 to $1,000.00 for me. I would tell him to send me half and keep the other half. I always wanted to take care of my little brother and he always proved himself to be on my side.

I got into lots of altercations at Milan; most of them would be from helping someone else out or to get others out of trouble. I was overprotective of my friends, so whenever I saw one of them being taken advantage of or being bullied I would get involved. I despised bullies. Often when Mom came to visit, my visits were limited. I'd be wearing a green jumpsuit, which meant I was in the hole for helping someone out. When an inmate was in the hole his visits were limited. Unfortunately, going in the hole interfered with the college classes I took. I was only able to finish nine college credits.

Once, while I was in Milan, a friend of mine, Chill had been attacked and had his throat slit. He didn't die, but that didn't negate the fact that the person who did it was trying to kill him. The prison officers knew that his throat had been slit from one side to the other. He had a towel around his neck so that no one could see the blood that was flowing from his wound. The prison put him in the hole and transferred him to another area of the prison knowing that his life was in danger there at Milan. I told Chill to go to medical before he bled to death. Then, I told him not to worry because the one who did that to him would be taken care of. The perpetrator got away scot free, though, without any consequences because he went into protective custody. That was the best thing for him.

My cellie's name was Lil Poo and he was from Highland Park, Michigan. He was about 5'6" and weighed about 120 pounds. He was a fighter. He never backed down from a fight even though he was small. One day, I got so drunk that I couldn't even stand up. I threw up all over our cell. Lil Poo helped me cleanup and even got the other Detroit guys to help him get me in the shower. I passed out in the shower; he came and got me out and back to the cell and put me in the bed. He knew that if the guard saw me like that or smelled my breath I would have been transferred. He was like a little brother to me. I looked out for him. Cordell would even bring Lil Poo's girlfriend up to see him, whenever he came to see me.

While at Milan, I had eye surgery on my left eye. I was blind in it because of the gunshot wound to my head. For two years, I was cross-eyed. It was pretty hard to take because I was accustomed to getting compliments on my eyes. Afterwards, I was cock-eyed. I woke up one day in prison and my eyesight had corrected itself. Miraculously, both eyes were normal, but I still had to have surgery on the left eye. The Kellogg Eye Center in Ann Arbor performed the surgery. After the surgery, I had to wear a protective patch over my eye for three weeks. They warned that if I was ever poked in it, I could go blind. During the time I had that patch on, Lil Poo got into a beef with one of the guys on my unit. He hung out with a dude from New York. They worked together in the kitchen. One day, they got into a beef because they were playing the dozens with each other. I suspect that Lil Poo got the best of him while playing the dozens. Some other guys must have geeked him up to go after him. The guy was a black belt in karate.

I didn't know he had gotten into it. We were in the yard playing cards and laughing and talking, when Lil Poo's co-defendant, Big Mark, came and banged on the table saying Lil Poo just had a fight. We jumped up to go and find Lil Poo because we all liked him and wanted to protect him because he was so small. However, it was time for the count and we were locked down on

152

the unit. Lil Poo was in one cell and he was alright, but he wanted to get back with the guy because the guy got some good hits on him. I couldn't fight with the patch on my eye, so I told a couple guys on my unit that they needed to go and handle the situation since the guy is on our unit. They wanted to wait until the lock down was over and everyone would be out in the yard. I tried to handle him on the unit trying not to make it a Detroit against New York thing. That situation might have turned into an all-out riot. The guys were hesitant to jump on the other man, I think, because he was a Black Belt.

I went over to holler at the guy, knowing if I was hit in the eye I would be blind and the surgery would have been in vain. Another inmate was over there telling him that he needed to make peace with Lil Poo and his boys because it was going to blow up in a major way. He saw me standing outside of his cell and I said, "*I just came over here to talk to you.*" So when the big guy left, I went into his room and put some pieces on him. I must have hit him 30 times nonstop. The reason was I knew that I didn't want him to hit me in the eye. I eventually noticed that he was knocked out in the corner of the cell. I made it back to my room in time for the count. After the count, we were waiting on the doors to open to go dinner. They let our unit out and to go to chow, I noticed in the chow hall that the dude I had beat up was standing around talking to about 12 guys. They pointed me out. So, I just sat in the chow hall thinking. "*I can't leave out of the chow hall until my boys get in here. The crowd I'm with ain't cut like me, so I need to wait for my other boys in the other units to get here so we can handle our business.*"

Cool Pop, a guy that I recognized, but didn't know that well, came and sat down next to me. He said, "*Hey Mike, come on and let's wait outside so we can see what they talking about doing.*" I said, "*I can't go right now because I don't know who is going to ride with me.*" Then Cool Pops said, "*I'll ride with you. Come on and go out with me because I got that thang with me*" (a knife). I asked, "*You got it on you now?*" He said, "*Yeah, I keep mine on me.*" I was amazed, that he is willing to do that. I knew that he was from Detroit, but we didn't have that kind of relationship.

The kitchen is one place where you don't bring weapons. Sometimes the captain, lieutenant, and the warden would be standing there and the guards could search an inmate at any given time to impress the top brass. I was shocked that he had his knife with him. I walked out with Cool Pop. We walked by the F unit, where my homies were — Boo, Dooley, Spoon, Big Chris, Flav, Moe, Gorilla Green, Bing, and Baby Keith along with some other dudes who were standing out there when the New York boys started charging me. They all rushed only me. I was fighting about 15 to 20 guys for about 35 seconds. It seemed like an eternity. I thought for a minute that my homeboys had left me stranded, but they hadn't. They were deciding which ones they would take. It didn't take long and my homeboys started handling their business knocking the New York guys out; not down but out! We laid down a thriller in Milan that day.

All of the guards ran over to where we all were. It seemed to me that they gave us a long time to fight. They were low on guards that day; and that gave us a good 15 minutes to do our thang. We scattered and went back to our units. I told everyone to be cool, leave it alone, we finished, we got away with it. The other Detroit guys on my unit wanted to go against the New York guys in *our* unit to create a name for themselves. I begged them to leave it alone because I was the spotlight of the whole incident and it would get me jammed up. They didn't listen and went at the New York boys again on the unit.

The guards came into the unit and started taking people to the hole. They took me to the hole. When they did, I knew that I was going to be transferred. There were about 13 of us that went to the hole from our unit and guys from other units went to the hole too, because they had done the same thing. It was Detroit verses New York. In the hole, I noticed that my hoodie had six or seven cuts in

154

it. That let me know some of the New York guys had shanks but they didn't go through my clothes. I was very angry. Within 30 days, I was transferred to Terre Haute, Indiana.

MERCY, MERCY ME

I was transferred to Terre Haute in 1993. On the first day I arrived, two guys had been killed in the kitchen. The entire institution was on lock down. There were about seven of us Detroit guys who were transferred to Indiana. We were put in the hole immediately. After about a week and a half, Cool Pop was made the porter on our side of the hole. The porter's cell stayed open for about eight hours a day. He could go in and out of his cell and talk to us. He was also the person who brought us our meal trays. It was a blessing to us, because if there were any extra trays we had first dibs before he gave them to the other guys.

The fried chicken served in prison is equivalent to a lobster meal on the streets. Fried chicken was only served about once a month. We were happy to have Cool Pop on our team. It was common practice for the other inmates to walk past the hole and shout out if there was anyone there from their cities. We would holler back if they called out our city to let them know to look out for us and to bring us something from the commissary.

One day, a guy known as Frank Nitti came by the hole. He had found out there were some Detroit boys in the hole. He said, *"This is Frank Nitti; anybody ever heard of me?"* I said, *"Yeah, I heard of you."* I had heard of him, because my father had a relationship with him. He asked, *"What have you heard?"* I yelled out, *"You know you was the godfather in Detroit."* Nitti laughed and said, *"Yeah, you right, what do y'all need? I 'll look out for you."* I said, *"Bring us some chips, honey buns and stuff like that. True to his word, he got it to us in the hole."*

While I was still in the hole, my mother, brother, and Linda came to visit me. My brother told me that he could tell that Terre Haute was different than the other ones they had visited me in. I asked, *"How can you tell?"* He said, *"We were about 80 miles out and we saw signs that said, prisoners in area, don't pick up hitchhikers. It was only five miles out when you were in the other institutions. You can even feel the tension in the air that this is an entirely different atmosphere."*

In Terre Haute prison, the visits were "NO CONTACT VISITS." I sat with my visitors, but I couldn't hug or touch them. In the other prisons, we sat at picnic type tables and we could hug and touch. In that prison we all sat in a row; I would have to sit in the middle and talk to them side by side, with no physical contact.

At that time, Terre Haute was the only federal prison that housed death row inmates. We found out that we weren't going to remain in Terre Haute because our security level was too low to be there. My mother said that she checked online and found out that Terre Haute was the closest institution to Detroit, other than Milan. The other prisons were eight or nine hours away. She said, *"You need to find a way to stay here if you want me to keep visiting you."* I tried to convince her that the prison was really for lifers and my level wasn't high enough to keep me there. She said, *"Well you need to up your level!"*

So, when I went back in the joint, I was still in the hole. There was a big guy from Indiana. He started talking about me. He made it his mission to try and belittle me every chance he got. He remarked that *"I wasn't nothing but a punk up in Milan,"* and that he wished he could have gotten next to me up in Milan. He knew that I couldn't get next to him because we were all getting ready to transfer to various locations. So, he was using that tactic to try to build a name for himself.

When we were locked down in the hole, we would be handcuffed behind our backs before our cells were opened to go to the showers or wherever. They only uncuffed us after we were locked into the shower. So, we were handcuffed from behind wherever we went and there was always a guard escorting us.

I would urinate in a juice carton and throw the pee in between the bars so it would land on this big dude, because I wanted him so bad, but I couldn't get to him. For some odd reason they took everyone out of the hole and put us into another room the size of a large high school classroom. He and I both knew that wasn't supposed to happen. I wanted to see what that guy was going to do after all of his disrespect, even though I already knew he couldn't hold his own. Not only that, but that was my ticket to up my level and stay at Terre Haute and keep my mom satisfied.

Big E was sitting on a bench watching TV so I walked up to him and I told him, "*I'm going to look over all of that mess you were talking.*" He said, "*Okay Mike, we was cool anyway, I was just messing around with you. We good you know we ain't like that.*" I said, "*Yeah fa sho man.*" He kept watching TV and I came from behind and hit him in the face. He ran in the corner, ducked his head, closed his eyes and started swinging like a windmill. I stepped to the side and hit him about three or four times. I knew that I connected when I saw him, run and fall into the huge fan on the unit. My friend took the base of the fan and hit him with it and another stomped him in the face. All of the extra wasn't even necessary, because I had already taken care of that guy.

The guards came in, separated us, and put us in a hole that must have been literally built for little people. The cell was about five feet high. The bed was a foot off the ground. I had to sit on the bed the whole time because I couldn't stand up and the door was made of steel and I couldn't see out of it. It was a very humbling experience. There were four of us from Detroit in there. We were yelling back and forth to each other. There was no porter, the food trays were delivered in silence. We were all afraid. We had to check on each other every now and then. It was mental abuse. We couldn't hear anyone down there with us, and it seemed like we were in a place that wasn't used that often in the prison. I prayed that they wouldn't forget about us because it felt like we were in a ghost town.

One by one, we had to go to see the lieutenant. I told the rest of the guys to let me take the rap because I needed my level raised. When I went to see the lieutenant, he said I know you all beat up that guy. I told him that it was a one-on-one fight. The guard was nasty and sarcastic and said, "*How could it have been a one on one fight? A guy that big would have whooped on you!*" He said that not because he was defending Big E, but because he weighed about 350 pounds. He was basically defending himself. I only weighed about 150 pounds at the time. Sarcastically I said, "*He couldn't have whooped me because most big people can't fight no way!*" He came back and said, "*You just lost 15 days of your good time.*"

Eventually, they transferred us to a different part of the hole where there were other inmates and we were able to go out into a small confined space for about an hour a day. It was like a breath of fresh air. They finally transferred all of us to four different locations. I was sent to Schuylkill, Pennsylvania Federal Correctional Institution. It was located on top of the Schuylkill Mountains near the Poconos.

Mom was very angry because I was nine and a half hours away. I told her that I tried my best to raise my level up but it didn't work. Linda drove up to see me by herself and I told her that I would give her $500.00 for coming. She kept pressuring me and asking me how I was going to give her $500.00 and where was I going to get it from? I told her that a girl who had been writing me every now and then would give it to me if I told her that I really needed it. Linda said, "*If you can get $500.00 from this girl, this means you have been keeping in touch with her for a while.*" So Linda got mad and cut me off. I was trying my best to be truthful with her. I really wanted to be a blessing to her, but if the truth be told, she was 100 percent right.

I had a good friend named James who was a ping pong expert. He said, "*Big Dogg (that's what they called me in Schuylkill) how are you and your girl doing?*" I said, "*It ain't working out.*" He said, "*I know,*

158

it's showing all over your face and you stressing about it. Do you want to walk and talk?" That was a common phrase where a person talks to another friend of his who was locked up. They'd walk the yard and talk together.

In prison, everyone has a special knack of tapping into someone else's heart. Prisoners are sometimes more effective ministers because they feel what you're going through, as they are locked away and are experiencing pain and hurt themselves. Ministry begins with, *"If you don't understand a person, you can't help them."* That's also how ministry fails. Many try to minister to people they don't understand.

In prison, you run into the best counselors and they will continually check up on you. There is a real emotional connection that people in prison understand far better than people out in the streets. It's a very loyal bond, because you have to talk people out of stabbing a correctional officer; you have to talk people out of starting riots; you have to talk people out of killing one another, you have to talk people out of depression and cursing out their loved ones. That is where counseling is most needed. Those guys lack a degree, but they share the same life experiences; so, they understand.

In the streets, people go to their pastor, psychiatrist, psychologist, and they call their friends, but they won't see them again until the next visit. In prison, you will see them again and again. If you see that person in the next hour, he will ask *"you how are you doing?"* It's that way because no one wants you to blow it. That person becomes his brother's keeper. It's a real brotherhood.

A guy named Red was on my unit. Red was solid, he was from New Jersey and he was a nice guy. He was shorter than me, about 5'10", and he used to work out a lot. We would shoot pool, too. His mother was getting high at the time and using the money that he would send to her. He still had money from the streets that he would give to her from time to time. He didn't want her to know that he had any money left, because she would blow it. He always called me to the phone to say hello to his mother. From speaking to his mother, I felt like I knew her, and she felt the same. I didn't know that Red was setting up a situation with me because I was cool with him.

One day, he told his mother, *"I'm going to have Mike to send you some money, because Mike is cool with me and he has money in the streets."* That made her think that he was out of money and that I was helping her out. She would always tell me thank you. That's just how the brotherhood was in prison.

June was another guy I met. He was from Brooklyn, New York. He was a beast on the basketball court, too. He stood 6'3" tall, was a very strong and very aggressive player. He was cool with an older guy on the unit that my father knew when I was a kid. His name was Moss. Moss eventually died in prison from an aneurism.

The only abnormal experience I had at Schuylkill was when I was called to the lieutenant's office. To my surprise there were two Pennsylvania County Sheriffs in the office and they had an envelope addressed to me. The letter was from Oakland County Friend of the Court. When I opened the letter it said that I was being sued for child support. I was shocked! I knew about the baby. I remembered in 1989, I was having a birthday party at a club and I saw the sister of the girl I was messing around with. Just like any other man, who would want a lot of women to come to his birthday party, I told her to come to the party and bring her sisters, too. She told me she was coming but her sister, Carol, was about to have a baby any day.

I had slept with Carol a handful of times, but I didn't get her pregnant. So, I asked, *"Who got Carol pregnant?"* She said, *"Dave is the father. You know her and Dave was messing around."* A couple of months after Carol had the baby, my cousin started dating Carol's sister. My cousin, just having a casual conversation with Carol said, *"Girl, you know this could be Mike's baby."* Because I was doing so good in '89, she switched fathers and started telling everyone that I was the father instead of Dave.

At that time, all my friends had children. I was the only one who didn't have any. I saw how they were financing their children, but they weren't fathers in their children's lives. I cringed at the thought of bringing children into this world and not standing up and being a father in their lives. For that reason, I paid for at least 25 abortions. Some of the women were truthful about me siring their kids; some were not, but I paid for their abortions anyway. I knew abortion wasn't right in God's eyes, but my motto was *"I refuse to bring a child into this world by any woman and not be in his or her life."*

Since Carol's baby was here, I took on the responsibility, because I knew that this little girl needed a father. I stepped up to the plate, even though I wasn't quite sure I was her father. When I got back to the unit, I called Carol, immediately. I threatened her after telling her what had just happened. I told her that if I found out the baby wasn't mine, when I got out she was going to pay for it. To my surprise, she told me, *"I was never the one who started that rumor. Your cousin, Jerry did."*

It's amazing, but I didn't get into any trouble in Schuylkill. That was the only institution where I wasn't sent to the hole for being a troublemaker. I only stayed in Schuylkill, Pennsylvania for seven months. After that I was transferred out to Loretto, Pennsylvania. Loretto was about seven hours from Detroit. I was getting closer to home.

SECTION EIGHT:

BLOOD TRANSFUSION

1994-1997

TROUBLE MAN

Loretto was one of the weirdest institutions I had ever been in. There were more than two people to a cell. Most of them housed 4, 6, 8 and 12 in each cell. When I was transferred, June, Killer, and Wise were transferred; we all rode on the bus together. On the bus ride, we all got closer to one another because we had a long time to talk and get to know each other. I specifically told June that I had got into it with some New York guys up in Milan just out of respect so he would know where I was coming from. He gave me much respect for being real with him. He told me, "*I always liked guys from Detroit,*" and I told him, "*I always liked guys from New York, but I had that one incident.*" We bonded on the way to Loretto. We were going to stick together.

When I arrived, I found out that I already knew a dude from one of the neighborhoods I used to hang out in on Six Mile called the Bronx. I knew another guy there who was all state in basketball at East Catholic High School named B.B. He and I roomed together. The joint was laid back, because it was run by a lot of D.C. guys and everyone there was quiet because no one wanted trouble from the D.C. guys.

Then we arrived. Sitting back and being quiet wasn't our style. Our crew consisted of a couple of Philly guys, and a couple of New York guys, me and B.B. He was the baddest basketball player in the place. They couldn't check him if they tried; however, Loretto was different from most institutions. Nobody was selling drugs in the entire place and it was nearly impossible to get any in. I found a way to get my hustle on, though. I took advantage of that situation. I was literally the only person selling weed in Loretto, and I was rolling in dough. Since B.B. and I roomed together, I would look out for him. My brother would sometimes bring B.B.'s son and girl up there to visit him because we all had become cool. I never smoked weed, but I was the lookout man for B.B. and June when they smoked weed.

After being in there from a while, a lot more D.C. fellas came in and trouble came with them. Even the guys that we were cool with started acting more aggressive and dogmatic as more D.C. guys were transferred in.

When we played ball, it was always our crew against the D.C. boys. One day, there were about 30 D.C. boys sitting on the bleachers while we played. A new D.C. brother fouled June real hard, and June fouled him back. The guy came up and had words with June. June grabbed him and push him up against the wall. The tension grew strong. There was an older guy who was looked on as the leader of the D.C. dudes. He ran onto the middle of the court and asked June if he was looking for a beef. June said, *"Naw, it ain't no beef, everything is cool."* The D.C. dude was so ugly and ruthless looking; it looked like he was born in a prison.

June ran down the court a few more times, thought about what that old dude said, walked to the bleachers and said, *"Let's do this!"* They both walked out of the gym into the hallway. About eight guys from D.C. walked out into the hallway. Killer, Smiley from New York, Hop from Philly, B and me went into the hallway, too. There wound up being about 20 guys total from D.C. in the hallway. June had his back against the wall, which is the normal position to stand in when you're outnumbered so that you're less likely to get hit from behind. June said, *"Let's go on and get it over with."*

The old head started talking and squashed the beef and everyone went their own way. The D.C. guys went one way and our crew went another way. Once we turned the corner, we broke off and went to get our knives, thinking the situation was going to end up real bloody. June was in a room with about 20 guys in an open space and he slept by the door. B and I went to check on him. June was asleep with his back toward the door. I said, *"June, you can't do*

164

it like that." June said, "*If they wanted some trouble, they would have did something, they don't want no beef.*"

I asked him, "*Why did you check him like that man?*" He said, "*I had to. I had to make my debut right, if I didn't we all were going to have some trouble.*" He made me think about myself and how I felt when I was in Ashland, Kentucky. June and I became the best of friends. I said to myself, "*I like this young guy. June was solid.*" There was still tension for a while, but eventually it died down. The fact is that there were more D.C. guys than there were of us, but they knew we were going to hold our own.

Most of the time, I played a lot of sports, which helped the time go by faster. I played football, softball, and basketball in every institution I was in. I started pumping a lot of iron in Loretto. I only had two years left. My friend Smiley didn't get his name by mistake. He always smiled. I never saw anybody do time as cool as Smiley and handle it just as well. Even on the roughest day Smiley always had joy. He was 36, six years older than me; he had already been locked up for six years, with six more years to go.

Well, one day I noticed that Smiley wasn't smiling. I asked him, "*What's wrong man?*" He said, "*Nothing*". I said, "*I know it's something wrong.*" I could see it in his face, just like James could see it on my face when my girl Linda stepped away. Smiley was married. He said that his son was getting too hard for his wife to handle. He had stopped listening to his mother and began listening to his grandmother, and Smiley's son would no longer take instructions from his mom.

He was at a party one day and his mother told him to come home and he refused, so the mother called his grandmother. His grandmother said she would go and get him. She went to pick up her grandson and, on the way back she had a fatal accident. Smiley's mother died and his son ended up on life support. Smiley got a letter from his mother and a money order the day before that tragedy struck. He had no idea that all of that was going on, either. He got a call from the counselor's office and they told him the bad news. The counselor told him that when they get the funeral arrangements they would let him go, but he would have to pay $2,000.00 to go. He had to pay for the two guards that would accompany him.

He called his sister and asked her for the money. She asked him where she should send the money. Later that day, Smiley's counselor called him into the office and told him that the church where the funeral was going to be was not approved. The church was in a drug infested neighborhood. I got the crew together and said, "*Let's tear this joint up!*" They said, "*Why?*" I said, "*Because they really are saying that none of us could go to our people's funeral! Any person dies in our family the church will more than likely always be in a drug infested neighborhood!*" We didn't tear up the place; we actually calmed down. There was no need to use them to take out our frustrations.

I had a Columbian friend named Righty, and he had a beef with a Mexican dude on the basketball court. The Mexican dude went and got the Mexican mob to come back and holler at him. I knew that Righty was indeed a real kingpin, which was recognized as a cartel. I was determined to get close to him, so I told Righty that I was going to handle the beef for him. He told me not to worry about it, but I wanted to do it because that was the gateway to my future. I thought that it was my purpose for being incarcerated–to get a big connection.

I walked over to the Mexican dude and told him, "*If you bother Righty, you going to have to bother me.*" Well, at that time they would rather risk trying to escape than bother our crew. With that simple warning, I squashed the beef. Righty told me that he would never forget me for what I did. I knew that meant that he knew he owed me one. Righty and I walked the yard every day, and I had a new homie and a motive on my mind.

I knew Righty was on a different level. In fact, Righty was brilliant. Once he told me, "*When you get back out there, make sure you*

166

get some white girls to make drug trips for you. I can get it to Florida, and you need to get it from Florida to Michigan." I told him, *"I wouldn't dare use white girls because if they get stopped they are going snitch."* Righty said, *"With all of the drugs I'm talking about, everybody would tell on you. The key is the police is not going to stop no white girls. They won't even have them under surveillance. Trust me, I know the game."* Then he told me to change my alias. He said, *"You black guys have alias like Pookie, Ray-Ray, T-bone. Get an alias of a real name, with real identification for that name like, John Doe for example and allow people to know you by that name. So, when you get in trouble they are looking for John Doe, but Michael Robinson has a passport to get out of Dodge."* I knew that Righty was in a different league. He shared other strategies with me, too. He told me to buy five or six houses with garages attached to them. So, when they drop the drugs off, they will be dropping them off in places where the Feds can't take pictures, watching you take suitcases out of the cars. That's just a handful of information that he gave me. I really thought that Righty's connection had to be from the Lord. (I must have been losing my mind!) Righty told me, *"I always wanted Detroit because I know you all can move some heavy weight in Detroit."* Detroit was known as a heavy drug trafficking city in America at that time. I was about to be one the greatest kingpins that Detroit had yet to see.

We were in the law library, one day. I told Righty, *"I could move 1,000 kilos of cocaine a week if the price was right."* Both of Righty's eyes grew big as golf-balls and he said, *"If you can move it, I can get it!"* Righty told me he had a guy in St. Louis that he was dealing with that was moving 100 kilos a week. He said, *"Now how is it possible for you to get rid of 1,000 a week?"* I showed him the map of the United States on the wall. On the map there was a black circle and next to the circle was the city of St. Louis. Every city that had a circle next to it on the map had a population over 100,000. Another example was a star next to the city, which meant that city had a population over 1,000,000. Detroit had a star next to it. So, I told Righty, *"If he can move 100 kilos in a week in a city of 100,000 people I can definitely move 1,000 kilos a week in a city of more than one million people.*" That argument sealed the job. Righty shook my hand and said, "*You're my man.*" I was determined that I wasn't going to let this connection go. Righty had a little over a year left and I had two years left on my sentence. To show you how blind I was and how far I had moved away from what was right, I really thought it was God working on my behalf. I could have easily made close to ten million dollars a week moving 1,000 kilos a week.

I reached out to Linda and began calling her again. She was dating a guy who was living with her. She told me that if he answered the phone just hang up. Instead of hanging up I would play it smart and ask for a guy, knowing that if I hung up, he would eventually figure out the phone was for her. I got tired of playing the game, so after a while, I just completely stopped calling.

One day, while I was in Loretto, I got a visit from an old preacher friend of mine who preached at Solomon's Temple when I was a teenager. He said that he was going to come and visit. I would talk to him from time to time on the telephone to get spiritual advice. He had been on my visitor's list for a few years. My name was called for a visit and to my surprise, Minister Gary Gay and Darryl Alston, whose wedding I was the best man at, were both sitting in the visitor's room. Oh what a happy day. I thought they had written me off. It felt good to see people I hadn't seen in a while.

1995 was an eventful year. It was the year O.J. Simpson was found not guilty, and the year of the first Million Man March. That same year, Congresswoman Maxine Waters was fighting tooth and nail for the crack cocaine law to be cancelled. She wanted the inmates who were incarcerated under that law to get immediate release for the time they served. Back in 1987, because of the government there was a specific law called the Crack Cocaine Law. It was a law that targeted the Black communities in the urban neighborhoods. If someone was caught with one gram of crack cocaine, it was equivalent to 100 grams of powder cocaine. So those little Black boys on the corner selling rocks were being charged like they were selling kilos!

Maxine Waters said on T.V. that not one Caucasian had been in the federal courtrooms for selling crack cocaine in eight years in one of the California districts since the law had been in effect. She accused the system, *"I want to know have you let them out of the back door when you arrest them or is it that you are targeting the Black and Hispanic communities?!"* We crowded around the television set, because most of those guys had crack cocaine charges. They were battling and battling and we were excited because if they won it would mean immediate release for some. Well, they lost and you could hear a pin drop. All of the Hispanics and Blacks hung their heads knowing that they had to do the time. It didn't affect me because I was incarcerated for selling powder; but my brothers were disheartened. I said to myself, *"If I'm ever going to be an activist for my people, now is the time".*

I stood in front of the big T.V. and I said, *"Hey yo! What y'all gonna do?"* They said, *"Ain't nothing we can do."* I said, *"They fought for y'all out there. Y'all brothers ain't gonna fight for yourselves?"* They asked, *"What we gonna do?"* I said, *"I don't have a crack case, but let's shut this joint down! We ain't the only institution that saw this. It's some other institutions that saw this and they going to war, and we're going to war with them!"* They said, *"What are we going to do?"* I said, *"We ain't going to work at Unicore tomorrow."* Unicore was the prison factory that was in every federal prison. In Milan, they made the bomb racks, in Oxford they made bombs, in Schuylkill they made office panels, in Ashland, Kentucky they made office furniture for every federal office or institution, and in Loretto we made walkie talkies. It was a multibillion dollar industry where they paid us pennies. It was slave labor through the government system.

"Unicore will be shut down tomorrow!" Somebody said, *"Those white people gonna go to work anyway."* I said, *"If they go, there will be some repercussions."* That night, we began to tear up stuff. We set

fires, tore up the equipment, broke windows, and because they didn't have a full staff, they really couldn't contain us. The next day all of the Hispanics and Blacks decided they weren't going to work. There were guards standing outside trying to help escort the white boys to their work sites. Our crew huddled up and we walked near the work site making our presence known. The white boys made U-turns and went back to their cells. We shut it down that day; without us working, those in charge lost a lot of money. We also knew that other penal institutions did the same thing. We were locked down the next day. Guards were dressed in riot gear, and the National Guard was called in. They came to our cells and said, *"Are you going to work or you cuffing up?"* Everybody in our room said, *"We cuffing up!"* They didn't have enough room to put us all in the hole so they started creating temporary solitary confinement areas. They would use classrooms, put up large steel doors, and put about 30 of us in there. We were sitting on the floor like sardines in a can. I know that the treatment was unjust, because it was very unsanitary; we were in that room for about five days without showers.

Each day thereafter, they interviewed everyone individually, and the number of people dwindled down. They even took some people to the local county jail because they didn't have enough room to support the riot. That was the longest I had ever been in the hole without being there to be transferred. I spent 145 days in the hole. I stayed like a trooper. My friends kept sending word to tell Mike to come out. I said, *"Nope, I ain't coming out. I'm going to stay in here until they transfer me because this institution is too racist!"*

Usually when you are in the hole, every now and then a priest or a nun would come and visit you and ask if you were alright, if you wanted any pamphlets to read, or if you needed prayer. Well I was out of control. I cursed the nun out, pulled my pants down and exposed myself to her all while I was cursing her out and calling her everything but a child of God. Twenty minutes later, the guards

170

came in riot gear, dragged me out of my cell and took me into a part of the prison I had never seen. I was naked and they beat me senseless. My arms were cuffed behind my back and were so high in the air with my face to the cold concrete that it felt like they were injecting something in my arm. I thought that they were going to inject me with something that would make me go crazy. I thought they had brought me down there to kill me.

One guy put his boot in my neck and said, "*N***er, we make our own rules here.*" They beat me and kicked me in the head. I was surprised that I was still in my right mind when I got back to the hole.

Back in the hole, I told everyone that we're going on a hunger strike and not to eat for three days. I told them that we were going to live off the water in our cell. The water would sustain us. I did it because I wanted to get the attention of the captain, the lieutenant and the warden. I told the guys that, "*Someone from D.C. is going to talk to us and when they do we are going to tell them that we want a transfer and we are going to kill ourselves, if they don't transfer us because this institution is too racist!*" The captain came and personally interviewed everyone in the hole.

Two Mexicans next to me in the hole wrapped their faces with some sheets and set their three inch mattresses on fire. I thought they were crazy. They said, "*Mike, man we gonna go hard! We got matches; let's burn this place down, just cover your face with the sheet.*" I yelled "*Mexico, don't do that!*" They said, "*No, man, we did it before!*" But, I wasn't trying to go that far!

The entire solitary confinement area was filled with smoke. I could hear them talking with muffled voices because the sheets were over their faces. I thought, "*They were really going hard and they were going to kill all of us from smoke inhalation!*" The guards drug them out and used fire extinguishers to put out the fire.

The captain came and got me to talk. I told him, "*This institution is racist, man.*" He told me things that blew my mind. He told me that they knew I initiated the riot and that I broke the window. I knew that there were some snitches on board and my crew had already gone back to the prison on the compound. He told me that the reason the prison was racist was that most of the guards had never seen black people before they started working in the prison system. I told him, *"You're the problem then, you shouldn't have hired them in the first place."*

Eventually, the prison denied my request for a transfer and sent me back to the unit. I shared everything that happened to me in the hole with my homeboys. I told them about the beating, and about the lieutenant calling me the "n" word. I told them about the food strike and how the Mexicans set fire to the hole. I was blown away when Killer told me what happened to him. He was transferred to the county jail during the riot. He was sitting in the back of the van, handcuffed and shackled. It was just the lieutenant and him in the van. He looked through the 12"x12" window opening into the front and noticed Lieutenant putting on black gloves as he drove down a dark, dirt road. Killer said he pulled up on an empty, dark road, stopped the van and started looking around.

Lieutenant got out of the van and opened the back door, while holding a 12-gage, riot pump, shot gun. He told Killer to get out of the van. Killer said he scooted way up into the corner of the van screaming, *"I'm not getting out the van! I'm not getting out of the van!"* hoping that someone would hear him. Soon another van with inmates in it pulled up. The lieutenant put that gun away before the other van got there. The guard in the other van told the lieutenant, *"Hey, we saw you turn off. Is everything alright?"* Lieutenant said, *"Yes"* and he closed the door and proceeded to take Killer on to the jail. Killer said, that he knew if he had gotten out of the van, the lieutenant would have shot him to death and the report to his mother would have been that he tried to escape.

While I was on lockdown, my mother came to see me, and she was told that I had been transferred out. She had driven seven hours from Detroit to come to see me. When I got in touch with her, she asked where I had been. She didn't know where I was, and I hadn't talked to her for more than 145 days. I didn't want to alarm my mother, but when she told me that she came up to see me and they refused to tell her where I was, I told her what had transpired. I told her about the riots, but I refused to tell her the rest.

Two months after I had gotten out of the hole, they told me I was being transferred to Ray Brook, New York. My cellie, B.B. was going home in a few months and the rest of the crew would all be out within five years. I made my rounds and got everyone's addresses and numbers so that we could all keep in touch. I believe that transfer was a setup for failure since I was going to a disciplinary institution, but I wasn't impressed. I had gotten used to the system and wherever I went I knew people and people knew me. I had been bounced around so much and my reputation had preceded me. My attitude was let's get home and leave this life behind while I still have my mom there waiting on my return.

REACH OUT, I'LL BE THERE

Ray Brook was a disciplinary institution in New York, but to me it was like all the other prisons I'd been in. I was already well known in the system. Actually, transferring to different systems made my time go faster. Ray Brook sits next to Lake Tahoe on a mountain. Going up the mountain on a bus is intimidating. The mountain was steep, and there were no rails on the side. When I arrived in March that year, I heard so many rumors of people dying driving up that mountain. So, I didn't want my family to try to come and visit me there.

I called my mom after I got there. She told me that she planned to come and visit me when the weather broke. My mother made a point to come and visit me at least once a month at every institution I was in. I told her not to come because it was too dangerous. I didn't want to risk any freak accidents since I was so close to going home. I told her I would see her when I got out.

After a time, Linda started writing me again. She was aggressive about us being together again. When I asked her about her boyfriend, she said, *"I don't know how I'm going to get rid of him, but I promise you that he is not going to be here when you get home. We are going to be together. Give me a couple of months."*

I was so happy to talk to her since I hadn't heard from her in over a year. In the meantime, I met another girl through my brother. Her name was Glory. Glory was my brother's girlfriend's sister. We had begun writing each other while I was in Loretto. She was very attractive. Honestly, my heart was with Linda, even though she hurt me. I never stopped writing Glory, even after Linda started writing me again. I was close to getting out, so I just told them that I would be out next year. I was trying to make preparations for a future.

At Ray Brook, my crew consisted of about six other guys from Detroit. I continued to play ball and work out hard on the weights. I worked out with my friend Red who I had met when I was in Schuylkill. He was getting ready to get out, too. We worked out together twice a day. I wanted my body and my mind to be tight. I was also trying to cut down on smoking. My boy B, from Loretto, was writing me and I told him that I got transferred. He sent me $20.00. He told me straight up that he wasn't getting any money.

The next month he sent me another $20.00. All of a sudden, he sent me $250.00 and let me know that when I got out everything was going to be set up there because he had improved. I knew that meant he was getting money. Our plan was to hook up with Righty when we got out; however, B had hooked up with his people again and he was saying forget Righty in so many words.

It felt good to know that B.B. was doing alright and when I got out, I wouldn't be going home to nothing. Not only that, but Linda and Glory were sending me money, too. Many other of my friends who had heard that I was getting out sent me money, as well. A lot of my other friends were sending me money at that time, because they knew I was on my way home. I knew that everything is going to be alright.

About 45 days before my release date, Linda wrote me and said she wanted to catch the bus to New York so we could ride back together on the bus. I called her and asked her what had happened to 'old dude.' She told me that he jumped on her really bad and she shot him five times, but he didn't die! She didn't have to go to jail because it was ruled self-defense. From that moment, I felt indebted to her. I was excited, and it was a done deal. We were going to be together.

One day while playing on the basketball court, I got into it with this big dude from Jersey who was supposed to be a standup guy. We argued about a call. After we calmed down a little bit he said, *"Man, I knew it was your ball, I was just playing."* I said *"What?! You were just playing? I quit!"* I didn't play ball anymore. He had pissed me off so bad that I was almost about to fight him. I was too close to going home; and I wasn't about to let anything keep me from getting out of there. I had 45 days left. After that incident on the court, every time he would see me he would nod his head and say sarcastically, *"What's up, Detroit?"*

I worked in the gym, and he did it again every now and then. I walked up to him once and whispered in his ear and said, *"You need to stop playing with me, man because I'm really trying to go home next month."* When I said that he swung on me, but I saw it coming and rolled the punch. He hit my shoulder and I hit him about five times. He was a big, muscle bound dude so he rushed me, grabbed me, and wrestled me to the ground. I was glad that we took it to the ground. I could box but he was swinging so wildly, had he hit me he probably would have broken something or knocked me out. So, we end up in a wrestling match. I just held on to him tightly. The guys yelled, *"Here come the police!"* That meant we needed to break before we got sent to the hole. We broke up but there weren't any police. It was a false alarm. The Big dude said, *"Let's go in the bathroom and finish it!"* Agreeing that we would finish it, I went to get my shank. I had only about a month to go. I was thinking," *he wouldn't have played me like this a couple years ago. He's probably thinking that I'm going to play it safe because I'm getting ready to go home. I'm going to deal with him like I just got locked up!"*

I lived on the second floor in my unit. The ceiling was made of tiles. We punched a hole in the ceiling, outside of our cell, as big as a 50 cent piece and then taped the hole up with a piece of white paper so no one couldn't tell there was a hole there. This is where we kept the knife. It was made of steel like a screwdriver. I went to my unit to get the knife out of the ceiling. When I tried to reach it, I hit it with my finger and the knife moved about seven inches further into the ceiling where I couldn't reach it. I thought, *"Dang! Now, I don't have a weapon."*

I grabbed my lock and my roommate's lock off of our lockers and I connected them to an army type belt. I put on my burgundy hoodie and walked back toward the yard with the belt wrapped around my hand, with both my hands in the front hoodie pocket. Going towards the yard, there were seven guys from New York talking, and they saw me walking by. They say, *"Hold on, Detroit!"* I knew the dude I was beefing with was from Jersey, so I aggressively say, *"What!?"* thinking they were going to try to get me to squash the beef. One of the guys say, *"Mike don't go out on the yard, the police are checking everybody."* When they said that, I knew they were really looking out for me. The police were checking because they knew something was about to go down. I went back to my room and they locked down the unit for about an hour. Wherever you are, you had to remain. If you are found out of bounds you get sent to the hole. I was out of bounds because I worked in the gym, but I was in the unit. Thank God they didn't send me to the hole. Usually when they think something is going down, locking down the unit is the best way to catch people in the wrong place at the wrong time. They are able to send the inmates to the hole to keep trouble from happening that way. Had they sent me to the hole, they would have probably left me there since I had just a few weeks to go. I made up in my mind then that I was going to go after him.

Red came to my unit door after the count because he wanted to squash the beef. He said, *"Mike, I can't get in it man. I'm from Jersey. That's my homeboy, you my man, and my hands are tied."* I said, *"I ain't looking for nobody to get into nothing."* Red said, *"Gone and handle your business, man but I know he don't want no beef with you."* I heard rumors that he had hit another guy from Detroit with a weight bar while he was at another institution.

After count, I received letters from my mother, Linda and Glory and I got two money orders. That made it hard for me to go out. When I read the letters, tears rolled down my eyes, because I knew that I wanted to go home. Still, I had to correct the problem with that dude. I didn't go into the chow hall, but I was in the vicinity of the chow hall, so I could catch up with him. Somehow, he crept up behind me and said, *"Hey Mike, Mike!"* I turned and pulled out the belt because I was about to bust his head open. He yelled, *"Hold on, hold on"*, he pleaded and apologized saying, *"I don't want no beef."* He continued to apologize. I could see in his eyes that he really didn't want any trouble. That is what kept me.

After that incident, I sat on my bed and I realized that God was watching out for me. It was God that had the boys in the yard stop the fight. It was God who had caused me to lose my knife in the ceiling. It was God who had the guards checking everyone going back into the yard. It was God who had me to receive the letters that day to soften my heart up. It was God who had that big dude catch me off guard instead of me catching him off guard. It was God who caused him to apologize and it was definitely God who caused me to let the beef go.

My counselor and I made my release plan. When a person was about to be released, the prison would allow family members to send clothes to wear home. I was bigger leaving prison than I was when I went in. I entered prison weighing 150 pounds. Leaving prison, I had grew to be 185 pounds. My brother, Cordell, sent a Nike outfit including tennis shoes, sweat suit, and jacket.

The day I was to leave, I felt butterflies in my stomach. I just knew in my heart that something was going to go wrong, and I wouldn't be able to leave. I was talking to some friends of mine, leaning on the pool table in the middle of the common area. They were trying to encourage me by saying, "*You going home man. Today is your day. Here is my number, keep in touch because I'm going to be in here for a while.*" I kept saying, "*Man, I don't feel it, I felt like some old case was going to come up and keep me from going home*". I had seen that happen to other people, though this was just another form of thinking you will be rejected again.

R. Kelly's song *I Believe I can Fly* came on the TV right at that moment. It was like God, Himself spoke to me through the words of that song. I yelled out, "*I'm out of here! I'm out of here!*" They said, "*We know man why you yelling it like that?*" I said, "*God just spoke to me through this song!*" My relationship with God may have drifted a long way, but I was still able to recognize that this was God speaking to me through this song. As soon as I heard R. Kelly say that '*I believe I can walk through that open door*', a female officer walked into our unit, walked into the office and closed door. She sat in there for about five minutes and she came out and called out Robinson! I said, "*That's me.*" She said, "*Are you ready to go, do you have your stuff?*" I said, "*I have everything, my photo albums, awards I won, and telephone numbers.*" She said. "*Let's go, I'm going walk you to R & D (Receiving and Delivery) so you can get dressed.*"

I had over $400.00 on my books and the prison gave me $100.00 cash when I was released. My case manager drove me in the prison van to the bus stop. He gave me my bus ticket and said, "*Do you want me to wait with you and make sure you get on the bus alright?*" I said, "*No, I'm alright.*" I really did need his help, but I just wanted to be free from anything associated with prison. Linda had already planned to meet me in Albany, New York. When I got to Albany,

Linda was standing there waiting for me. She ran over to me and hugged me. She was wearing some spandex tights, boots and a pull over hoodie, with a leather jacket. I really needed her. I didn't know how to catch the Greyhound bus.

I was paranoid! I thought the Feds were trying to arrest me at every bus station. I kept telling Linda that the Feds were watching me. She wondered why I thought that. I told her because all of those people have walkie talkies and I was afraid to stand next to them. Linda said, "Those are phones Michael, cell phones." I didn't trust the people on the cell phones. We road from bus station to bus station.

I had to stay 40 days in a halfway house. I had to report to the halfway house 36 hours from the time I got out. I had a lot of layovers, but I made it to Detroit in about 15 hours. I had more than 16 hours to play around with before I had to report. I remembered seeing the Detroit sign as we traveled down I-94. I yelled out on the bus, *"I'm back in the D!"* The people on the bus thought I was crazy, but I was so happy to be home. We got back in Detroit about 11:00 p.m. I spent time with her for a couple of hours and then I called Cordell and he came to the house to pick me up. Linda was angry about it; but I wanted to go and see some of my friends, that I could catch up with who were awake at that time of night. I went by Pastor Gary Gay's house, who came to visit me while I was in jail. I knocked on their door about 1:00 a.m. When they saw me, they screamed and yelled; because they were so happy. Afterwards, Cordell and I went for a long ride through Detroit. He had a lot he wanted to share with me. One of the things he decided to tell me was that he and Carol had become pretty close during one of the years I was incarcerated. He said that she said she was going to marry me when I came home. He then told me that she was working at a topless bar, making a lot of money. Cordell said she used to hook him up with some of the girls from the bar. She allowed Cordell to use her apartment to spend time with the girls. He knew she was doing that to get close to him.

One day while Cordell was at Carol's apartment, he found some papers on her dresser from the Oakland County Friend of the Court. Cordell said that Carol had me down as the father of her other baby, as well. He said, *"I just wanted you to know that."* Hearing that really blew my mind. There was no way I was father of her other baby, because I would have had to have gotten her pregnant while I was in prison. I told Cordell, *"Don't worry about it; they probably just need some help financially. When I get on my feet, I'll look out for them."*

SIGNED, SEALED, AND DELIVERED

Early that morning, Cordell came to pick me up and take me to breakfast before I had to report to the halfway house. That halfway house was run like a tight ship. I heard rumors that before I got there the staff was relaxed and people paid them to be able to leave. They did have super tight rules. A person could go to church on Sunday; but they could only be gone for a total of four hours and had to bring back a church bulletin as proof.

The Detroit drug game was run by people like me who had served time in prison. For the most part, the dudes who ran it when I went to prison had fallen off. Because I had did my time in a federal prison, it was like I had been to the Ivy League Drug University of the world. My friends who were in prison with me, seemingly formed a bond: the no man left behind mentality. They would come to the halfway house to see me and make sure I was alright. Even though they couldn't get in, they would bring me cash between $1,500.00 and $2,000.00. They really looked out for me. Everyone who had made it home before me was doing good. It was just a matter of time before I got mine.

Linda had a hookup. She knew somebody doing credit card scams. It enabled me to go shopping and buy thousands of dollars' worth of clothes. I was looking good and had a pocket full of money. I saw a bright future ahead of me.

A girl I knew owned a beauty shop on Six Mile. Since I was in the halfway house I was responsible for getting a job. We set it up so that it looked like I worked for her making $200.00 a week. I had to pay $50.00 a week to the parole officer and a few dollars to the lady who was making the check stubs up for me. She covered for me when my parole officer would call. She would tell him that she sent me to the beauty supply store, then she'd call me, and we would call him back on a three way so that the beauty shop number would show up. He wasn't easily fooled. He would tell me, "*You sound like you are talking from far away, it sounds like you are on a three way call.*" My parole officer was the head parole officer at that time and he was about to retire. He told me that he only took high profile cases. I asked him, why did he have my case because my case wasn't high profile? "*I have your case and I see that you acted a fool in prison and I'm here to straighten your black a$@ out!*" He also said, "*I see you were found not guilty for a homicide case back in '89, and I see which attorney you had.*"

I'm going to tell you how the government looks at this. The government looks at it like you did the crime, and you hired a good attorney, so if you ever got caught in a crime they have a right to kill you because you have this on your record. I said why can't they look at it like what really happened. I was innocent and I hired a good attorney because I didn't want to go to jail for something I didn't do. I felt like I had the worst parole officer in the world. I did my time; and I was still under tight surveillance from my parole officer. I wasn't going to let him win, though. I was going to outsmart him sooner or later. I just needed to tighten up my game.

I only had like 40 days in the halfway house and then two weeks of home release with a curfew. After that, I was finished. Once I was done, I moved in with Linda in her apartment in Southfield. I always used my mom's address. My parole officer kept bothering me about the beauty shop and said that he wanted to see some real check stubs. I finally went and got a telemarketing job and managed to work that system, too. Nevertheless, I had a real job and he couldn't say anything about it. He would even come up there and see me sitting at my desk answering my calls and then leave. He started to lay off of me once he did that a few times.

I decided to get in touch with Righty. He told me to buy long distance calling cards and I could use the phone booth to call him. He told me to never call him from the same phone booth twice. Righty had been home for a little while and he was getting his guys back working again. Righty told me to grind up on some money because he wanted to show his guys that I had some money. I called my friend Deuce because he was making some money. He was really happy about that connection. He told me that he'd had a big connect like that years ago when I was locked up. He said, "*I made so much money that it scared me. I didn't know what to do with it. I had to break it off because I caught a real big case and I had to pay a whole lot of money to get out of it; and I beat the case. The feds tried everything they could to get me. You need me to help you because I didn't have anyone to help me through it.*"

Since my brother Cordell used to play ball overseas, he had a passport. I couldn't leave the country, but I was going to send my brother and Deuce to South America to get everything started. In the meantime, I called my man B, because he knew Righty, too. Righty said that he would sell me a half key of heroin for $15,000.00. That was unheard of. B said he would loan me the money to get the heroin and we would turn it into $90,000.00 within the next few weeks. Righty was going to have someone to meet us in Florida with the heroin.

We hired two guys to drive the heroin back for us. We were going to pay them $1,000.00 each. B and I rode in one car while our drivers rode in the other car. B had money, so he bought a plane ticket to fly back. That left me to drive back alone. I picked up Cordell in Jacksonville, Florida. He had flown down there, so he could help me drive back. We all made it back safe and sound. We got to the spot to hook up some of the stuff we had bought, and we found out it was fake! At that exact moment, Righty turned into a slime ball in my eyes. I called him. He said, "*Just like you know everything about basketball in your country, we know everything about drugs. Don't hold this incident against me. I will make it right.*"

Righty was very angry about what happened. He said, "*I'm going to have someone to fly out there tomorrow and give you every dime back.*" For some reason, I thought that he was lying. True to his word, Righty had someone to fly up to Detroit and give me back every penny. I gave B the money I owed him. We both agreed that Righty *was* a man of his word; and I was determined more than ever, to do business with him. He had proven himself.

YES, HE LOVES ME

Linda and I were living together, and we had great plans. I was also trying to make up for lost time in the joint. I couldn't help myself. I was playing the field. I was clubbing and hanging out, buying everybody drinks and letting the city know that I was back. Eventually, Linda finally got tired of my foolishness and we broke up.

I had to swallow my pride and ask my father if I could move back in with him. I had to keep a job; I was working at a video warehouse factory for minimum wages and I was working like a slave. There were about 200 to 300 employees. I knew a supervisor who worked there, and I would pay her to let me leave. She'd punch me out at the end of the shift. I would go and hang out at a couple chicks' houses until my shift was over and then go back home.

We kept pushing the date back for Cordell and Deuce to go overseas and meet with Righty. I was hanging out at the bar drinking one day, and this butch looking girl came up to me and asked me if I had a car. I said, "*Yeah, why do you want to know that?*"

She asked if I wanted to mess around with her girl. Her girl walked up and she was drop dead gorgeous! I asked the girl, *"What do I have to do to get the full treatment?"* She said, *"You have to give my girl $100.00."* I gave her the money and went to the car. The streets were different when I came out of the joint. Women pimped other women. Her language and her body movements reminded me so much of Linda that I decided to ride out to Linda's house. I saw her car in the parking lot. I knew she was there and that she wouldn't answer the bell. I threw some pennies up to her window on the third floor where she lived. I saw a curtain move but she didn't answer the door. I thought to myself, *she's in there with some dude.* My mother started paging my beeper over and over again. When that happened, I knew Linda had called my mother and told her that I was outside of her apartment trying to get in.

I rushed back to the bar doing 80 mph before I responded to my mother's call. I called her from the bar so that the caller ID would show where I was. I convinced her that I was at the bar and not at Linda's. Afterwards, I got in the car and went right back to Linda's apartment. That time I was determined to get it. She had me twisted! When I got there, I rang all of the buzzers except for hers and somebody buzzed me in. I got to the third floor and just kicked the door in. There were two guys in her apartment. One guy was sitting on the sofa watching TV. He jumped up and said, *"Hey man, I don't want any trouble!"* He ran out of the door without warning his friend. Linda and her new boyfriend were in the bedroom and they didn't hear the commotion. I got to the bedroom door and kicked it in, too. The man she was with was taller and thicker than I was. He grabbed me and manhandled me pushing me and slamming me down and finally got me to the front door and slammed me out of the door. It was like an answer to prayer, because when he let me go, I started putting those pieces on him. As I was punching him, he was making noises and hollering. Blood was coming from his face. I thought that I had broken his nose. I ran back into the apartment and grabbed a knife and said to Linda, "*I'm going to kill them because I see that's who you want to be with!*", but I was bluffing. I wanted to know if things were serious between them. I wanted to see her response. I wanted to know if I had a shot or if she had given her heart to him. Linda, stood in the doorway and said, "*Please Michael, just leave, I've already called the police.*" Linda had called my mother, Cordell and the police. I dropped the knife and said, "*I'm out of here.*" She really loves this dude. As soon as I did that, the Southfield police rushed into the apartment. Reality hit me when I saw the police.

I knew that I had messed up and I was going back to prison because I was not supposed to have any contact with the police. I was on a four years parole. Cordell got the call and he was on the eastside. He drove at top speed all the way to Linda's house. By the time Cordell arrived, he saw about ten police cars and he thought I had killed someone. Later, he told me that he said to himself, "*Dang, he just got out of prison and now he's about to go back!*"

The police took me to jail and charged me with 'breaking and entering and two counts of assault and battery.' I was on four years of parole, and I was about to go back to prison. I knew that the next time they saw me on the streets of Detroit, it would be in about 25 years. Look how fast somebody can get in trouble by acting a fool. I got out on bond the next day. Cordell called my parole officer. The parole officer told Cordell to tell me to come and see him when I got out of jail. Cordell begged him not to lock me up. He pleaded, "*I know my brother got drunk and went and acted crazy, but that's not him. Please don't lock my brother up.*" He told Cordell, "*Tell him to come and see me and I'm not going to lock him up.*"

Cordell told me what he said and told me to go and see him. I said, "*Naw, he lying, I'm not going, I know how this system works!*" Cordell said, "*No! He said he wasn't going to lock you up!*" I said, "*Do you think he will tell you the truth?*" I didn't trust that parole officer, but I went anyway to see him.

When I got to my parole officer's office, he sat me down and said these words, *"When I went to your house, I saw how you were raised. I saw how nice your house was and how nice your lawn was manicured. I knew that your father made you take care of the lawn, when you were a kid. I remembered that you told me that when you were younger you attended Bishop Bonner's church. Even though I never liked that church, I know Bishop Bonner, and I knew that he ran a tight ship. I've watched you and I know that you are a good-hearted guy and a good young man."* Then he said, *"I have a master's in psychology, and you are one of the best fellas I ever had an opportunity to be their parole officer. That is why I harassed you when you told me that lie that you worked at the beauty shop. I knew you didn't work at that beauty shop. I believed that I was assigned to be your P.O. to bring some order into your life."*

He said, *"When you get some liquor in you it ain't no telling what you will do!"* When he said that, tears began to roll down my cheeks as I thought, *"I was 32 years old, sitting in his office crying like a baby, because for the first time in my life I realized what had been missing. It was a father."* That conversation was one that I should have had a long time ago with my own father. I thought, *"how can he recognize all of this in me and he just met me, and my father never saw it."* He encouraged me to get it together. He had the goods in his hand to put me away, but he gave me another chance. He told me, *"Most people go back to prison within six months. If they can stay out past the six month period, they can make it."*

At the time I was at my six month period. He said, *"If I was a white parole officer, I would have sent you back to prison. Do you want to know why?"* I said, *"Why?"* *"Because, I wouldn't have taken the time to study the person you are."* All this time I thought I had the worst parole officer and he turned out to be a blessing in disguise. We talked for over an hour; he even pulled Cordell into the office and talked to us both.

IF THE TRUTH BE TOLD

Love is an action word. It's a verb, because it must be given out to fulfill a hunger. The Bible says: "God so loved the world that He gave…" Love is far more than a conversation, because love mollifies a wound, heals the broken hearted, sets the captives free. Love always comes ready to alleviate the pain of others by doing all within its power. That's why the scripture tells us God is love and every good and perfect gift comes from above. My parole officer was given to me by God Himself because God is omniscient; He knows everything. God already knew I was going to violate my parole before I ever did. So, He had predestined me with supernatural help, far past the devil's assigned time of destruction. What an awesome Father we have in God, who can make a way when there is no way.

David said, "*God is my strength: my refuge, my present help in a time of trouble…*" I was definitely in trouble, big trouble even though His word had manifested itself in my life.

SECTION NINE:

MY FATHER'S BLOOD

1997 - PRESENT

LORD JESUS, HELP ME

On Devil's Night, I was on the phone on a three-way call talking to some relatives of mine when all hell broke loose. They asked, *"Where is your father?"* They knew that my father and I had a rocky relationship and we never saw eye to eye. I told them, "He should be home any minute now." It was around 3:00 p.m. Suddenly, I heard noises at the side door of the driveway. I was sitting in my parent's room in a chair while I talked on the phone, I said, *"Speaking of the devil, I guess he's coming in now."*

Next, I heard the glass on the side door shatter. I said, *"Hold on it sounds like somebody is bothering my mother or father!"* I put the phone down and ran to the door. Cordell was asleep upstairs. As I ran to the side door, I passed the kitchen window and my heart dropped because the DEA was in the driveway trying to bust down the door. They were hollering *"Police, Police!"* I yelled, *"Please don't knock down my mother's door, it's a dead bolt, I have to use a key to open it!"* They continued hitting the door with the battering ram and telling me to hurry up and open it. I didn't want to stand in front of it because it could bust me in the face. I tried to open the door from the side without standing in front of the door and at the same time alert my brother to what's going on.

I knew that Cordell was asleep upstairs, so I yelled out his name to wake him up. *"Cordell, Cordell wake up, wake up!"* All I thought was, *"if they get in and they run up the stairs he would jump up out of his sleep by reflex, to defend himself, which could get my brother killed."* Finally, Cordell ran down the stairs in his underwear yelling *"what's up Mike!?"* I yelled at him to get on the floor. *"Get on the floor and put your hands out!"* He said, *"What's going on?!"* I said, *"Shut up and lay on the floor with your arms out, so they can see your hands! It's a raid."* I had been in raids before so I knew how to respond.

One of the most frightening situation I had ever encountered in my life was a raid. It's because all of your rights are violated. You're overtaken by a gang of 10 to 15 people who break into your house with high powered weapons ready and willing to kill you.

Soon, I was laying outstretched on the kitchen floor and Cordell was laying on the hallway floor. I saw infrared lights pointed all over my brother's body. So I yelled at the officers, *"He's down, ain't nobody else in here! Put the cuffs on him! He's down! Nobody else is in here!"* I was trying to show the officers how to conduct the raid without anybody getting hurt, especially my little brother. The officers were running through the house and Cordell kept asking, *"What's going on Mike?"* I told him to be quiet and just stay down. I then asked the police, *"Please get a dog and don't tear up my mother's house!"*

My mom and dad hadn't returned home yet, but I knew that they were about to walk into a nightmare. The phone was still off the hook so Mary and my cousin, Pam heard everything that was going on. They listened to the entire raid. They handcuffed me and Cordell and sat us down on the living room sofa, while they ran around looking for drugs and tearing up my mother's house. Mom and dad walked into the house and I put my head down. The police didn't handcuff them but asked them to wait in the kitchen. Those policemen's whole demeanor changed when my parents walked into the house. I was never so happy to see my father come home.

I began to feel God was trying to relay a message to me through that experience. I had just gotten into trouble at Linda's house and now I was in trouble again. Grace was prevalent that day. Its presence was real. It was like God was saying, *"I'm giving you enough grace to make a decision and if you don't make the right decision, I'm going to slam the door on you!"*

I decided at that moment. I bowed my head in the midst of all of the commotion and in a small whisper I said these words, *"Lord, if You get me out of this, I promise I'll serve You and I will never look back."* I knew I was in a position where a lawyer couldn't help me, and my parents' hands were tied. Only Jesus could help me. It was out of man's hands; it was a task that only God could perform. I needed my heavenly Father to work a miracle. I had made so many wrong decisions in my life that I felt the same way the prodigal son felt when the Bible said he came to himself. I knew that play time was over. It was *praying* time.

A woman police officer said, *"The search warrant says Michael Robinson."* I looked at Cordell and said, *"Tell her you are Cordell, and I'm going to verify it. They are not looking for you."* Cordell looked at me and said, *"C'mon dog, I ain't no snitch! I ain't going out like that!"* I whispered to him, *"Bro, this ain't snitching, both of us don't need to go to jail, if you go downtown you're going to have a case. Tell them who you are!"* He said, *"For real."* I put my head down again and I said, *"Lord, I promise you, I will serve you, I promise you I will serve you!"* The hell with an attorney; I need Jesus as my lawyer! Cordell knew I was in trouble because he overheard me say, *"Lord, help me Jesus!"*

The woman officer said who is Michael? I said, *"I am"*. She said, *"Stand up, young man"* to Cordell. Cordell stood up and she took the handcuffs off of him. She looked at me and said, *"Stand up,"* and she removed the handcuffs from me, too! Me of little faith, I kept my hands behind my back thinking those were her personal cuffs, and they were going to put some more cuffs on me to take me downtown. The police woman noticed my hands behind my back, and she said, *"You're free to go."* It was amazing to me that I was free to go and they had confiscated $20,000.00 out of my mom's house. Yes, it was drug related, but I didn't have any drugs in the house. It didn't make sense that they didn't take me to jail!

The police walked out of the door, but I knew that I would be indicted by the federal government based on the fact that they raided the house. I just didn't know why they raided my mom's house, but the moment they left, I started paging Deuce. He never called me back. I began thinking he had something to do with the FBI coming to my mother's house. I paged one of Deuce's closest friends and he called me back. I told him, *"Meet me somewhere. I need to talk to you about something."* I was going to get some answers or else. Little did I know, that he was coming to get some answers, as well. I didn't know at the time that Deuce was in jail and they had raided four other houses at the same time they were raiding mine. The Feds had finally caught up to Deuce. Thank God we never moved forward with the South American connection or my brother would have been locked up, too. The Feds had pictures of me having conversations with Deuce. They probably raided my mom's house after they pulled my record and saw that I was fresh out of prison.

I met Deuce's friend at a McDonald's at 9:00 that night. Although it was Devil's night, the Lord still had power. I had victory on Devil's night. The dude I met that night thought I had snitched because Deuce was in jail. I thought Deuce had snitched, because I hadn't heard from him. I asked him where was Deuce and he told me that Deuce was locked up. I told him that the Feds just raided my house. He was surprised! We didn't know what was going on. I called my parole officer and told him that the Feds raided my house for no reason. The parole officer said, *"Don't worry about it. I didn't lock you up before so I'm not going to lock you up this time. Just report on your regular day."*

I really made up my mind to turn my life around. When I was a child, I heard that you have to be careful what you say, because what you say the devil can hear and will try to stop your plan. So, I didn't tell anybody that I was finished, nor did I tell anybody that I was going to have one last fling that weekend, because on Monday, I was going to surrender to God, totally. I was going to fast Monday, Wednesday and Friday and seek God for direction.

That weekend, I smoked marijuana and I wasn't even a marijuana smoker. I got drunk and I spent time with several different women. It was all out of my system. Monday, my new life began. I fasted and prayed for an hour in the morning and in the

192

evening, and I did the same on Wednesday and Friday. I lay out on the hard tile floor upstairs crying out to Jesus. On Friday, He baptized me in the Holy Ghost again, with the evidence of speaking in tongues. From that day forward, I did not look back. I disassociated myself with everyone I knew in the streets. I was MIA. It wasn't that I didn't love them; I just could not be around them at that time in my life because I wasn't strong enough to fight off temptation. I was baptized with the Holy Ghost and with fire!

Everyone who came around me knew that I had that fire and that I was crazy about God. I would walk to a church that was close to my mother's house for Bible class on Tuesday night. The next night, in the cold, I would walk to another church for Wednesday night Bible class. I went to prayer at Straight Gate. I was hungry and desperate for God. My mother would let me use her car to go to Pastor Gay's church on the eastside on Sunday. I couldn't get enough of God's presence.

I had a court date coming up regarding the incident at Linda's house. If those two witnesses came to court I would have a case. Linda already said she wasn't coming but the other two guys were subpoenaed. Linda said, "*Mike, they weren't street guys and they are afraid of you, so they are coming to court.*" I was afraid. I walked to the church for Wednesday night Bible class. After Bible class, the Pastor asked if anyone needed prayer. Nobody said anything. I would sit in the back of the church because I felt so unworthy. I waved my hand. The Pastor said, "*Come up here, son.*" He told the congregation, "*Lets pray for this young man. Is your prayer request spoken or unspoken?*" I said. "*Pastor, I want to speak this thing. I have a court date tomorrow and if the two witnesses show up you won't see me again because I will go to prison for a long time.*" The pastor and those church mothers prayed like never before.

I went to court the next day. My brother and I only had $3,000.00 left from the money we made in the streets. I had to give it all to the attorney. After giving the attorney that money, there was nothing left from the past. The money I made never really did me any justice and I never started what I wanted to do, but at that moment, I knew I was in a place of refuge and nothing mattered because I felt safe in the arms of Christ.

My court time was 9:00 a.m. I sat in the courtroom until about 9:40 a.m. Thank God that the two witnesses didn't show up. I was happy that the case was going to be thrown out, but, to my surprise, the prosecuting attorney said he wanted to change the time to 1:00 p.m. and that they were going to go to the witnesses' jobs and get them. I looked at my attorney and said, *"They can't do that, can they?"* He said, *"I'm afraid they can."* I returned back to court at 1:00 p.m. The witnesses must have skipped work because they didn't show up at 1:00 p.m. either. The prosecuting attorney was so mad that his face turned red as an apple. I said, *"Lord, I told you, I'm going to serve you."* I walked out with a clean slate.

I went to see my parole officer and I told him, *"I'm saved; I'm going to let Jesus drive this car the rest of the way. I've been driving too long. You see, I would allow Jesus to be the co-pilot, and at times He would have to snatch the wheel. Since we had switched seats, I was riding with Him!"* My parole officer knew that Jesus had changed my life. He said, *"Like the old folks used to say, I see a glow on you, I see a difference."* I felt like God used my parole officer to be a part of the changes in my life.

I was living for Jesus. I was saved, but I was still addicted to smoking cigarettes. I only smoked about three or four cigarettes a day, but I couldn't stop. God told me to go on a seven day fast and I would be able to stop. I went on the fast, because I knew that if I fasted for seven days, I didn't smoke for seven days. During the fast, I kept counting down to the eighth day, so that I could smoke a cigarette. I was craving a cigarette so bad that I couldn't help it. On that eighth day, God told me to fast for seven more days. He instructed me that I could eat, just don't smoke, and He let me know that He would help me. I don't know how much it helped, because I still wanted to smoke every day. I had just enough energy not to smoke. I determined that nothing was going to stop me from smoking after those seven days. When I came to the end of them, God reminded me of a book I had read in prison. It said that if you do anything for 21 days you can make or break a habit. So, I pushed it seven more days. I couldn't wait for those seven days to end because I said to myself, *if the habit is gone I can smoke and get away with it and it won't bother me anymore.* God said to push it to 30. I pushed it to 30 and I said, *"I don't care what happens, I'm smoking!"* On the 29th day, I went to the store to buy a pack of cigarettes with the intent to fire up on the 31st day. I got mad because the desire was gone. I said, *"God tricked me."*

I went to God and I said, *"I don't think You were honest with me because You said if I fasted for seven days, You would help me. I thought you were a God who cannot lie".* God spoke back to me and said, *"I am a God that is line upon line, and precept upon precept, I give a little here and I give a little there. I never give the whole vision to any man. I didn't tell you that you would have to go 30 days because you wouldn't have been able to handle it. So, I gave you only what you could handle at the time."*

During my journey I began to see how the Father's love really was, and He started to teach me how to trust Him. At the time I wasn't working, and I was looking for a job. I read an ad in the newspaper that said employment was available at Metropolitan Airport. My mom drove there so I could fill out an application. After I filled out the application, I asked the lady, *"Where do I put the application?"* She told me to put it in that box. I looked and saw the box was full of at least 200 applications. She said, *"The box is filled with over 100 applications every day."* When she wasn't looking, I stole the applications and only left five in the box along with mine. I tucked the applications in my coat and walked out.

My mother was waiting in the car for me and she saw the applications. She said, *"What are you doing with all of those applications?"* I told her, *"I stole them because everyone is applying for the same job".* My mother said, *"You're either going to do it God's way or you're not!"* So, I had to go back into the office and sneak them back into the box when the receptionist wasn't looking. After all of that and with all of those applications, I knew I was the least qualified, but thanks be to God, they hired me! God showed me that He was in control and that I had to trust Him. God was being a Father to me. He was showing me the relationship between a father and a son. God was showing me that He would turn my mess into a miracle. Yes, He was teaching me how to trust Him. I had real trust issues because I didn't think I could depend on my natural father and it spilled over into my ability to trust God. Often times we relate to the Father how we relate to our natural fathers. I believe that God was showing me the Father that He wanted me to be. God began to give me what I would ask Him for. Sometimes I would have to wait. It was at those times when He showed me how to wait and be ready when it comes.

YOU KEEP ON BLESSING ME

My job at the airport was fueling the airplanes. The devil would talk to me at times all the way to work and back. I was making $8.00 an hour. He would taunt me and say, *"You making a five-dollar bill, two singles and four quarters, for a whole hour's worth of work."* Then he would say, *"There was a time when someone could talk to you for one hour and hustle you out of a couple hundred dollars, but now you only making a five-dollar bill, two singles and four quarters for a whole hour's worth of work."*

I felt like giving up, because I could picture myself back on my feet again, driving a decent car, living in a nice home, and having the nice wardrobe that I was accustomed to having. I needed a boost. I needed a head start. There was only one thing that kept me from giving up, and that was that the Bible says that faith comes by hearing. It doesn't say it comes by what you heard. It says it comes by hearing, which means constantly hearing. Mom had a cassette tape in her car, by the late great legendary, Church of God in Christ

196

Presiding Bishop G.E. Patterson, entitled, "Hold On, Help is on the Way!" God had a plan every step of the way.

I listened to the tape going to work and going home from work. If I listened to it without hearing the choir singing and the beginning scripture, the message lasted about 26 minutes. There was just enough time to hear the whole sermon all the way to work from my parents' house and I would listen to it again on the way back home from work. That sermon was a faith builder. My faith was coming to life. Every time the message was preached it was like God spoke to me telling me, *"Hold on son, don't give up and don't quit, because help is on the way!"*

One day, a friend of mine had been paging me over and over. I avoided answering and returning his calls at first. Then, I decided to stop at the phone booth on my way to work to call him back. He told me that he had a plan and he needed some help. He said he had $5.00 and $10.00 plates to make counterfeit bills. Then he told me that something told him to call me. He said he makes about $20,000.00 a week, but it leaves him exhausted. He said if I helped him to make the counterfeit money we could make at least $40,000.00 a week. He needed help and he told me again that something told him to give me a call. I knew *that* something was the enemy, but I continued to listen, because I desperately needed some money. I held the phone for at least eight seconds after he finished talking. I was thinking until he said, *"Mike, Mike are you there?"* I was contemplating what I should do.

He told me that the way he got rid of the money was by buying kilos of cocaine with it from some guys in Tennessee. He said that he had to pay a few thousand more than normal for them. It didn't matter because the guys weren't getting real money anyway. Listening to him and holding that phone contemplating what he propositioned made me want to say yes. My flesh, my entire being, wanted to give in to that temptation, but the Spirit of God in me said, *"NO!"* When I finally spoke, I said these words, *"If it didn't come from God, then I don't want it."* I meant what I said, too. If I was going to trust God, I knew that I had to trust Him all the way. I was all in. I hung up the phone and realized that for God I live and for God I would die.

I neglected to put down that I was incarcerated on the application at the airport. I hadn't been truthful and after working there for a couple of months, my past caught up with me. Eventually, I was released and unemployed again. I was going hard for the Lord to maintain my salvation and to keep my sanity. So, my week was full of church services. On Tuesdays and Wednesdays, I would walk to Bible class at churches in the neighborhood. I would also go to a church on Thursday night for midnight prayer from 12:00 midnight to 2:00 a.m. On Friday nights, I would go to Straight Gate for prayer. I would even go to Emmanuel's Temple church on Mondays for noon day prayer. I was fully covered. I was in church every day of the week. As loyal as I was to the streets, I was even more loyal to God. A change had taken place in me. I was praying my way through.

Every Sunday, I would attend Deliverance Temple of Faith under the leadership of Pastor Gary because it was the only day my mother would allow me to use her car. I was loyal to the ministry because Pastor Gary was loyal to me. When I was locked up he came to visit me, and I appreciated it. He was a junior pastor at Solomon's Temple before he became pastor at Deliverance Temple of Faith. When I received the Holy Ghost, I joined his church and was faithful.

The first sermon I preached was in his pulpit. It was entitled, "It's Your Choice". I studied a whole month for that message. I took notes. I wanted that message to be just how I prepared it. I thought I did a perfect job. When I got up to preach Pastor Gary anointed me and prayed for me. The church held about 80 people, but there had to be about 125 people in the church the day I preached my first sermon. Half of them were people that I knew from the street. My old crew had come to the church to see if ole Mike Robinson was serious with God or playing a game. A lot of my friends and girls were there. I hadn't seen them in a long time. Somehow the word had gotten out. I believe that they came to see a show, but the Holy Ghost was about to take over.

I had made up in my mind that I was going to preach this message perfectly. All I had to do was glance at the papers and preach every word on the paper. I was a little nervous and a little shook up, but I got really nervous when I got up to the pulpit and discovered that I had left my notes at home. I shared with the congregation that I left my notes. I told them that I had a plan and God had another one, and that I would have to depend upon the Holy Ghost. My text was from Joshua 24:15, *"As for me and my house, we will serve the Lord."*

I preached so hard, I didn't even know who I was. My friends knew at that moment that I had been changed. The whole church went up. The people were shouting and dancing and crying and I knew that God had used me. A friend of mine by the name of Lovell Cannon called me on the telephone and said, *"What I want you to do, I want you to go to Solomon's Temple and get the same training that I got. You need to sit up under Bishop W. L. Bonner for a while, so you can get some balance in your life."* He was saying in so many words that I was too hard headed and too rebellious and that no one could tell me anything. I needed to get under someone that I would honor and respect and who could teach me. At that time, I was all over the place, preaching and giving my testimony wherever I was asked to go. I really wasn't *submitted* to any leader.

I decided to take Lovell's advice, because I respected him and I really respected Bishop Bonner since he had always been a father figure in my life. I honored him as a true soldier in the Lord. I went to Solomon's Temple on a Friday night. Bishop Bonner was one of the few pastors who would lay hands on everybody in the church, and there could be more than 2,000 people in attendance. That night, as usual, Bishop Bonner was laying on hands. After the service, I walked up to Bishop Bonner and I said, "Bishop Bonner I know you don't remember me." I hadn't seen Bishop Bonner since 1985 when he preached my brother's funeral. It was 1999, fourteen years later and as I shook his hand he looked at me. As he looked at me, he gripped my hand tighter and said, "*I know you, you are a Robinson.*" I almost burst into tears. I thought to myself, "*This is my spiritual father!*" I knew at that moment that Pastor Lovell had heard from the Lord. I told him, "*Bishop Bonner I really need to sit down and talk to you, so I will make an appointment with your secretary because I know that you are very, very, busy now.*" He said, "*Son, do you have time tonight?*" A tear rolled down my face. I said, "*Wow, this is confirmation that this was a divine appointment right here.*" He said, "*Son if you got time. I have time. Let me finish greeting the people and we can go into the office and talk.*"

When we sat together in his office he simply asked, "*What is it, son?*" I said, "*I really want to be a member here, Bishop. I'm called to preach, but I feel that I can't be free here because the people know too much about my past. The people knew that my brother and I were in the streets selling drugs. You preached my brother's funeral after he was shot and killed. They knew I had been shot, that I was on Michigan's Most Wanted and that I had been in prison. As much as I want you to be my leader, I know that the church would always condemn me here and I wouldn't be free.*"

Bishop looked at me and said, "*Son, I'm the Pastor of this church. If anybody condemns you in this church, whoever it is, bring them to me, and I will put them out of this church!*" I knew that Bishop Bonner wasn't being completely honest with me. I didn't believe he would put anybody out of the church if they gave me any trouble. I also knew that Bishop Bonner was giving me his stamp of approval to be free from condemnation in his house. When he said that I felt like the prodigal son. He let me know in so many words that he had my back.

He was a real spiritual father. He tried me, and he tested me. He told me that they had prayer on Saturdays at 6:00 a.m. He said, I want to see you on your face lying next to me at 6:00 in the morning. I was on my face the next day at 5:45 a.m. When he came out of prayer, he began singing *Blessed Assurance*. Then he looked at me and nodded his head as if to say, "*You're here and you kept your promise!*" Shortly after that, we reestablished the most powerful father and son relationship I ever had.

TRUST IN HIM

I started going to different job fairs because I needed employment. I also needed a car and a place to stay. I needed money. I didn't have a pot to piss in or a window to throw it out of.

One day, I saw on the television that there was a prophet coming to Straight Gate church. Straight Gate was one of the largest churches in Detroit. They advertised the prophet as a true man of God. My cousin, Kathy was saved, too; we used to visit different churches all of the time. So, she and I went to Straight Gate. The prophet preached a powerful message, but after the message he did stuff that really annoyed me. He asked for seven people to come up to the altar to give a thousand dollars. I didn't have a Chinese yen in my pocket.

Four people walked to the front and got envelopes from the prophet to give the thousand dollars. There were three envelopes left. He said, "*If you don't have the money now, don't worry about it. Have the faith to believe that God will bless you with it this week.*" Then he said, "*I speak this thing into your life.*" I decided to go up and get an envelope. I said to myself, "*I want to see how God is going to bless me with this money. The only way I'm going to give $1,000.00 is He's going to have to bless me with $10,000.00.*" So, I took the envelope and placed it in my Bible in the 28th chapter of Deuteronomy. I remembered my Pastor, Apostle William L. Bonner preaching from that scripture a lot. He called it the blessing plan.

I didn't get the $1,000.00 blessing that week. I held onto the envelope, but I felt that the prophet's words had fallen to the ground void. I discredited him as not being a true man of God. I was scrutinizing leaders at the time. I would look for ways to judge them.

That next week on a Friday, my brother and I were sitting in the driveway in his car. We had a disagreement and I got out of the car to go into the house; he handed me $100.00. I walked to the door to go into the house and he blew the horn and waved me back to the car. He said, *"Here goes nine more hundred dollars; put that with it. You can use that to put down on a car. I won some money in Vegas this week."*

I was being tested. I didn't think I had to give the $1,000.00 to the church because the prophet said I was supposed to get the money the previous week. I called a couple of people who I respected and they said, *"No, I wouldn't put that in church."* I called Sherry, who was like a spiritual big sister to me. She told me, *"Mike that's a test."* I asked her, *"What would you do?"* She said, *"I don't know what I would do. I don't think I would do it if I was in your position, but I know what you are supposed to do. If you do this, God is going to bless you."*

I went to Straight Gate that night, as usual, for Friday night prayer. Straight Gate was not having prayer that night. There were about twelve people in the prayer room making programs for another event. The devil knew that I was right next to my breakthrough and he was trying to stop me. I told them that I was there to drop some money off. I told them the story about the prophecy and how the money didn't come that week but it came the week after. I pulled the envelope out with the thousand dollars in it and the people said they couldn't take the money; I would have to bring it back on Sunday.

I grabbed the money out of the envelope and I said, *"Ma'am, if I keep this money until Sunday I'm not going to give it to the church."* I was already thinking" *I don't want to give it to you anyway!"* I slid the money down the table and said, *"Y'all can split it, because I know what*

I'm supposed to do. I'm getting this off of me." The mother ran and grabbed the money and said, *"Oh Lord, at least fill out the envelope because when Pastor hears your testimony he's going to want you to come down and tell your testimony on the air."*

When I gave them the money, it felt like a burden lifted off of my shoulder. I went home and told my mom. While I was talking, my brother came in and overheard the conversation. He was angry, and I understood, because he was trying to help me. He pulled me to the side and said, *"I know you saved and all that, but I need to tell you something that's very important."* He said, *"There's a thin line between faith and foolishness. I hope you were walking in faith because I ain't got no more money for you to give to those churches."*

I went on a fast. I said I was going to fast until the Lord gave me a job. My normal routine was to meet God at 10:00 in the morning and pray for about an hour. I would lay in my mother's den on my face. It was Monday and I was planning on going to a job fair at Cobo Hall at 1:00 p.m. I made up my mind to pray from 10:00 a.m. to 12:00 Noon, and afterwards I would take the bus to the job fair. The phone started ringing while I was praying. My mother answered the phone and she tapped me on the shoulder and said I want you to take this call.

It was a manager at General Motors who was over a department in six different locations. He went to school with my brother. He said, *"Hey Mike, I'm going to hire you. Can you meet me at the plant at 2:00 p.m. tomorrow? Dress professional; wear some khaki pants, a business shirt and some black shoes. I need you to dress like a supervisor, because that's who you are."* Won't God do it!

I met him at the plant and I had to complete all of the employee paperwork. He knew my situation. I said to him, *"I have one problem."* He said, *"What's the problem?"* I said, *"Every time I fill out the application if I put down I've been convicted they don't hire me. If I lie on it, they find out and fire me."* He said, *"That ain't your problem. You don't even have to complete an application. Just fill out these W-2 forms."* I didn't even have to lie. God was teaching me how to trust Him.

Thirty days later, they had a one-day sale for Chevy Tahoe trucks. They were zero down, standard trucks, nothing extra. I got there late, and they told me to come back the next day to complete the rest of the paperwork. I went back before work the next day and completed the paperwork. The salesperson was in the office talking for a long time and I was waiting at the desk and the enemy was talking to my mind. I was on the verge of doubting by listening to the enemy's voice. God was teaching me to trust in Him. He was showing me how great a Father He really is.

The sales person came back with another sheet of paper for me to fill out. She said, *"I need you to complete this form again."* I said, *"For what?"* It was 1998. She said *"We have a 1999 Chevy Tahoe. It is fully loaded and the people refused to take it so we are going to give it to you for the same sale price."* It had leather interior, bucket seats, DVD, sunroof, everything was automatic. I didn't even have to give a down payment. It was a blessing. God was teaching me how to trust in Him and not in man.

When I looked around, I was making about $20.00 an hour with all of the overtime I wanted. I had a brand new, fully loaded truck, and would soon move into my own place. That $1,000.00 seed opened doors and I took quantum leaps. My brother saw the hand of God on my life. He knew that I was not walking in foolishness, but it was faith. I had hope. God kept me. I was working the afternoon shift. Women would call me, but by the time I got off work, it was too late to go by their houses to get into any temptation that the devil would bring my way. Don't get it twisted, I wanted to go to their homes, but God was keeping me.

I was getting tired of visiting different churches and the pastors inviting me up to the pulpit to tell my testimony. It made me feel like that was all I had to offer. I wanted to know the word and be a preacher of God's word and give my testimony by choice, and not by force. I decided to go to Bible College at Solomon's Temple under Bishop Bonner. It was called Berea Bible College. I would go into the ministers' meeting on Wednesdays and on Sundays, too, as the minister would delegate the ministerial duties. Those ministers had been preaching for 10 to 20 years. I felt like a kindergartener sitting in a room with high school students. I felt inadequate. I felt intimidated and, at times, I felt like quitting.

Whenever the ministerial duties were given out, no one would volunteer for baptizing newly converted Christians. There were only two of us who were willing to accept that responsibility. We baptized everyone who would come to the altar for baptism for at least two years. We would make jokes that the other ministers were afraid of the water. The truth of the matter is all of the other ministerial duties were jobs where they could be seen, such as leading prayer, reading the scripture, introducing the soloist and exhortation. Those were the ministerial duties that were done in front of the congregation, while the ministers who baptized were hidden from sight. I was being trained on the back side of the desert like Moses. I needed to be there, because I was hotheaded, and I needed to be humbled.

I called my friend, Pastor Cannon, who was my God sister Kitty's brother, to complain about having to baptize every Sunday. He said, "Keep doing what you doing; you're getting the greatest blessing." I didn't always want to baptize because I had to change clothes and we would always be the last people to leave the church. I wanted to go to dinner and since I was single, I wanted to talk to the women after church. God kept me celibate by keeping me in the baptism pool. I was learning how to serve. My Father was making me.

At the ministerial meetings, I felt so far behind the others because they knew the scriptures inside and out. I wanted more from God. That influenced me to want to travel to Jerusalem and go to an accredited Bible school. At Friday night services, two young preachers would be allowed to preach. Although, I had favor with

Bishop Bonner, I didn't have favor with the people over the youth ministers. I wasn't in the clique. So I would probably only get an opportunity to preach every five months at the church.

God opened up another avenue. One day, my brother and I went looking for my uncle who was an alcoholic at the time. The people in the neighborhood kept telling us that they hadn't seen him in a long time. Finally someone said, *"Did you check down at the NSO shelter?"* The Neighborhood Services Organization (NSO) shelter was considered the worst shelter in the city of Detroit. We didn't think that he would be in a shelter because he always had a place to stay, but we decided to go to look for him at the shelter. We found him there. His hair had grown out so long that we couldn't even recognize him. My brother said, *"Mike you need to call down here and see if you can preach to these people."* That is where the true work of God is. So, while the young people were preaching at the church, I was preaching at the shelter. People were being filled with the Holy Spirit. I was doing what I saw my pastor do. I was praying and laying hands on people in the shelter. I was getting experience at the shelter and the hand of God was on me. People were being healed, delivered and set free. When I would get an opportunity to preach at the church, the congregation could see growth in me. God was indeed training me on the back side of the desert.

One day, while I still worked at General Motors, I was talking to the security guard at the vending machine and I overheard them call *"Man Down"*. The security guard took off running in that direction and I took off running behind her. We got to a secluded place in the plant and saw a man in his mid-sixties, lying flat on his face in a puddle of blood. They let me stay because I was with them when they first found him. They taped off the area and called the paramedics. The paramedics arrived and put the defibrillator on him. I had my hand on his shoulder and I was praying in tongues. The paramedics kept telling me to move my hand. The female paramedic was agitated with me because I was in the way and praying in tongues. I began to pray louder. She whispered to me, *"You can stop praying now, because he is already dead and we're getting ready to take him out of here."* I said, *"Lord, you did it for Lazarus. Will You do it for him?"* I kept praying. They turned him over and he had already made a bowel movement. I kept praying, *"In the name of Jesus, Lord do it, show Your power!"*

They were about to put him on the stretcher and the female paramedic pushed my hand off of him. I put both of my hands on him then. The moment they put him the stretcher, God instantly brought him back to life. He started coughing and stood straight up on his feet, like nothing had happened! They said that he was clinically dead for 35 minutes. No one could believe it! Everyone in the plant started calling me the miracle man because God used me to raise a man from the dead! Jesus' name was being proclaimed more than ever in the factory. Non-believers became believers. I know for a fact that God was using me in that plant. I told everyone on my shift something about Jesus.

IF THE TRUTH BE TOLD

On the streets of Detroit, I would sell drugs to any and everybody that I would come in contact with. When I became a citizen of the Kingdom of God, I made up in my mind that I was going to tell everybody about how good God was. Jesus said, *"Go ye into all the world and preach the gospel to every creature."* I was looking for creatures. I think that's the problem with American spiritual leaders today. Preachers are only interested in believers; they ain't looking for creatures anymore.

MY MIND IS MADE UP

I wanted to take a trip to Israel and visit Jerusalem; however, because I was still on federal parole, I wasn't even allowed to leave the state let alone the country. I talked to my parole officer about it; he went through loops and hoops to honor my request because he saw the change that had taken place in my life. I was granted permission to go and I found myself on the plane traveling with a group of people from our church organization. Dr. Spellman, the trip coordinator, had been to Jerusalem 38 times! Sherry, my spiritual sister, came through again and paid for my flight to New York.

Walking through the streets of Jericho, Jerusalem, and sailing across the Sea of Galilee made the Bible come to life. For instance, the scripture that says, God owns the cattle on a thousand hills. Everywhere we went, there were cattle on literally a thousand hills. I saw a field of wheat and the tares looked just like the wheat. I was baptized in the Jordan River and Dr. Spellman and I baptized everyone who went on the trip with us. There were more than 30 people who went. I visited the upper room, and I felt the Holy Spirit so strong that I was filled all over again speaking in one of God's heavenly languages.

I visited the place where Jesus was crucified. I went to the pool of Bethesda. I visited Mt. Carmel where Elijah killed the false prophets. I went to Bethlehem to the house of David. I had many experiences that were too numerous to talk about, but that Jerusalem trip changed my life. Again, God was grooming me, orchestrating my steps, teaching me, and showing me who He was. Our relationship got stronger, and He showed me how to trust Him.

After my trip to Jerusalem, I decided to go to ministry school in South Carolina. I quit my job in 2001. I gave it all up and entered W. L. Bonner Bible College in Columbia, South Carolina. People said I was crazy, *"You have a criminal conviction, don't quit your job."* By the time I was to enter Bible College, I knew that my Father was talking to me. The Lord had showed me that He wanted me to make another sacrifice. I discussed my decision with other ministers and missionaries. They, too, advised me not to quit my job because I had a good job and had just gotten out of prison. Some even let me know that other people wished they had my job. I knew that my Father didn't speak from a heart of fear. God taught me to know His voice by listening to the religious people's responses. He said do the opposite. They responded in the natural to a spiritual situation because they had no faith.

Complacent and religious folks will help you learn to hear the voice of God for yourself. Those people had been in the same place for so long that they were afraid to walk by faith. Often times, I would ask people who had been in church a long time, their opinion and when they gave it to me, I knew that God wanted me to do the opposite. They were religious people and they were stuck in the boat. If I just hung out in shallow water, I wouldn't have to trust Him, but if I launched out into the deep, I would *have* to trust Him. I had previously trusted numerous people who had crossed me. I would be absolutely crazy not to try trusting my Father God.

I took time to think about it and realized I didn't have anything to lose. I decided to quit my job and not let anyone stop me. I said to myself, "*I'm an ex-convict, I'm just out here. What's the worst that can happen to me after all that I have been through in my life? I lost my brother, I've been shot in the head, and I've been to prison. You don't get punished for making a godly decision.*" I had come to far **not** to trust Him!

When I told my boss my decision, he said that he would purposely wrongfully fire me so I could draw unemployment. He said, "This was the best I can do because I can't give you a leave of absence." The cost of living was higher up North than it was in the South. I was making more money drawing unemployment than people who worked and had degrees. My unemployment was supposed to last for six months. I don't know what happened, but my unemployment lasted for 18 months! I got two extensions. I realized that I couldn't lose when I trusted in God.

My mother won a lawsuit for $100,000.00 and she decided to give Cordell and me $30,000.00 each. I begged her not to give me anything, but it was only because I had been rejected my whole life. Rejected people love to give, but receiving is a hard pill to swallow. She said, *"God told me to do it."* She said, *"I know the money that you were making out there and I hope this will encourage you."* The things that happened to me encouraged me and it let me know that my Father was with me. He continued to teach me how to trust Him.

I was never a great student academically. In school, I was considered kind of slow, but in Bible College, I made the Dean's list every semester I was there. I was not working so I used the time to study. God taught me how to develop good study habits. I was determined to do well. He showed me how to discipline myself. I wrote out a daily schedule from the time I got up until the time I went to bed. I would pray for three to four hours a day and study for five or six hours. I even had an hour for rest and recess. I was fully focused, because my Father was my teacher.

I had favor with Bishop Bonner at Bible school, but we didn't have one-on-one mentorship because of his busy schedule. All of the up and coming ministers at the school came from a background of preachers. They had in-house counsel. I was the only person in my entire family, at that time, who was a preacher and I didn't have a personal role model in my family to rely on. I felt slighted and alone. I needed one-on-one mentorship.

Bishop Ronald Carter from New York, the one we called godfather, and the same one who Tony lived with for a while, reached out to me. He found out I was saved and in Bible College. He took me under his wing and never condemned me, even though he knew my past. He even put me on one of his daughter's Buddy passes. She worked at the airlines. He said, *"That will allow you to fly out to my house once a week for free and I'm going to mentor you as a father does a son.*" I didn't have any classes on Saturdays and Sundays. I would get to him on Saturday and he'd sit down with me in his office and show me how he prepared his sermons. I would fly to New York every weekend for free and stay in his house, without charge. That was a blessing and an answer to my prayer. God had sent me a mentor.

There were two professors at the college, Fred Rubin and Bradford Berry, who became mentors to me, too. They allowed me to preach at both of their churches. Bishop Carter allowed me to preach at his church, also. I was coming up through the ranks. God knew where I lacked, so He gave me more than enough. I will never forget that once a month Bishop Bonner would anoint everyone at the college during the church services, and everyone who came from out of town. The out-of-town students, who were mostly pastors, would come for a week because they were in the long distance learning program. The church would be filled during the anointing service.

Bishop Bonner was very demanding and took full authority in those services. One particular night, Bishop Bonner was anointing a man, the man's head rested on his shoulder and Bishop Bonner had his hand on the back of his head. Bishop looked over at the other ministers standing around and I was standing with them. He pointed in my direction, but I just knew he wasn't talking to me. I was the lowest man on the totem pole. He aggressively pointed again in our direction. Many of the bishops and pastors were pointing fingers at themselves asking, "*Are you pointing at me?*" He pointed again at me and said, "*Come here!*" I walked over to him and he said, "*I want you right here, whenever you see me praying for people. I need you right here!*"

That statement literally changed my life. I knew that he didn't need me. I was considered a trial sermon ministry student, and he was one of the most anointed men of God that I'd ever seen in my entire life. He was the Presiding Apostle over the entire organization – The Church of our Lord Jesus Christ of the Apostolic

Faith. Yet, he wanted to pour into me. I didn't quite understand why he wanted me to be with him, but God began to show me. *"I want you, because there are some things that he has, that I want you to have."*

There was always somebody that held the anointing oil for Apostle Bonner when he prayed for people, but little did I know that God had the oil on me. I watched him closely, like a hawk. Wherever he walked, that's where I walked. I watched how he would pray for people and then start walking as if God was talking to him, giving him further instructions. Spontaneously, he would point people out in the audience and prophesy to them. I noticed that he was a demon buster. He treated the devil like he was a stray dog that had jumped the fence in his yard. He took authority over the devil, without fear and would command him to go and the devil would leave!

Though I had favor with Apostle Bonner, that wasn't the case with people. There were a couple of us young guys who would stick close to Apostle Bonner and we were faithful. The dates we were to preach were changed without notice. Things were done vindictively to hurt us. One time my friend, Randall White and I decided not to go to the Friday night service. We were going to the gym to preach to the men there. At the Bible College, they had open recreation for the men in the neighborhood. We went and preached to the neighborhood guys at the gym, because we had been taken off the preaching schedule without notice. When we finished preaching at the gym, over 40 people followed us to the church to be baptized.

One night, I had a dream that Apostle Bonner was preaching in his church in Detroit. I was still in South Carolina, at the time. I was sitting on the pulpit alongside other preachers. Bishop Bonner looked about 15 years older and he was smaller in size. In the dream, he looked like he could pass away at any moment. Toward the end of the message, he called for me to come to him. He put his mouth on my mouth and blew in my mouth and fell out and died on the pulpit. I woke up and wondered what it meant. I never told anyone, but I always searched for the interpretation of the dream.

When I returned from Bible College, I was sitting in the Ministerial office with the other ministers, but rather than feeling like a kindergartener among high school students, I felt like a ninth grade student sitting among a bunch of kindergarteners. I knew then that God was showing me how to trust Him more. There were a lot of people in the church who knew the word of God, but they didn't know the Author of the book.

I'VE GOT AN ANGEL

Cocoa brown skin sun kissed by God Himself is the best way to describe her. I noticed her at a few church conventions. As elegant as royalty she reminded me of fine china – the kind you don't eat on, but adorn for display in a lighted china cabinet to behold its beauty. Although I'd spoken to her, she didn't respond like she was interested. In the back of my mind, I thought either she didn't like me, or maybe she was married. I was still in ministry school and I was being pressured by the older church ladies and missionaries to find a wife and get married. They also wanted to be able to be a part of the selection process, so any woman I met would have to pass their scrutiny and meet with their approval.

I made up in my mind that I was going to rebel and that I wasn't going to marry anyone from my home church in Detroit. They kept trying to match me with who they wanted. Every selection I came up with was criticized. I was discouraged enough already; I definitely wanted them to stay far away from my personal business. Once, when I was flying to New York, I met a woman from Louisville, Kentucky at the airport. She was saved and let me know that she was over the singles ministry in her church. She flew all over the country instructing teachers on their teaching methods. Her mother was a preacher. The church mothers and missionaries didn't approve of her, either. They said, *"No, she might end up being a preacher, too."* A woman in the pulpit was taboo and could possibly be a threat to the ministry in their eyes. I couldn't win for losing.

I was back home because I had become a part of the long distance learning program and traveled to South Carolina once a month. My roommate knew I was looking for a wife and he told me about a girl who went to his church. He said, *"She's dark- skinned and I didn't know if you are attracted to dark-skinned girls?"* My first instinct was to tell him that I didn't need him to hook me up with anybody; however, as he continued to describe her, I thought it may be the girl that I had been trying to get to know. I knew that she attended his church, so I told him, *"Okay."* He was going to give her my number and get her number to give to me.

Her name was Michelle and we started talking on the telephone. I was in Detroit, and I no longer talked to the girl from Kentucky, because Michelle was the girl I had been interested in all the time. Michelle was in my organization and we agreed with the same biblical teachings. We would talk on the phone for hours like teenagers. I was about 38 years old at the time and fell totally in love with her. Everything I wanted in a wife, she was. For instance, she could cook, she could sing, she was athletic, she said she played softball and even golf at times. Michelle taught Sunday School, and she dressed nice. You name it, she did it. I told her everything about me; including that I spent time in prison. I wanted to know if she liked me for real. I started flying back and forth to Jacksonville, Florida to visit her.

One time, Bishop Bonner allowed me to teach a workshop at a convention in Cincinnati, Ohio. The title of my workshop was, *"Think Outside the Box."* It was supposed to be 2 ½ hours long. I had never taught anything over 45 minutes in my life. I was just a young preacher coming up through the ranks. The day that I was supposed to teach the class, I had forgotten my notes. My brother was my biggest supporter, so I called him early that morning, and asked him to fax the notes over to the hotel. I had a little over an hour to study before my workshop.

I invited Michelle to the workshop and she came. There were about four other workshops being taught at the same time. I don't know what happened, but people began coming into my class from the other classes. There was standing room only. Michelle was so impressed by the whole thing. To top it off, that was the best workshop I ever taught. I was shocked and amazed at the level of information the Holy Spirit delivered through me that day. I knew it was God. My class was the talk of the convention. I received so many preaching engagements just from that one workshop.

My professor, Apostle Bradford Berry, stood outside the classroom for the last 40 minutes of the workshop. There was no better teacher than Apostle Berry. I modeled his style of teaching so much that I would talk and teach just like him. He was my role model. He was so very proud to see how God used me that day. He played a major role in my life, always encouraging me because he wanted me to do well.

Michelle and I had already talked about marriage. After she attended my class that day, it sealed the deal. I believe she thought I was the next thing smoking in the ranks of the organization. Michelle was nothing like the other women that I previously dated. She never drank, smoked, or hung out. She never got high or partied. Michelle was raised in the church. That was exciting to me, because most of the women I dated previously were familiar with the street life. She also didn't have any children. That was a plus to me. Up until that point, my life was so dysfunctional that I never thought I would marry someone as innocent as Michelle. They often say that opposites attract, she was totally opposite to what I was accustomed to.

We spent countless hours on the telephone since our relationship was long distance. We talked on the phone when she was at work and when she got home from work. There were times when we fell asleep on the telephone. From our conversations, she appeared to have a great prayer life and to be a faithful woman of God. She was closely knit and connected to her pastor and church. She was very active in ministry and very well respected by others. I thought I was the most blessed man in the world because to me, Michelle was completely flawless. She complimented me and my ministry. I couldn't wait to let those missionaries and church mothers see the lady that I had chosen. I found someone who met and exceeded their standards with flying colors.

Michelle's family had no doubt heard a lot about me, especially after that workshop I'd taught. Her family wanted me to fly out to their time share in Orlando, Florida to meet them. I knew that Michelle wanted her family to approve of me. I was already preparing for marriage. I was purchasing property, fixing it up and renting it out. I even went to a very nice jeweler and bought her an engagement ring. I wanted to buy her a nice class diamond. I had already decided that when I went to meet her family in Orlando, I was going to ask her to marry me.

I landed in Jacksonville, Florida and Michelle picked me up from the airport. I asked her immediately, "If I were to propose to you Michelle, how would you want me to do it? Would you want me to propose to you in front of your family?" Michelle said, "*I would prefer that you would propose to me in a private setting just between me and you.*" So, I looked at her and said, "*Let me ask you this before I ever decide to propose to you. Do you love me?*" She said, "*Yes, of course I do.*" Immediately, I got down on one knee and I said, "*Do you love me enough to spend the rest of your life with me?*" She chuckled and then she started crying. She said, "*YES!*" When we got to Orlando and her family saw the ring, everyone in her family was happy for her, but they had to feel me out. Something in me believed that she really wanted me to propose to her in front of her family. Either way, her dad and all four of her brothers talked with me individually. Afterwards, I could tell that they accepted me. We had such a good time. All of her brothers were good men, had good jobs, wives and beautiful children. They would get up and cook breakfast, lunch and dinner. I must have gained ten pounds on that trip. It was nice to fit right in with them, too. I looked up and had a whole new family.

While I visited with them, we set our wedding for the following year, May 1, 2004. I travelled back and forth to Jacksonville as if I had a business there. Honestly, I did have some business there and I wasn't going to let her get away. After spending six years in prison, getting saved and being celibate for another six years. I believed in my heart that Michelle was a divine connection from God, because I waited. Florida was called the sunshine state, but I was honored that she agreed to move to Detroit and experience the harsh winters, when she had never experienced snow a day in her life.

As our wedding day approached, I became afraid. I had never been married before. At the last minute, I had to fight with issues from past relationships and disapproval from friends and family. Some people were upset that I didn't marry who they wanted me to marry. Some who were supposed to attend our wedding, decided not to come. I felt so pressured that I almost didn't want to walk down the aisle; however, I still had great support. Michelle's family paid for the entire wedding, reception, food, everything. I had over 30 people from Detroit to fly into Jacksonville, Florida for our wedding along with friends from our church organization who also flew in to celebrate our wedding with us.

Right before the wedding, Apostle Berry saw me sitting in the room with the wedding party and he motioned for me to come out and talk to him. *"What's wrong with you?"* he asked. Like most men, I tried to hide the pain and frustration and I said, *"Nothing, I'm alright."* He said, *"I see stress all over your face. This is supposed to be the happiest day of your life."* I said, *"Apostle Bonner, isn't here and now I **know** he's not coming. I don't even know whose going to marry us?"* I also didn't know Michelle had pressures of her own to deal with regarding our upcoming wedding.

Apostle Berry took charge. He took me into another room, counseled me and mollified the situation. Apostle Rubin was there also. It was amazing that every time I ran into stressful situations or unfair matters that occurred in my life or ministry, those two were always my greatest supporters. I felt blessed above measure and the stress dissipated. I thought that the enemy was doing everything in his power to stop our wedding, but when it was over, I knew I had made the right decision and had begun a new chapter in my life.

Seven months prior to our wedding, I was sitting in service in Detroit. Apostle Bonner leaned over to me and said I need to talk to you about something that is very important. After service, I asked him what he wanted to talk to me about. He said, *"There is nothing to worry about. I will talk to you when I get back from South Carolina."* Apostle Bonner was a stern man. He was all or nothing. He comforted me by saying that there was nothing to worry about. He left for South Carolina in September and returned to Detroit in November. He never mentioned anything; however, after his birthday celebration, he pulled me into his office.

"Son, I've got a church in Ypsilanti, Michigan. You told me to bless you before I leave this earth and I'm blessing you. I'm sending you there to take over that ministry because the pastor is going to retire soon. The Lord showed me that you are the person that He is going to use to take that ministry to another level."

Right after Michelle and I were married, we jumped right into pastoring a church. We didn't even have a honeymoon. That was stressful to Michelle because she was thrown right into being a pastor's wife.

When we started pastoring the church, there were about five people coming to the church, including Michelle and me. We had a lot of work to do. I would bring car loads of people to the church letting them know that I was preaching in Ypsilanti. Before I became a pastor, I was the only young minister who preached on a

Sunday morning at Solomon's Temple. Preaching to 2,500 to 3,000 people was a big difference from preaching to 10-15 people.

After I became the pastor of the church in Ypsilanti, the congregation began to grow. We would have events and invite our fellow churches in the organization to attend and support. Through fasting and prayer, I received a word from the Lord and shared it with Michelle. I told her that we would concentrate on building the ministry in the Ypsilanti community. I told her that we were going to stop inviting other Christians to support our events, because God called me to "... *save that which was lost.*"

I followed the leading of the Holy Spirit and invited an evangelist from Ypsilanti to be the keynote speaker for our women's conference. Our goal was to reach out to the churches and the community in Ypsilanti as that was the part of the vineyard the Lord placed us in.

I've learned over the years as a pastor that the objective of most churches is to disciple members from other churches. They like to recycle membership; however, my job was to find the lost sheep. So, for the women's conference, we put out all of the chairs. Usually, we'd only put out 25 chairs for service. On that day, we put out all 125 chairs and we filled up the entire church!

God told me to reach the unreachable. We went to the college campuses, and started a ministry there. The millennials, ages 17-33 started coming. We setup shop at a local Starbucks and started teaching Bible class once a week. We reached out to anyone who would listen. Drug addicts and Jehovah Witnesses were being baptized in Jesus' name. Lesbians, atheists, and Lutherans were being converted to Christianity. A couple of Catholics left their churches, stopped praying to Mary, and started worshipping Jesus. Those people were saved and baptized in the Holy Ghost and became committed members of Ypsilanti Community Church.

One night, I had a dream that a bright light appeared in the sky. It was rapidly approaching the Earth's surface. It looked like it was hundreds of thousands of miles away. At first, I didn't pay any attention to it, though it was noticeable, but, the closer it got to Earth the more the light transformed and looked like the face of a lion inside of the intense light. The light continued speeding toward the Earth and soon covered much of the sky. God revealed to me that the light represented the coming of Jesus, the coming of the Lord. I began to yell and holler. I sprinted all over the city banging on people's doors. I was telling people that Jesus was coming, get ready! Get ready! I knew that I didn't have enough time to do what I was assigned to do. I felt like I let God down, on my assignment. I began yelling, *"No! No, Lord don't come back now. The people are not ready!"* In reality, I was at fault.

Thank God it was a dream. We as leaders have an assignment other than filling up our churches and teaching saved people new doctrines. God showed me to base our ministry totally on soul winning. If that's not the primary purpose, He is not in it. If we can de-program people's minds from traditions and rituals, then we can re-program them to do the great commission. There is something that my pastor, Apostle Bonner always said, that his pastor told him. *"Add thou to it."* That meant add more souls to the Kingdom. He also said, *"If you ain't fishing, you are just another tradition."*

TROUBLE DON'T LAST ALWAYS

When I became the pastor at Ypsilanti Community Church, I struggled with the former administration. Apostle Bonner needed someone to pastor the church, yet I experienced major opposition from the previous church board. Apostle Bonner had already given me my instructions, but conflicting information remained. A lot of lies were told on me; however, this just kept me praying and fasting. Though I was in another spiritual fight, I had no doubt God had placed me there. Those struggles turned me into a prayer warrior. I always considered myself a soldier, ready for war or battle at any given time. As pastor, I had to learn to fight a different way.

Everything that could go wrong, went wrong, including court proceedings. It became a horror movie. Horror is the only way to express what I went through. My name was being slandered, other pastors in the community shunned me because of the lies that were told on me, all in an effort to turn people within the organization against me. I was even talked about in the City of Ypsilanti. God was with me because the judge ruled in my favor. Those people who tried to destroy me meant it for evil, but God meant it for my good.

Throughout the whole ordeal, Apostle Bonner would always tell me to meet him at the prayer meetings. He was showing me how to get a breakthrough on my knees. I learned at the beginning of my ministry that I couldn't fight with fists, guns, or knives. I fought many battles on my knees. I was a prayer warrior.

The Lord spoke to me even while I was struggling with the church board. He showed me that something was missing in ministry. I didn't want a stereotypical ministry where people came to pray, sing three songs, preach a message and say the benediction. I wanted to do exactly what Jesus and the apostles did in the book of Acts. I was determined to pastor a ministry that flowed with signs, wonders and miracles. That spiritual desire kept me on my face seeking God. I had been to hundreds of churches but to me, something was missing. I'd heard good preaching, and singing, and sat under good teaching. I had the Holy Ghost, but I needed the power activated. I was tired of talking about it, reading about it, and not seeing the manifestation. I bumped into miracles here and there, but I wanted it to be a normal occurrence in the ministry. Suddenly, I recognized what all of the battles were about...the enemy wanted me to give up and quit. I was close to seeing the manifested power of God. I was a glory chaser and didn't give up easily. So, the devil declared war on me and the ministry. He had a battle on his hands.

There were about 11 people in our ministry who suffered with different ailments and sicknesses. So, I instructed the church to go on a 21-day Daniel fast, eating nothing but fruit and vegetables and praying three times a day. I went on an absolute fast. We all prayed that everyone would be healed. Eight months before the fast, a friend of mine, Minister Andre, wanted to introduce me to an anointed evangelist whom God used on many different occasions showing signs, wonders, and miracles. He told me that he had never seen anybody with an anointing as strong as that young man. Andre and I came up through Solomon's Temple together. I started naming other ministers and pastors whose ministries we had witnessed. He still affirmed that no one else he had seen was that anointed.

He said, *"The only person he knew that I knew who was on a level like that guy was Apostle William L. Bonner"*. I was amazed, and I didn't believe it. I thought that type of anointing came with many years of salvation. Religion taught me that to be anointed to perform signs, wonders, and miracles meant one had seniority, a title, and grey hair. I called the evangelist on the phone. When we spoke on the phone, he sounded like a cool guy. He said he would love to come to minister at the church. Every time I would look for him to come, something would come up and the date would change. That was going on while our church was on a fast and we were looking for God to heal everyone who was sick. I received an unexpected phone call from the evangelist and he apologized for the other times he couldn't make it and he said if I didn't mind he would come the very next Sunday. He asked me a question no one before him had ever asked me: *"What area do you need me to minister in?"* He named areas like people receiving the Holy Spirit, salvation, healing, deliverance, and he named some other areas. I said healing. I hadn't ever seen that brother once in my life, I was trusting in the word of my friend and stepping out on faith.

222

The evangelist told me to expect him about 25 minutes after service began because he was coming from Detroit, which was approximately a 35-minute drive. People I'd never seen but who followed his ministry came to the church. His brother came in with his wife. He looked like a preacher, so I invited him up into the pulpit. He whispered to me, *"Hey Doc, he's is my brother. Have you ever heard my brother preach before?"* I said, "No, I haven't." He said, *"People are going to be falling out, jumping around and laid out all over this floor. He is about to tear this whole church up!"*

True to his word, the evangelist came in about 25 minutes after service started carrying his robe. We escorted him into the office. I asked him if he needed some time and he said, *"No, just let me put my robe on."* He preached from Acts 10:38 - how God anointed Jesus Christ of Nazareth with the Holy Ghost and with power, and He went about doing good and healing all who were oppressed of the devil. After he preached, he asked everybody who needed to be healed to come up to the altar. He laid hands on some, and blew on others. People fell out under the power of the Holy Spirit. I recognized that he had a very strong anointing on his life. My brother, Cordell had a slipped disc in his back. I knew I could get an accurate reading from my brother.

After service, I asked him what he thought about the service, and if he thought that the preacher was real or a fluke. Cordell said, *"That brother was real man. He has a strong anointing! When he blew on me, my back was completely healed!"* Everyone in the church who had a sickness was healed that day. I thought God was going to use *me* to heal them, but He didn't. It didn't matter. I was still happy. God had answered our prayers. The evangelist hung around after service and talked to me for about 40 minutes. We laughed and talked like we had known each other for 40 years. That young evangelist was a man of power and I wanted what he had. He said, *"Man, let's hang out. We can hang out on every Monday and go and get something to eat."* I said, *"That's a deal."* When Monday came, I didn't call him because I felt I was unworthy. I let about eight

Mondays go by without even picking up the phone. One Monday around noon, the evangelist called me and asked what I was doing and if I could meet him at the pancake house. I said sure. We met and I found out that he had just started pastoring and he was having service at a hotel in Southfield. I began to go to his services at 3:00 p.m. and I witnessed miracle after miracle.

He told me that it was easy to flow in signs, wonders and miracles. *"I'm going to give you some books and things to read and you just have to allow it to change your life."* He told me to read a book by Dave Roberson entitled *The Walk of Power and Walk of the Spirit.* He told me to read *Believers Authority* by Kenneth Hagin, too. Every time I told him I was finished with a book, he would give me another one. He told me to come to as many services as possible so that I could watch him flow in the anointing. I was a good student because I was hungry. My uncle had set me up to preach at a men's revival in Inkster, Michigan. My life was changing. I was in the habit of praying two hours a day in the Holy Ghost and I had just come off of a ten-day fast before the men's revival.

The pastor had just preached at my church that Sunday and I had a four o'clock engagement to preach as the keynote speaker. He and I talked after service as usual, then I went over to Inkster to preach at the church I was invited to. My message was entitled, *"That was Then, but This is Now!"* After I finished preaching, I did something I had never done before, I looked at all of the people and some were in wheelchairs, some carried oxygen tanks, and some were carrying canes and walkers. I asked, *"Is there anybody who came in here sick, but wants to leave healed?"* I had said to myself, *"I'm going to see if this stuff works that I'm doing".* No one came up but it looked like at least 50 people needed to be healed. I said it again with emphasis, *"Somebody needs to be healed in this church."*

One lady was sitting in the middle section on the end seat with a walker. She walked down the middle aisle very slowly. It took her about five minutes to get to where I was. She was about 80 years

224

old and frail. One could tell that the people in the church knew her condition, because you could hear a pin drop. The people stood up to see what was going to happen. I asked her, "*What do you want God to do?*" She said I need two brand new hips, but I'm too little to have the surgery. I just need this pain to go away." I said, "*God will give you two brand new hips right now!*" I didn't know where I got that message from. She chuckled, and said, "*That would be something.*"

Out of respect to that dear sister and because I was at a visiting church, I told my wife to put her hands on both of her hips. Then I said, "*when I put my hands on my wife's hands you are about to have a supernatural hip replacement!*" I prayed, "*By the power of the Holy Ghost give her two brand new hips in the mighty name of Jesus! Give her this creative miracle, Father God!*" After I prayed, I grabbed both of her hands and said, "*Raise your right leg and now raise up the other leg. Faith without works is dead. Now walk around the church.*" She reached for her walker and I grabbed it and threw it about seven feet away! I said you won't need this anymore! She took about 15 steps, the church began clapping and she began running around the church screaming, "*I got it! I got it!*" After that about 35 people came up to the altar for healing. Something happened to me, too, that had never happened before. I felt like a heavy jacket had been placed on me. I didn't know at the time that it was the gift of faith. I had never felt like that and I didn't know how long it would be on me. I told the people, "*If you want God to do something for you, you had better tell me while this is on me.*" Everything that I spoke came to pass right there. Everyone who got in line was healed. A woman was healed from arthritis and throat cancer, people left their oxygen tanks, people jumped out of wheelchairs. I was on the right path now and it was what I was searching for. I wanted to be a man of power, a man who could operate in signs and wonders under the power of the Holy Ghost. I knew that my friendship with that pastor was a divine connection. From that moment on, the ministry took a turn and we began to see miracles right in our church. I was in a place where it was easier to get them healed than to leave them in their sick condition. I wanted sick people to come to my church because I knew that God would heal them. I started wearing that jacket everywhere I went. I knew that I wasn't walking alone.

I CAN DO ALL THINGS THROUGH CHRIST

Consistently, I began praying in the Holy Spirit on a daily basis for hours a day. I fasted even more and started seeing the results of spending time with God. There was a young man who came to our church. He had been diagnosed with AIDS. He went into the hospital and was in ICU on life support. I visited him often. The doctors had given him a couple of weeks to live. I was visiting him one day and God told me to anoint him with my saliva. I questioned God. I said, *"What? My saliva?"* God said what comes out of the mouth comes from the heart. God was showing me my heart was pure.

The young man was asleep. So I spit on my hands. I knew that I couldn't be caught doing that. If his loved ones saw me they would never let me pray for him again. I looked around the room. I rubbed my hands with spit on his face as if it was anointing oil. I left and I didn't go to visit him the next day. The enemy had been beating me up talking to my mind all day. I had faith when I prayed. Michelle and I went to the hospital the day after that. We didn't have to check in at the desk because I knew his room number. When we got to his room, he wasn't in the bed. The devil spoke to my mind and said, *"He's dead."* I walked by the room went back and peeked in again. I still didn't see him. I decided that I would leave and wait to hear from the family because I was not going to ask the nurse or the doctors what happened.

As we were leaving, I heard a voice say, *"Pastor Robinson."* I walked back to his room and saw him sitting in the chair watching TV. I had totally missed him before because I expected him to be in the bed. He looked good and he wasn't hooked up to any machines. He said, *"Pastor Robinson, I'm waiting on the nurse to come and move me to the other floor."* They were moving him out of ICU! If I had never seen God move before, I saw Him move on this occasion.

During one of our worship services, one lady drove from Virginia, she was diagnosed with skin cancer and God healed her. Another man drove from Tulsa, Oklahoma just to be in one of our services because he heard that the power of God was moving. On another occasion, a young man came up and he was crying during the altar call. I asked him what was wrong, and he said the doctor gave him six months to live and that he had full blown AIDS and that he had three months left.

He said, *"Pastor I just want to live. I want to be healed."* I asked God to forgive him for his sins, I rebuked the demonic sphere of AIDS. I told that demon of AIDS to let him go. *"You won't have him"*. I released the healing power of God to manifest Himself in his body. The young man fell out under the power of the Holy Ghost. A couple of months later he called my cell phone crying. I didn't know how he got my number, but he told me who he was. The way he sounded I thought something went wrong. He said Pastor I want you to know I got my doctor's report. He said this is what the doctor said, *"I am 100 percent AIDS free!"*

So our church began having healing services once a month and the Lord started moving. As many people who came in sick, that's how many people went home healed. Ypsilanti Community Church became a healing epicenter.

There was a revival in Washington, D.C. There was an older Evangelist by the name of C.S. Upthegrove. He was a part of the Voices of Healing, a group that consisted of Pentecostal healing revivalists such as A.A. Allen, William Branham, Jack Coe and R.W. Shambauch. I got to the revival late, so I met my friends at the restaurant after the service and Evangelist C.S. Upthegrove was there with them.

They began talking about all of the miracles that they had seen and witnessed throughout the year. They told us how they saw gold fillings manifest where cavities were in people's mouths. They talked about how the Shekinah glory of God would come and rest in the services. They talked about how gold dust and angel feathers would fall in some of the services and how people would instantly lose weight in some of the services. I had never seen miracles of that magnitude before. I actually thought they were making up stories.

God orchestrated the service that next night. My brother and I had front row seats. Signs and wonders are for the unbeliever and I didn't believe that God would do some of those things they said. I didn't think that God operated like that. It was too spooky for me. I knew He could heal. I knew He could save. I knew He could deliver, but I didn't believe the rest of it. That was going too far.

There was a lady there who must have weighed about 200 pounds. She had congestive heart failure and she needed to lose some weight right away. She told C.S. Upthegrove that she needed to lose 40 pounds. He said, *"Daughter you're going to lose that weight tonight!"* The man of God laid hands on the woman and put his red mantle on her. Instantly, she started losing weight. I saw it with my own eyes. I said to myself, *"with God all things are possible"*. I became a believer.

At our services in Ypsilanti, when we were still having healing services, a young woman saw angels. Every time I laid hands on the people, the young woman said she saw angels go right through the people snatching the sickness out of them. Evangelist C.S. Upthegrove prophesied that the Lord would give me seven times the anointing that was on his life and he laid his mantle on me and I fell out under the power of the Holy Ghost. Later on that evening, he gave me his information and told me that he would love to come to the church and preach for me. It was a year later when I called him, because again, I felt like I wasn't worthy to have a man of his stature at my church. One day, I wanted to have a revival and I decided to give him a call. C.S. Upthegrove simply said, *"Yes, Son, I would love to come to your church and minister."* I didn't know that God was putting a new mentor in my life.

In Bible College, I always longed for a father or grandfather in my family who preached the gospel like most of the other students and God always put great godly men in my life. C.S. Upthegrove began to call me, mentor me, and spend quality time with me. He called me once and told me that he was praying for me. He said, *"I wanted God to show me where the little preacher was at. Whatever you are doing son, keep doing it, because God said you are right where He wants you. You are in the center of His will."* Meeting C.S. Upthegrove was a divine connection. I was exposed to a greater anointing of healing. I saw legs growing out, gold fillings replaced cavities. God was smiling on us because people were coming from out of state just to be set free from demonic bondage.

One day, a woman from Toledo, Ohio had seven tumors in her body - three in her neck and four in her back. God healed her from every last one of those tumors in her body. During our service, they were totally dissolved. We began to see and visualize miracle after miracle. There were so many that several books couldn't describe how powerfully God was moving among us.

My first cousin had serious health challenges for many years. She called me over to pray for her. She was living in total darkness in her room. When I went to see her, she told me not to touch any light switches because she would be in unbearable torment, if I did. I felt my way to her bed and I began to curse that evil spirit of infirmity from her. We both felt the awesome power of God move in her bedroom. When I left she told me to turn the lights on. I told her, *"No, because you told me what damage it could do to you."* She said, *"When you began to pray, I saw a halo over your head that was so bright that I knew God was healing me"*.

The Lord told me to write down every scripture in the Bible that had the word 'glory' in it, and He would show me His glory in a brand new dimension. I obeyed the voice of God and I also went on a 40-day fast, eating nothing and just drinking water, like Jesus did. When Jesus fasted for 40 days the Bible clearly stated He ate nothing for 40 days. Many scholars believe that He drank water. It was a very challenging fast for me. I lost 68 pounds. My wife and I drove to Moravian Falls, North Carolina. Many in that small city believed God opened Heaven to bless the people in that exact location because some missionaries had prayed there for many years for more than 12 hours a day. So many men and women of God, and so many prophets had seen angels, been healed, and heard the audible voice of God. They had many godly encounters at Moravian Falls. So, of course, I went there thinking I might see an angel or have some kind of encounter with Heaven.

When we got there, we stayed at some unknown motel. We went to the small falls that could easily flow from a section carved out in a normal sized front lawn. We prayed, we worshipped, and prayed in the Holy Spirit only to go back to our motel room somewhat disappointed. Before I fell asleep, I got on my knees, and made a complaint to my Father God. I said, *"Lord, I came this far expecting to hear or see an angel and my trip has been in vain."* About 30 minutes later, I head God speak to me and He said, *"You're looking for an angel to appear. From this day forward, I want you to look for Jesus to appear to you."* That was all I needed to hear my Father say to me. Although I had never seen Jesus with my naked eyes, I was constantly looking for Him, and I've seen His manifestation on so many different occasions.

When we started to travel back home, I almost died. I was on day 38 of my fast when I started bleeding from my bowels and it didn't stop. Later, someone told me that my body was feeding on itself. But I had come too far to end the fast that was called the 'prophets fast.' I guess it was called that because Moses, Elijah and the Lord Jesus Christ were the only ones recorded in scripture who fasted for 40 days. I got into the bath tub and prayed to God. I prayed, "*Father God, if it's my time to depart this Earth, I'm ready, but if you still have work for me to do, heal my body*". The tub was drenched with blood, but I could hear the voice of God in my spirit man saying, "*Son, I still have much work for you to do.*" I took a shower, got into my bed, and fell asleep. After the 40-day fast, God had even increased the anointing far greater than before. Gold dust fell in some services and I even began to see feathers around the church. The Lord started doing strange things and special miracles which brought many souls to Christ.

A lady was going to get her foot amputated. It had turned black. She said the doctors asked her if she wanted to continue to take medication or if she wanted them to remove her foot. She told them that her foot was literally killing her and to rid her of the pain she wanted them to remove it. There was an open wound on her foot that wouldn't close. It was the size of a silver dollar. Her best friend told her to ask me to pray for her. When she came to the church, she asked me not to touch her foot because it would force her to scream. I told her, "*When I touch it I promise you won't feel any pain*". I laid hands right on the open wound and released God's healing power. She said that she didn't feel any pain. The next morning, she called and told me that the open wound had closed up and her foot had returned to its normal color. That wound on her foot had been open for more than a year; her foot was black for more than a year. When she went to her doctors, they didn't find anything wrong with her foot and didn't have to amputate it. Later, she told me that the doctors were treating the wound as if it was cancer when in truth she had been bitten by a spider.

Several people with herpes had been healed also. We've seen God literally grow out legs that were shorter than the other leg, some two or three inches shorter. Two ladies were healed who were both partially paralyzed from major strokes. One young fella had a hole in his heart and God healed that 12-year old by closing the hole in his heart.

I truly believe that my Father God can do anything. At a few healing and miracle services, I would ask the people to walk past my shadow and watch God heal them from whatever sickness or disease they had, and yes, Jesus would meet me at my request. I figured if it could happen for the Apostle Peter in the book of Acts, why wouldn't God do it in my ministry? My Father allowed His glory to continuously flow within our ministry. I am a true believer that with God all things are possible.

My wife and I were leaving the grocery store late one evening and a car came from nowhere from the driver's blind side. We both shouted "*Jesus*" and the car literally drove straight through us supernaturally with the help of God's angels and no one was hurt in either car. Yes, the car drove through our car as if it was a ghost car!

I went to a conference in Marietta, California and Ed Dufrane, a prophet who walked in miracles, was the conference host. While I was there, I was able to visit another prophet whose name was Dick Mills. He prophesied over my life and laid hands on me. He said that my ministry will always flow with signs, wonders and miracles. He also said that I would raise the dead.

Seven months after that conference, I was back at my church and our church mother died right during church service. There was a nurse at the church who took Mother's pulse, and wrote down the time, telling me that we had to clock her out at 1:32 p.m. because she was dead. My faith went to the basement. I couldn't believe it; not in the church. I told my wife to tell the praise team to kick it into full gear. I told the church "*if you can pray in tongues, pray in the Holy Spirit right now.*" But, I still had little faith. I whispered to the Lord, "*Father, what am I to do?*" He said, "*Don't lay hands on her. Grab her by the mouth, put your mouth on her mouth and I will breathe through you.*" As I grabbed her mouth, I still didn't have any faith, but that same weighty jacket came on me and my faith went to the mountaintop. I breathed into her mouth and she came instantly back to life. The church went up in praise. They went crazy! Mama is still with us and kicking strong. She is 96 years old at the time of the writing of this book.

FATHER, CAN YOU HEAR ME?

My natural father had taken ill. He was diagnosed with Alzheimer's and he began to experience serious memory loss. My mother was trying her best to take care of him, but it was too much for her. We had a family meeting and decided to put him in a nursing home. I would check my father out of the nursing home and would bring him to the church every time we had a revival. I was looking for my father to be completely healed. Every time C.S. Upthegrove would come to town, if my father didn't make it to the revival, I would take Evangelist Upthegrove to the nursing home so he could lay hands on my dad. It seemed like the more I tried to get a breakthrough in that area the further I would be. My dad's sickness gave us both a chance to spend time recreating the love that Christ wanted us to have toward each other.

God began to show me that although we didn't have the best relationship, He had allowed my father's heart to be hard toward me to help make me into who I am today. There were times when I would wash my father up, change his diaper, and feed him that he'd say things that would touch me like, *"Thanks, son."* I knew then that God had placed forgiveness in his heart. God was also working in my heart. He gave me a clear revelation when Jesus was on the cross and the Roman soldiers were whipping Him. Jesus yelled out, *"Father forgive them for they know not what they do."* God showed me that throughout the years my father could only show the love that he knew how to give. If he had known better, he would have done better. That knowledge helped me to understand the true meaning of forgiveness. People can only love as much as they know how to love. While I was taking care of my natural father, I began dreaming about my spiritual father, Apostle Bonner.

I woke up from a frightening dream, and I remembered that I'd had that same dream before. I dreamt that my pastor and spiritual father, Apostle William L. Bonner was preaching a message and at the end of his message he pointed at me and told me to come to him. He grabbed me by my chin, put his lips to my lips and breathed into me, fell out and passed away. The dream was the same. He was still that elderly man from the first dream. Only this time when I had the dream, it was years later and Apostle Bonner had caught up to the age that he was in the first dream. From that dream, I knew he was supposed to at least lay hands on me before he made his transition. I shared the dream with a close pastor friend of mine. He said your dream means that God is going to give you a double portion of what Apostle Bonner has. I asked him why he thought that. The pastor replied, *"Because he breathed his spirit into you twice."*

Apostle Bonner was very sick and had just gotten out of the hospital. I drove to the eastside of Detroit to get him to lay hands on me. I went to the church to see him and they would not let me into his office. For some unknown reason his ministers were stopping people from visiting him. Maybe they did that because he was too weak, or people were trying to get him to do favors for them because they thought he was about to pass away. I wasn't trying to take advantage of him. I just needed him to touch me one more time, to lay hands on me. I understood the church's position. They were trying to protect him. I went back a few more times and they kept telling me that he wasn't available, even though I'd see his car parked outside.

One thing I know, is when you're after something that God has for you, you can't take no for an answer. The next time I went to see him, they said that he was in South Carolina. I jumped on a plane to South Carolina. I was determined that my apostle was going to lay hands on me. I knew there was something he had that God wanted me to have. I remembered in the beginning when I was young in the ministry, he told me to watch him every time he was in the prayer line. He wanted me to be with him.

I went to the church in South Carolina. I told them that I had to get Apostle Bonner to lay hands on me. I told the pastor and the secretary that I'd had a dream. I told them the part of the dream where he blew in my mouth and I knew that Apostle W. L. Bonner was supposed to lay hands on me. I was having the same problems there trying to see him as I did in Detroit. Eventually, they let me go through. I told Apostle that I had trouble getting in to see him in Detroit, so I flew to South Carolina to see him. I told Apostle that I wanted him to lay hands on me. He replied, *"Son I can't do it here, you have to wait for the service tonight. Can you stay for service tonight?* I said, *"Yes sir, I already planned on it.* He said, *"Wait until the fire is burning."* That meant wait until the anointing was high.

As persistent as I was in the streets and as sold out as I was to the devil, I was just as persistent and sold out to Jesus in the Kingdom. On the streets of Detroit, I would do anything to be accepted and now by me being on God's side, I would do anything for His approval. That night in the service, Apostle gave me an impartation. He spoke to me and said, *"The Lord is going to put in you what I got in me!"* Apostle Bonner lived for three more years after that.

The Lord was removing one spiritual father and giving me another one in Evangelist C.S. Upthegrove. Our relationship increased. When he would come to town, we drove around for hours and talked. He would tell me to pull up in various parking lots and we would sit quietly in the car. He would say, *"Let's not talk. Let's just hear what the Lord would say".* He brought me a handheld tape recorder, and he told me to record what God gave to him to tell me. I would record him for hours. When he knew that God had given him something to tell me, he would tell me to pull out the tape recorder. I would pull it out. He said, *"I have travelled all over the country and preached in all types of mega churches. All of the places where I have preached, and mostly every pastor who called me, didn't want me; they just wanted the miracles that I would do at their churches...but you want me, son."* That blessed me. I never forgot that. We became so close that I would fly to his home in West Palm Beach, Florida to visit him from time to time.

He would allow me to go to some churches with him and allowed me to testify and share a few words. He was opening doors for me. He ministered to me and took me under his wing. I saw things happen to me in Ypsilanti that had never happened before.

On April 7, 2015, Apostle W. L. Bonner passed away. That was a very sad and touching moment for me. Although I knew he would make his transition one day, it just seemed as if that day would never come. Suddenly, all I had were memories of my spiritual father. What a great man he was, and I think of how God really used him. I remembered the countless anointed messages he preached and the thousands upon thousands of people that were baptized with the Holy Spirit who sat under his ministry that reached other nations throughout the world. I remember the many sick people who were healed through that great man of God. In Liberia, West Africa, 500 people were filled with the Holy Ghost from God using him to preach one message.

He had over 500 churches under his leadership, and he asked little ole me to help him in every prayer line when he was anointing the people of God. He would come to my college dormitory and pick me up in order for us to have lunch together. He wanted me to be the chaplain of the Youth Council Group in Detroit, and in Columbia, South Carolina. He personally assigned me to be over the Outreach Team in both locations. Then, he sent me to pastor the church in Ypsilanti, Michigan. What touched me the most from my spiritual father, Apostle W. L. Bonner, was that he anointed me and prophesied in my life saying *"God is imparting in you a double portion of what He gave me, son. So, use it."* He did that before he made his heavenly transition. I have truly inherited something from my father. I had the opportunity and privilege to be a pallbearer at my spiritual father's home going celebration. What an honor.

Sixteen months after my spiritual father, Apostle W.L. Bonner passed away, my biological father made his transition. A few months before my dad made his departure, I was asking God if he was ready, spiritually. God sent a prophetess to tell me *"Stop praying for your dad. God is ready for him to spend eternity with Him"*. That was indeed a prophetic answer that gave me confirmation that my father was heaven bound.

On the morning that he passed away, my mom, Michelle, my brother, along with my cousins Michelle, Linda and me, went to the nursing home. Seeing my father there, deceased, reminded me of all the things he did when I was a kid. He played sports so well; he was a deacon in the church. He wasn't the best husband by far to my mom, and he wasn't close to being the best dad to me, but, he was there. He stayed. Some fathers leave and never come back. My father stayed. His presence made a great impact on many young boys in our neighborhood. Standing there looking at his corpse, I could hear the Lord speaking to me, saying, *"I hardened his heart against you to make you into who you are today."* God was actually telling me that it was the harsh treatment that my father had toward me that He used to make me strong, tough, and compassionate all at the same time. Through it all, I learned to survive under any condition or circumstance. I learned to have compassion for others, and I learned how to protect myself and others, as well.

So, my father was used many years ago to prepare me to be a pastor. If I would never have been hurt, I wouldn't be sensitive to the pain of others. If I would never have been homeless, I wouldn't know how to minister to homeless people. Thank God I was incarcerated, because I have a great love for the ones who are imprisoned. I can easily love the young man who is having run-ins with the police, the drug addict, and the drug user. I give all of the credit to my father, Mr. James Robinson, for being the master teacher.

I'm a pastor who has had experiences in all phases of life and I overcame the devil by the blood of the Lamb, and the word of my testimony. I truly believe that Jesus paid a price for everyone that's ever been born in this world to have salvation. I also believe we have to pay a price for someone, too. I paid a price, so some child could be mentored and counseled; so that he or she will never have to experience the life I lived. Some pastors have the truth with no experience. I have the truth with experience. I thank God for my father, who has been one of the greatest blessings in my life. He helped navigate me to become the man of God that I am today. I had the opportunity and privilege to eulogize my father's home going celebration, which was another great honor.

C.S. Upthegrove made his transition 17 months after my biological father had passed away. When it rains, it pours. There was one thing after another. I have never seen a man who had the stature of C. S. Upthegrove. He never had a bad word to say about anyone. He truly walked in love and humility. There was no one he could not reach. He shared so much of himself with me. He ministered on the same platform as A. A. Allen, Oral Roberts, William Branham, Kathryn Kuhlman, Jack Coe, and W.V. Grant just to name a few. He even traveled to Lagos, Nigeria to minister at T. B. Joshua's church, but his love for God's people was beyond measure. At his age, he ministered countless hours to God's people. Through his ministry, I saw so many miracles. Thousands were healed from all manner of sicknesses, and all manner of diseases. He was a one-of-a-kind person. What I loved most about him was that he anointed me one day and prophesied in my life. He said, *"God is going to impart into you an anointing that's seven times stronger than the anointing that's upon my life."* I just thank God for him taking the time to mentor me, counsel me and prophesy in my life. He referred to me as being his favorite son in the Gospel.

He always reminded me never to say negative things about people in the Body of Christ. One of his quotes was, *"The Body of Christ is the only army that's willing to kill their wounded soldiers."* Unfortunately, we do. If the church sees another saint hurting, they will finish him or her off. C. S. Upthegrove was indeed one of God's generals on the battlefield. I thank God Almighty for allowing him to become my spiritual father during the years we were blessed to spend time with each other. I was blessed with the privilege and opportunity to do the prayer at his home going services. What an honor.

Now, I always knew Carol's daughter was not my biological child; however, I was willing to step up to the plate and not leave her fatherless. One day, I received a subpoena to go to court because Carol and her mom had gotten into an altercation that resulted in Carol's daughter being stabbed. The state brought in a social worker for the case. The social worker wanted me to allow the state to take custody, only because they felt the grandmother only wanted custody for financial gain.

Well, I tried to adopt her and get full custody of her. Surprisingly, the court told me that she was old enough to make her own decisions about her whereabouts. I didn't understand how an 11-year old child could make such a decision. I wanted to be a father to her because she needed a male role model in her life. Through it all, I tried. I was paying child support, trying to spend time with her, and even attempted parent counseling. Every time we were supposed to go for counseling, they gave the counselor an excuse for not meeting. Out of over a dozen times, we only met twice.

Finally, I came to the conclusion that I wasn't able to get custody of her and that everything I had tried failed. I signed on the dotted line and gave up my parental rights to her maternal grandmother. Through it all, hopefully the finances were used to help an innocent girl have a better life. In the midst of all that happened, I learned how painful it was to be fatherless. My greatest lesson from this was how to become a loving, spiritual father to countless young people who need a father figure. This is indeed an honor.

MY FATHER'S BLOOD

I opened my Bible to John 3:16 as I was preparing to preach the message. Then, I noticed that the word 'begotten' is two words in the Greek - mono and gene. 'Mono' means singular, original, only or one. 'Gene' means DNA, it means blood; it's a short term for genetics. If that scripture was quoted in the original text it would read something like this, *"God loved this world so much that He gave His son, who had His only original blood type"*. That is the very reason that the only way we can get to the Father is we have go through the Son. Jesus cleanses us with His Father's Blood. So, when we become born again, we become *re-gene-rated*. God blessed me with one natural father who had made some natural deposits in my life. He blessed me with two spiritual fathers who made many spiritual deposits in my life. Now, I see the reason I have the opportunity to walk in the exact footsteps of Jesus Christ - I have my Father's Blood, DNA, and genes! Soon, I began to realize that I am just as much a son of God as Jesus Christ is.

That's why Jesus said, the works I do, you shall do also, and even greater works than He did. That's only because once we became sons of God the Father, He changed our spiritual bloodline from Satan's corruptible seed or DNA to the exact same incorruptible DNA as Jesus Christ has from His Father's blood.

II Corinthians 5:17 says, *"If any man be in Christ, he is a new creature. Old things are passed away, behold all things are become new."* I can truly thank Jesus Christ for baptizing me with the Holy Spirit. Now I have "My Father's Blood." I am qualified to walk in the exact same miraculous power of my big brother, Jesus. The Bible says, *"...as He is, so are we in this world."* So, I'm unstoppable with His blood flowing through me. I have all power to heal all manner of sickness and all manner of disease. That is why Jesus was so often moved with compassion. Compassion is defined as one who is willing to do anything in their power to help alleviate another's pain. That is exactly what Jesus did in His every day ministry.

I looked back over the years and realized that I had not used compassion in my life until now. In the past, I wanted a return for what I gave. Now I know my return comes from my Father. God was always teaching and preparing me to be more compassionate, and how to move in empathy. God gave me a heart of compassion to pastor His people for such a time as this.

So, through it all, my Father God was teaching me through Toya, how to become a true father to the fatherless. Regardless of the nature of any case, every child needs a father in his or her life to bring them real structure, discipline and the strengthening of life to them. Through my biological dad, God showed me that many children feel rejected and need a father's compassionate side, as well as his victory cheer when they feel like quitting and giving up. Through Apostle Bonner and C. S. Upthegrove, God taught me that to be a strong leader, pastor and spiritual father to the Body of Christ, I must carry a strong anointing, seek the wisdom of God, flow in signs, wonders, and miracles, keep the faith, and maintain a great prayer life. My Father God was literally equipping me throughout the years with everyone He sent into my life. Every person who influenced me was there by divine appointment and by divine assignment.

Looking back, I must give glory to my Father God for shaping and making me into who I am today. I'm so glad He kept me and trained me up in the way I should go. When I get old, I will not depart from how my Father trained me. I've been fully transformed by My Father's Blood.

ACKNOWLEDGMENTS

I would be remiss without taking the time to pay a debt of gratitude to those who have assisted with this vision coming to pass. First and foremost, I want to acknowledge the leadership and guidance of the Holy Spirit to help complete this project. I am confident that multitudes of lives will be converted from the reading of this book which outlines the compassion and mercy of Christ, which is never limited when searching for and saving a sinner.

I thank God for surrounding me with family and friends who somehow believed that I could write a book. They assisted in this day coming to pass through their consistent, unwavering prayers and encouragement. To Michelle, my wife, who willingly followed me from the sunshine state of Florida to Michigan's unpredictable weather, to not only support my vision, but has put up with my every day craziness!

To Tonya Simpkins-Allen, Tonya Roberts, and Rachelle Arnold-Lee who were an ever present help in this entire process. To Wyman Jenkins and Eric X for being the big brother figures who provided the inspiration that was needed for completion. To "Jazz", my God-daughter, for always providing timely encouragement. To my big brother and little brother at the same time, Cordell, who has always rooted for my success. To my niece, Misty, you have a special place in my heart along with my nephew, "Lil Kordell", who has referred to me as his "Ace Boon Koon". To Aunt Eloise, I will never forget how you opened your home to me, providing me with a place to stay and call home when I had nowhere to go. There are truly too many others to name here…you know who you are!

I am thankful for the divine alignment of Britany and Chris Slater, who through their creative efforts, were able to develop a book cover that represents *My Father's Blood* perfectly. To my editor and publisher, Dr. De'Andrea Matthews, for sharing her expertise, work ethic, and effort in this project. To Angela Coleman, who assisted me with penning my testimony of God's grace, mercy, and *His* plan for my life.

I am ever so grateful to Pastor Calvin Landrew for affording me the opportunity to minister my father's eulogy at his church. It was through this that I was able to heal and honor my father one last time. To my mother for always believing, caring, loving, and *praying* for me…her prayers were not in vain. God hears and answers a mother's prayers.

Last, but not least, to Apostle Dr. James. I. Clark, Jr. for being with me in the beginning by mentoring me throughout Bible College, and is still with me today as my presiding apostle. Sir, you are appreciated.

I always had an intrinsic desire to use my hands. I wanted to pursue boxing as a sport. I wanted to learn how to play the organ. I was a gifted artist, even earning a scholarship for my talent. None of these came to fruition. Yes, it was disappointing, and even devastating at times. Sometimes, what we see as devastation is preservation. God had intended all along to use my *hands* to touch *His* people. He could have picked anyone, but He chose me.

~Pastor Mike

ABOUT THE AUTHOR

Raised on the streets of Detroit, young Michael Robinson was indirectly groomed to become a well-known hustler and drug dealer. Answering the call of salvation at a young age, Michael would soon fall away into a life of crime due to his tumultuous relationship with his father. This breach inflicted crippling emotions of rejection, depression, oppression, and rage within him. His life's experiences took Michael down paths of violence, selling drugs, abusing alcohol and serving 78 months in the federal penitentiary.

On the verge of going back to prison, he gave his life completely over to God and did a 180-degree turnaround with the help of the Holy Spirit. In 2004, Pastor Mike married Lady Michelle. In 2005, he was ordained and sent by his spiritual father, Apostle William L. Bonner, to pastor Ypsilanti Community Church. Affectionately known as "Pastor Mike", he currently serves the Highland Park Police Department as a chaplain. Pastor Michael C. Robinson is a man of faith which is evidenced by the many healing and special miracles manifested through his ministry. An anointed man of God, Pastor Mike humbly engages the presence of Jesus, allowing the Holy Spirit to change and charge the atmosphere for miracles!

Made in the USA
Columbia, SC
16 June 2018